D1645157

A Tragedy of Errors

A Tragedy of Errors
The Government and Misgovernment of Northern Ireland

KENNETH BLOOMFIELD

LIVERPOOL UNIVERSITY PRESS

First published 2007 by
Liverpool University Press
4 Cambridge Street
Liverpool L69 7ZU

British Library Cataloguing-in-Publication data
A British Library CIP record is available

ISBN 978–1–84631–064–5 *cased*

Typeset in Monotype Dante by
Koinonia, Manchester
Printed and bound in the European Union by
Biddles Ltd, King's Lynn

For Elizabeth,
Caroline and Timothy

Contents

CHAPTER ONE

A personal perspective

When I read Modern History at Oxford in the late 1940s, there were relatively few well-known and reliable works about the history and politics of Northern Ireland. The 'special subject' options available in the final year of the course did not include – as they do today – a study of the recent history of the Province.

As a by-product of the turbulence to come, we now have available a huge variety of accounts: biographical, autobiographical, journalistic, polemic or sociological. We are able to read the accounts of a wide range of eminent historians, journalists or protagonists. It would be tempting to conclude that yet another book would simply add a further cairn to the mountain of controversy and analysis.

I would not have put pen to paper if I could not hope to offer a distinctive perspective. The son of English parents who settled in Northern Ireland in 1929, I bring to the consideration of controversial events no overwhelming baggage of inherited loyalty or affiliation. True, I am associated with the Protestant tradition; baptised into the Church of England, confirmed in the Church of Ireland, but also at various times a member of Methodist and Presbyterian congregations. My 'baggage' is essentially British; but while I personally remain at ease with Northern Ireland's position within the United Kingdom, I have always been comfortable with the concept that ultimate status should be determined by majority opinion, that peaceful advocacy of an end to partition should be regarded as a wholly legitimate political activity.

I have never been a member of any political party. In spite of this I can, I believe, validly claim to have been closer to political events in Northern Ireland throughout a most turbulent period than any outside observer and most political protagonists. Now and then I was a subordinate player in important events; more often a privileged and fascinated spectator.

Between 1956 and 1991, save for relatively brief intervals, I was involved in a close working relationship with the political leaders of Northern Ireland.

My appointment in 1956 to be Private Secretary to the Northern Ireland Finance Minister, Captain Terence O'Neill, led on in time to my senior role in the Northern Ireland Cabinet Office under the last three Unionist Prime Ministers – O'Neill, Chichester-Clark and Faulkner. Thus, the first half of my career was spent under the old 'Stormont' system, whereas during the second half I worked more or less closely with successive Secretaries of State: Whitelaw and Pym, Rees and Mason, Atkins and Prior, Hurd and King and Brooke. It had also been my painfully brief privilege to serve the short-lived power-sharing Executive of 1974 as, in effect, its Cabinet Secretary.

Thus it was that I attended the fateful 1973 conference at Sunningdale, experienced to the full the shame and agony of the Ulster Workers' Council strike, sat alongside successive Secretaries of State at meetings of the Inter-governmental Conference established under the Anglo-Irish Agreement of 1985, and took part in negotiations with the United States Administration to establish an International Fund for Ireland.

If this prolonged personal involvement in or close to political events has been one of the motives for undertaking this analysis, another has been my very direct exposure to the cost of 'the troubles'. In a modest way, I and my family had been placed at risk like so many others. Since the Semtex bomb attack on our home in 1988 destroyed bricks and mortar rather than life or limb, we could be counted amongst the fortunate; nevertheless the pain in losing the home in which one's family has grown up can be imagined.

While I was, of course, conscious of the suffering endured by Northern Ireland while still serving as a member (and ultimately the Head) of the Northern Ireland Civil Service, it was ironical that a more comprehensive insight would await my 'retirement'. This arose out of successive Government commissions to consider the impact of 'the troubles' on its victims, first of all in a broad sense as Victims Commissioner and thereafter in the more specialised fields of Criminal Injuries Compensation and the still continuing efforts to recover the bodies of 'the disappeared'.

These activities fully brought home to me the extent and complexity of the costs, whether in human, financial, economic, social or political terms. Of course we had not been a Rwanda or a Kosovo, but in our small community the ongoing conflict over three decades had left few communities or families unaffected.

With a declared PIRA ceasefire, with genuine movement on the front of decommissioning, with renewed efforts to restore devolution impending and with a rejuvenated Belfast bustling with activity and new construction, it is not surprising that advice to look forward rather than back should have a growing appeal. For myself, however, I believe profoundly that we need to understand what happened, why it happened and whether (and if so how) it might have been avoided, moderated, or brought to an earlier and more favourable conclusion.

Above all, I am concerned that grave misjudgement may flow from the assumption that the so-called 'peace process' is the only game in town. I would identify not one but four distinct processes, which are, of course, interrelated.

I would define the 'peace process' as the business of bringing paramilitary violence and criminality to an end, with the collateral advantage of scaling down the expensive and sometimes repressive State apparatus required to combat it. No one can deny that real progress has at last been made on this front, albeit only after dreadful human and material losses across the community. On the other hand, some paramilitary organisations have yet to renounce or abandon violence, the true extent of 'disarmament' is ultimately unprovable and essentially a matter of trust, and the relationship between serious ongoing criminality and paramilitary factions is obvious.

Alongside this there is the related matter of the 'political process'. Here the hard fact is that efforts to restore stable devolved institutions since the demise of the old Stormont Parliament have so far fallen far short of the ambitions of their sponsors. The multiple tasks of building confidence and reaching agreement between bitter political rivals, persuading their respective supporters to stand by such an agreement, and not merely forming but maintaining a stable and coherent devolved government, have so far proved too testing.

Then there is what one might call the 'international process'. For decades one could identify the question of Northern Ireland as the one major issue undermining good Anglo-Irish relations. The nadir of this relationship was marked by the sacking and burning of the British Embassy in Dublin. In the end real headway has been made on this front. Revisions of the Irish Constitution following on the Good Friday Agreement dealt at last, after inordinate delay, with the fundamental question of majority consent for any move to Irish unity. With a growing spirit of cooperation between Britain and Ireland, the 'Irish question' has also been much diminished as a major irritant in Anglo-American relationships.

The greatest grounds for continuing concern, however, relate to the 'community process'. Sectarian segregation is still deeply entrenched; physical separation between hostile communities remains inevitable in too many areas; contentious marches and parades heighten tension and reinforce animosity.

It is, then, timely to consider how Northern Ireland has been governed or misgoverned since 1921, and how it stands today after so much suffering and sacrifice. The 'troubles' have been very costly indeed for all concerned whether in political, social, economic or purely human terms.

But was it, perhaps, unavoidable? Were we all the puppets of historical inevitability? I do not believe so. I believe that many of these agonies could have been avoided with more wisdom, foresight and courage all round. In the chapters which follow I shall attempt to sustain that argument, as I look in turn at the several roles of the British state, the Irish Free State and Republic and the domestic Governments and parties of Northern Ireland itself.

CHAPTER TWO

The British dimension: union, devolution and direct rule

The course of events between the Act of Union and the onset of partition has been so well recorded and analysed by generations of historians that I need not describe it in detail. For all of the nineteenth and the early years of the twentieth century, Britain agonised about its handling of its Irish inheritance. The late onset of Catholic emancipation, the experience of famine and emigration, the constant swings of policy between coercion and concession, and the eroding resistance to afford Ireland or most of it real Home Rule or independence; all contributed to a progressive alienation of much of Ireland alongside a growing fear by Ulster Protestants of submergence in a predominantly Catholic state.

The Government of Ireland Act, enacted in 1920, followed a 'stay' on constitutional development imposed for the duration of the First World War. The legislation, accepting the reality that Ulster could not conceivably be coerced – having regard in particular to the suffering of its sons at the Somme in 1916 – sought to establish, within the framework of a continuing United Kingdom, separate Parliaments and Governments for 'Northern Ireland' (six counties in the north-east of the island) and 'Southern Ireland' (the remaining twenty-six counties including three in Ulster) respectively.

It was a very strange anomaly in the outcome that Home Rule was, however reluctantly, accepted by that community within Ulster which had traditionally opposed it, and that, when finally offered it, that community in the rest of Ireland which had sought it for so long was no longer ready to accept it. Because the new powers of government and administration had to be both offered and accepted, the Act of 1920 was never to operate as those who framed it had hoped or intended. It was certainly not designed to be an instrument for the total separation or exclusion of Ireland from the United Kingdom. Nor did it envisage – even in the context of Ireland's continuing involvement in the United Kingdom – a final, permanent or irrevocable separation between the two parts of Ireland as the Act defined and distinguished them.

It is very important to remember that the Act of 1920 was a 'Government of Ireland', not a 'Government of Northern Ireland' Act. The customary Explanatory Memorandum published with the legislation envisaged the possibility that in the event of a majority of members elected to the House of Commons in question failing to take the oath required of them, one or other (or perhaps even both) parts of Ireland would 'refuse to work the Act'; and this, of course, is precisely what happened in 'Southern Ireland' where events rushed forward towards the establishment of an Irish Free State.

Section 2 of the 1920 Act, however, had provided for the setting up of the so-called 'Council of Ireland', which from the outset was to be responsible throughout the whole of Ireland for railways, fisheries and measures to deal with contagious diseases of animals (the last far from an esoteric responsibility when one considers the recent implications of foot and mouth disease close to the Border). In the longer term, though (and using the language of the Act itself), the Council was to be established

> with a view to the eventual establishment of a Parliament for the whole of Ireland, and to bringing about harmonious action between the Parliaments and Governments of Southern Ireland and Northern Ireland, and to the promotion of mutual intercourse and uniformity in relation to matters affecting the whole of Ireland, and to providing the administration of services which the two Parliaments mutually agree should be administered uniformly throughout the whole of Ireland.

One thinks immediately of the abortive Council of Ireland provisions in the Sunningdale Agreement of late 1973, of the topics discussed by the Intergovernmental Conference established under the Anglo-Irish Agreement of 1985 and of the cross-border machinery set in place under the Belfast (or Good Friday) Agreement. This provision of the 1920 Act, like the provisions for a Parliament and Government in 'Southern Ireland' never took effect. Its terms, though, indicate very clearly indeed that, if the 1920 Act was pragmatically partitionist, it was aspirationally unitary.

The failure of the 1920 provisions in 'Southern Ireland' led to the establishment by Sinn Fein authorities of a provisional Government with its own armed forces in the field. The British response followed a pattern all too familiar in the interrelationships between the two islands. Just as, during the nineteenth century, the responses to Irish demands for reform and autonomy had alternated between coercion and concession ('killing home rule by kindness') so the Irish push for independence was met initially by the mailed fist, with the Auxiliaries and Black and Tans reinforcing the more conventional security forces of the Regular Army and the Royal Irish Constabulary and Dublin Metropolitan Police. It was a relatively short but brutal war, marked by atrocities on both sides, with the position of those in Ireland who had remained loyal to the Crown peculiarly unenviable. Faced by adverse reaction and publicity both in Britain and abroad, the wily pragmatist Lloyd-George changed course and decided to meet, and negotiate with, representatives of Sinn Fein. I would observe that when a British Government states with peculiar emphasis that it could never in any circumstances contemplate this, that or the other, one should then make preparations for just that contingency. The English (and I am wholly of English blood myself) have at their command a peculiarly patronising variety of self-satisfaction, and assume that references to 'perfidious Albion' embody a spectacular misjudgement of their impeccable qualities. Lloyd-George, of course, was far from being an Englishman, but had demonstrated throughout his career a singular agility in political manoeuvring. A favourite story about him relates to the time when a major issue in Wales was the proposal to disestablish the Anglican Church. Introducing him in what he intended and even believed to be a flattering way, the chairman of a great open-air meeting had intoned: 'I know there are many people in this great audience who would believe the Bishop of Llandaff is the greatest liar in Wales. But we have a match for him tonight, in Mr Lloyd-George.'

The negotiations in London were a fundamental turning point. If Lloyd-George and his colleagues were reasonably well informed about actual or potential divisions amongst the Sinn Fein leadership, as they certainly ought to have been with an extensive intelligence apparatus at their disposal, they should have viewed the absence from the delegation of Eamon de Valera with the gravest suspicion. The motive of any leader in holding aloof from negotiations is generally to allow himself a double option. If his delegates achieve all he would wish for, he can share in the adulation accorded to them. If they have to compromise – as negotiators inevitably and invariably have to do – he has the option of recommending rejection and hanging his own negotiators out to dry. If Lloyd-George was a fox, Eamon de Valera even in his youth was a wise owl. The 'Treaty' negotiations in London illustrated that reality, which was all too apparent on many future occasions when bitter opponents were to meet in an attempt to reconcile or compromise their difficulties. It may be possible, by power of argument or threat of overwhelming force ('instant and terrible war') to bring those facing each other across the conference table to sign or otherwise endorse some agreed conclusion. But that will only be the first stage of a process whose ultimate outcome cannot be taken for granted. The 'spin' placed on the agreed document when the parties leave the table may show huge ambiguities or differences in interpretation. Understandably each side will want to emphasise a partial if not a complete 'victory'; if not the attainment of ultimate objectives, certainly a substantial move towards them. But will the parties purportedly represented at the table be prepared to live with the agreement reached in their name? Even if the negotiators had been given unambiguous status as plenipotentiaries, they may subsequently be disavowed and disowned. If an agreement requires subsequent approval in some final elected or other forum, it may be impossible to secure majority support for it; or even if there is majority support, the process of debate may lead to splits and divisions, with consequences all the way from political friction to outright civil war.

It was not perhaps surprising that Lloyd-George sought to finesse some crucial issues. While he could not coerce the infant Northern Ireland to enter a newly born Irish State, he could and did hint at movement likely to place pressure upon it; hence the idea of a Boundary Commission which could be presented to Craig and the Unionist leaders as involving no more than a slight adjustment, and to Collins and the Irish delegates as holding out the prospects of deep erosion of a territorially modest entity. Lloyd-George's central aim – not unlike that of a number of his successors – was fundamentally to extract Great Britain from the mess, confusion and bloodshed of Ireland.

The Treaty was signed; Northern Ireland exercised its option not to throw in its lot with the new Irish Free State; the Treaty itself was accepted by the Irish Parliament (the Dail) only after bitter debate and a political split leading to a brief but bloody Irish Civil War, and leaving a legacy which dictated the course of Irish politics for decades. Thereafter, the relationship of the United Kingdom with the Irish Free State was changed fundamentally. There were still some outward, symbolic (but nevertheless highly controversial) symbols of relations with the Crown and the 'mother country', but in reality untrammelled executive and legislative power in the twenty-six counties passed into the hands of those elected by the Irish people.

The ongoing relationship with Northern Ireland and its institutions was of quite a different character. In the past some very distinguished scholars have made a fundamental and surprising error in describing those institutions – both in their legislative and their executive capacity – as 'subordinate'. Here, we have to be very careful about the use of terms. In its grant of powers to Northern Ireland, the Government of Ireland Act had reserved to what were then called the 'Imperial' authorities sole responsibility for such matters as the raising of military, naval or air forces or involvement in relations with foreign countries, while an intermediate category of powers had been withheld for the time being, but was theoretically open to transfer in the future. All other areas of government were 'transferred' to the new authorities in Northern Ireland. In the course of time, and not very surprisingly, these lines of division proved to have distinctly fuzzy edges. To take a single (but very important) example, the Northern Ireland authorities had no power to raise or maintain a military force. Yet the new police service of the Province, the Royal Ulster Constabulary (RUC), inherited the essential paramilitary and weapons-carrying characteristics of its all-Ireland predecessor, the Royal Irish Constabulary. In Continental terms, these forces were closer to being a gendarmerie than a civilian and normally unarmed equivalent of the English 'bobby'. Moreover, the regular police came to be supported by a local militia, the Ulster Special Constabulary.

On the other hand, even within its defined powers the new Parliament of Northern Ireland truly was, in the classic sense, a 'subordinate' legislature. Section 75 of the Act of 1920 had asserted that 'the supreme authority of Parliament of the United Kingdom shall remain unaffected and undiminished over all persons, matters and things' in Northern Ireland. This clearly entitled the United Kingdom Parliament, at any time it chose, to alter the scheme of Government for Northern Ireland or 'invade' the area of matter 'transferred' to the law-making authority of the Northern Ireland Parliament. It has to be appreciated, too, that the legislative process of the Northern Ireland Parliament itself required for its completion the grant of Royal Assent. The procedure is succinctly described in a Treasury document of August 1953:

> The Royal Assent to Bills is given on Her Majesty's behalf by the Governor. Every Bill submitted to the Governor for the Royal Assent is accompanied by a certificate from the Attorney General of Northern Ireland that all its provisions are within the powers of the Northern Ireland Parliament. The Governor, if so directed by Her Majesty, must reserve a Bill for the signification of Her Majesty's pleasure. Copies of Bills are sent to the Home Secretary so that he may consider whether any advice should be given to Her Majesty.

The term 'Governor' can mean or imply any number of things. In a colonial situation, he could be the real head of the executive Government of a substantial territory. In a school or (as I was later to find myself from personal experience) in a great public corporation like the BBC, the Governor and his colleagues may bear the ultimate responsibility for everything but in practice rely heavily on the professional management of the organisation. In Northern Ireland the Governor, appointed by the Crown, had the role of exercising the executive powers of the Crown in respect of all matters falling within the sphere of the Parliament and Government of Northern Ireland. The Ministers of the Government of Northern Ireland formed an Executive Committee of the Privy Council for Northern Ireland to 'aid and advise the Governor in the exercise of his executive powers'. In reality, the relationship of a Northern Ireland Governor to a Northern Ireland Cabinet was from the outset similar in character to the relationship between the monarch and the United Kingdom Government. It was clearly contrary to developing constitutional practice that a person without any democratic mandate should exercise real executive power. On the other hand, the arrangements for considering the Royal Assent to Bills passed by the two Houses of the Northern Ireland Parliament clearly left open the possibility that such Assent could be withheld indefinitely, on the advice of the United Kingdom Government conveyed by the Home Secretary. This provision did not relate just to questions of vires, that is to say whether or not the Northern Ireland Parliament had exceeded the constitutional powers granted to it, albeit on their face validated by the Attorney General's certificate. It rather afforded an open-ended opportunity to consider whether Royal Assent should be withheld, perhaps indefinitely, on the grounds that the legislation in question did not serve the wider public interest as interpreted by the Government in London.

This fundamentally important ability to weigh the wisdom as well as the validity of Northern Ireland legislation came to the test in 1922. The Northern Ireland Government, faced with a great deal of dissent and disorder at the level of local authorities, had introduced and carried through the Northern Ireland Parliament a Bill to abolish proportional representation at local government elections. Michael Collins, who had made a markedly favourable impression upon Winston Churchill during the Treaty negotiations, then appealed to Churchill against the enactment of a measure which he saw as likely (and indeed intended) to reduce Catholic and nationalist representation in local government. As a result of these representations, Royal Assent was for a period withheld. This action brought about an early crunch between the United Kingdom and Northern Ireland authorities. The Government in London was fearful that the delicate fabric of the Treaty could fall apart, plunging it once again into the morass of Irish politics and administration. But Craig and his colleagues in Belfast were prepared to play 'hardball'. They made it clear that the withholding of Royal Assent from a piece of legislation clearly within their constitutional powers would bring about their resignation from office and the prospect of resuming direct rule, at least of this part of the troublesome neighbour island. Collins himself, meanwhile, was killed in the course of the ongoing Irish Civil War, the Lloyd-George coalition was becoming increasingly fragile, and so, after a delay of two months, the contentious Bill received its Royal Assent in September 1922.

Not only was this form of overt action, or the threat of it, not repeated, but also progressively the authorities in London were to impose upon themselves a convention that legislation impinging on powers transferred to the Northern Ireland Parliament would only be introduced with the approval of, or indeed at the request of, the Northern Ireland Government. Again, to quote the Treasury document of August 1953:

In practice the United Kingdom Parliament refrains from legislating on matters with which the Northern Ireland Parliament can deal, except at the request and with the consent of Northern Ireland. It is recognised that any departure from this practice would be open to objection as impairing the responsibility which has been placed on the Northern Ireland Parliament and Government, and stultifying the purpose for which the United Kingdom Parliament confers discretion and responsibility on that Parliament and Government.

This extreme diffidence in taking advantage of the saving provisions of Section 75 of the 1920 Act was to have the serious long-term consequences of misleading some important Northern Ireland political figures about the reality of ultimate power. When pressures for reform in Northern Ireland mounted in the late 1960s there were to be those who would argue that the theoretical power saved by Section 75 had withered from desuetude and that any attempt to breach such a well-established convention would be unconstitutional. These people failed to appreciate that a convention was no more and no less than an embodiment of an underlying sense of what was good and useful. If Parliament could amend its own laws, it could certainly depart from its conventional behaviour. It was, of course, patently the case that some theoretical powers preserved by Parliament could never be, would never be, exercised. The Canada Act, for example, could be repealed in the same way as any other United Kingdom statute; but in practice there could be no question of Britain attempting to reassert executive or legislative authority in Canada. However, Northern Ireland was certainly not a dominion but a part of the United Kingdom.

The executive power, the power to govern, was coterminous with the power to legislate of the clearly subordinate Parliament. Did it follow, then, that a Cabinet of Ministers in Belfast headed by a provincial Prime Minister was also a subordinate Government? Here, I draw a clear distinction between a client Government and a subordinate Government. Any Government unable to fund its expenditure from locally raised taxation and money borrowed upon its credit, or reliant in the last resort upon external forces to secure peace and order, has some of the characteristics of a client Government. It will depend for adequate resources upon the continuing goodwill of another Government, and in times of disorder on a willingness to commit national manpower to ensure its security. In Northern Ireland it rapidly became apparent that there was no prospect, over the long term, of raising enough taxation locally (or obtaining tax money raised centrally but 'attributed' to Northern Ireland) to maintain a decent standard of services and meet, through a so-called 'imperial contribution', a share of the cost of operating services on a national level. The utter dependence of Northern Ireland upon Treasury goodwill became more and more apparent, and long before the more recent troubles, soldiers of the British Army had been required to buttress the local police in coping with the 1935 sectarian riots in Belfast.

Yet the Northern Ireland Government was not subordinate in the sense of having to respond to lawful orders of the British Government of the day. Nor was, say, the local Ministry of Education a sort of branch office of its Whitehall equivalent. Parliament could, of course, at any time impose some such constraints upon the Northern Ireland Government, but had not chosen to do so. In the last resort, however, the British Government of the day was in a position to exert a powerful influence or even pressure behind the scenes. Such incidents occurred from time to time, but with no great frequency. Strong Treasury pressure upon the Northern Ireland Authorities obliged an unwilling Northern Ireland Government during the 1930s to undertake a general revaluation of rateable properties and to accept more local responsibility to meet the growing costs of education.

I myself was to be a witness to another of these episodes. During the 1950s, when I was serving as Private Secretary to successive Ministers of Finance at Stormont, a member of the then Northern Ireland Government, perhaps influenced by sectarian considerations and demographic trends, sought to depart from a well-entrenched practice of keeping parity with Great Britain in the cash social services available to citizens. The vehicle for doing this was to be legislation to reduce the rates of family allowance available to large families (believed to be largely a Catholic phenomenon). In addition to local opposition (and not just from Catholic circles) it was indicated discreetly from London that a very poor view indeed would be taken of such an initiative, and the Northern Ireland Government abjectly retreated. However, not every confrontation ended in a retreat by the Northern Ireland authorities. The United Kingdom Government had expressed great concern about the provisions of the 1930 Education Act, including some reservations about its constitutionality under the 1920 Act, but when the Stormont authorities held their ground, Whitehall baulked at the ultimate sanction of withheld Royal Assent.

The fundamental fact was that the United Kingdom Government, from the establishment of the Parliament and Government of Northern Ireland, lacked both the will and the capacity to monitor and understand what was happening within this part of the nation, and where it might lead. Westminster, paralysed for years by endless Irish debate and obstructionism, showed little enthusiasm to be involved again 'over there'. Ministers at the Dispatch Box in London were not willing (or in reality able) to answer questions about matters for which they had transferred responsibility to Belfast. Indeed, the Chair and Table Office would decline to allow such questions to be tabled.

Perversely, the United Kingdom Government was arguably less well informed about developments in this patch of its own territory than it was about the more remote dominions and even many foreign countries. In Canada or Australia or New Zealand there would be a substantial British mission, led by a senior United Kingdom diplomat with the title of High Commissioner and the rank of Ambassador. From such sources, the London Government could keep itself continuously well informed about every aspect of politics and economic and social life. In foreign countries, Ambassadors and their staff would play a similar role and in many cases would be supplemented by information obtained through intelligence channels. It was not, of course, necessarily the case that the availability of wise and experienced advice would lead to wise governmental decisions. No warning notes from the Berlin Embassy were likely to penetrate the imbecilic complacency of Neville Chamberlain. Apart from official sources of information, the British public could draw upon a diverse media still committed in many cases to in-depth reporting and commentary on serious and complex issues.

In the case of Northern Ireland, physical proximity to the British mainland (on a good day I can discern from my home in County Down the coast of Scotland) was not accompanied by proximity to the unrolling of events. There were, of course, 'imperial' civil servants in Northern Ireland, dealing with matters in areas withheld from the Northern Ireland Government, such as income tax, customs or the civilian support of the armed services, but none of these – many of them, of course, of local origin in any case – had a political reporting role. The most senior appointee of the Crown in Northern Ireland, appointed on the advice of the Home Secretary after consultation with the Northern Ireland authorities, was the Governor. Since I served for a time as Deputy Clerk of the Northern Ireland Privy Council (in right of my role as Deputy Secretary to the Northern Ireland Cabinet) I had some degree of exposure to successive Governors, their functions and roles. Many of these were ceremonial in character; the plumed hat at the State Opening of the Northern Ireland Parliament accompanied by an artillery salute or the social evening at Government House Hillsborough, with normally subfusc civil servants ornamented with Orders and decorations appropriate to their rank and precedence. One assumed that, even though the Governor was acting as surrogate or viceroy for a constitutional monarchy, he was entitled to the traditional role outlined by Walter Bagehot, 'to advise, to be consulted, to warn'. I cannot know to what extent any of the Governors sought to advise or warn the Government of Northern Ireland. All I can say for sure is that, as a senior civil servant in the close counsels of Northern Ireland's last three Prime Ministers, I never had any sense of the Governor as a significant factor in their plans or calculations. Only in the last of the line,

Lord (Ralph) Grey, a professional colonial administrator of New Zealand origin, did I detect any marked contribution to the body politic as distinct from an ornamental contribution to the more showy side of governmental activity. Grey, in my view, was a 'class act', wiser and more experienced than many, if not all of the local politicians. No doubt from time to time successive Governors visiting London would call upon the Home Secretary of the day and chat about the state of affairs in Northern Ireland. This could be no substitute for a professional and continuous source of official reporting on the development of events.

In any case, the Governor was in no position to know in detail what was going on. A great deal of the high-level dialogue between Belfast and London was conducted along the axis joining the Stormont Cabinet Office with the Home Office. The responsible division was the residuary legatee of a strange rag-bag of functions not falling neatly within the main areas of Home Office responsibilities for the prisons, the police, immigration and nationality and so on. Headed by an Assistant Secretary (not a rank of any great seniority in the Whitehall system) the Department handled the relationships of the United Kingdom Government with the authorities in Northern Ireland, the Channel Islands and the Isle of Man, as well as esoteric responsibilities for vivisection, the registration of London taxicabs and the state management of public houses in Carlisle. There was, of course, a most fundamental difference in status as between Northern Ireland, on the one hand, and the Isle of Man or the Channel Islands, on the other. Northern Ireland remained a part of the United Kingdom; the other jurisdictions were dependencies of the Crown outside the United Kingdom. Now and then the Home Secretary himself, or a junior Home Office Minister designated by him, would get involved in some Northern Ireland business. Actual visits to Northern Ireland were infrequent; neither pressingly sought on the United Kingdom's side nor much welcomed or invited on the Northern Ireland side.

Perversely, the Northern Ireland Government, with its much more modest human resources, was rather better placed to keep a finger on the pulse of the relationship with its 'big brother'. While no member of the Home Civil Service with a role of political reporting to the Government in London was based in Northern Ireland until very late in the day, the Northern Ireland Civil Service had posted to the Home Office a 'Liaison Officer' charged with the duty of keeping in touch with the proposals under consideration by United Kingdom Departments which might affect Northern Ireland, and of facilitating consultations and exchanges of information between the two Governments. In the immediate post-war period the serving Liaison Officer was A.J. Kelly (later Sir Arthur Kelly, Secretary to the Northern Ireland Cabinet), whose racy manuscript reports back to Belfast recorded encounters with the

Home Secretary, Herbert Morrison (whose grandson, Peter Mandelson, was to be Secretary of State for Northern Ireland many years later). In spite of historic Labour Party sympathies with aspirations to ultimate Irish unity, those Labour Ministers who had served in the wartime coalition under Winston Churchill were conscious of the wartime benefits which the use of Northern Ireland bases had conferred upon the allies, while Eire had maintained its traditional neutrality. Nor was the sense of obligation to Northern Ireland diminished when, in 1949, Eire withdrew from the Commonwealth, drawing from the Labour Government in the Ireland Act 1949 a statutory affirmation that 'in no event will Northern Ireland or any part thereof cease to be part of Her Majesty's dominions or of the United Kingdom without the consent of the Parliament of Northern Ireland'. Of course, while such an affirmation could be regarded as reassuring, and indeed necessary to clarify Northern Ireland's position on Eire's departure from the Commonwealth, the acute could observe that the positive affirmation had an implicit corollary, in that departure from the United Kingdom was not ruled out in the event of the Parliament of Northern Ireland consenting to it.

Not until the obvious and grave deterioration of the situation in Northern Ireland in the late 1960s was any significant movement made to ensure that the United Kingdom Government would be better informed. An initial step was the installation of a direct and secure 'hotline' between the desk of the Northern Ireland Cabinet Secretary (Sir Harold Black) and the Home Office, to be followed in August 1969 by the dispatch to Stormont Castle of a first 'UK Representative' in the person of a senior diplomat and trusted adviser to Harold Wilson, Oliver Wright. Wright, later as Sir Oliver Wright to serve as a British Ambassador in Bonn and Washington, was a 'heavy hitter', soon established an extensive range of contacts, and had direct access to the Northern Ireland Prime Minister of the day, James Chichester-Clark. On his departure in March 1970 he expressed the clear view that Britain had tended to neglect Northern Ireland in the past, while Northern Ireland had been determined to go it alone; this in his view had been bad for both parties. Between August 1969 and the onset of direct rule, Wright was to have two successors, Ronnie Burroughs (later Ambassador to Algeria) and Howard (later Sir Howard) Smith whose later career would include terms as Ambassador in Moscow and Director General of MI5. By March 1972 the United Kingdom had, at a location called 'Laneside' at Craigavad in County Down, in effect a mini-embassy under Howard Smith's direction, with all the accompanying apparatus of secure communications. If not too little it was certainly, by then, a great deal too late. For years successive United Kingdom Governments, unassisted by the radar of any effective local representation, had peered at Northern Ireland, if at all, as through a dense fog.

All of this was happening while a vast amount of routine business continued between the two Governments. Much of this, of course, was not conducted along the Home Office–Northern Ireland Cabinet Office axis, but on a bilateral basis between individual Northern Ireland Departments and their Whitehall counterparts or opposite numbers. Amongst these relationships, much the most significant was that between the Northern Ireland Finance Ministry and the Treasury.

The state of the local media did not contribute to a greater understanding of underlying tensions and difficulties. The *Irish News* was widely regarded amongst the majority community as a semi-official organ of nationalist politics and Catholic religion. The *Northern Whig*, the venerable *Belfast Newsletter* (then controlled by the traditionally unionist Henderson family) and the widely read *Belfast Telegraph* were seen as firmly in the unionist camp. Even under the distinguished and high-principled editor Jack Sayers the last-named moved no further than towards the style of unionism promoted by Terence O'Neill. Well into the post-war era, the local BBC lived on complacently comfortable terms with the unionist establishment.

At this point it may be convenient to summarise the most cardinal of errors, from which so many other trials and disasters were to flow. In spite of their ultimate authority for Northern Ireland, as for all other parts of the United Kingdom, successive British Governments from 1920 onwards left the Province in very large measure to its own devices, utterly failed to react to evidence of mounting tensions, did very little to keep themselves informed about developments virtually next door, seldom used their ultimate power to initiate Westminster legislation, or to use the power of the purse and other means of influence. Even under the Wilson-led Labour Government the main pressure for intervention came from back-benchers like Paul Rose. If the introduction of direct rule in 1972 was a reaction to failure, it was not just a local failure but a national one.

It is now necessary to examine in greater detail the events surrounding the deployment of the Regular Army in aid of the civil power, and the subsequent developments leading up to the prorogation (and eventual dissolution) of the last Stormont Parliament and the onset of direct rule.

Under Clement Attlee's post-war Government, Labour Ministers continued to be influenced by the contribution of Northern Ireland to the war effort. The attitude of the Conservative Governments of Churchill, Eden, Macmillan and Douglas-Home which succeeded the Attlee administration was at least equally influenced by the close relationship which had long existed between the Conservative and Ulster Unionist Parties. Although never formally merged or amalgamated, these two were 'sister parties' to the extent that leading unionists could on occasions hold positions of influence in the

Conservative Party and Government. Sir Hugh O'Neill (later Lord Rathcavan), who was to enjoy the unique distinction of the membership of three Privy Councils – of the United Kingdom, of Ireland and of Northern Ireland – had been the first Speaker of the Northern Ireland House of Commons, then as MP for North Antrim had held office briefly as Under Secretary for India and Burma. Sir Knox Cunningham, Bart, another Ulster Unionist MP, was to serve Harold Macmillan in Downing Street as his Parliamentary Private Secretary (PPS). Those who hold this position at the centre of the governmental system can play varying roles, depending upon their own talents and the personality and attitude of their master. The PPS can be an influential policy adviser, or an invaluable link between the Prime Minister and the wider party in Parliament, or the kind of elevated office boy the Americans call a 'gopher'. Cunningham, a Cambridge boxing blue of heavy build and unreconstructed opinions, fell into the Archbishop Marcinkus category of personal aide. Other Unionist MPs served on, or even chaired, specialist committees within the Conservative Parliamentary Party. Most Tory members were comfortable with these relationships. The relatively polished, if somewhat limited, MPs on the Unionist benches were, by and large, the sorts of people who – with different birthplaces and accents – might well have sought Conservative seats in Surbiton or Guildford. They were not at all like the abrasive and unclubbable men who were later to replace them.

The beginning of a sea change became apparent after Harold Wilson took office as Labour Prime Minister in 1964. While there was little sign of any eagerness, on the part of Home Secretaries like Sir Frank Soskice, to give any priority to the situation in Northern Ireland, a group of back-bench MPs, such as Paul Rose, Member for a Manchester constituency, began to seek – and on occasion to find – ways of raising 'the question of Ulster' on the floor of the House of Commons, in spite of all the conventional constraints, and this process was greatly reinforced by the election of Gerry Fitt as MP for West Belfast in 1966. The Northern Ireland Labour Party (once again a 'sister party' rather than a local or national party) and various representatives of minority nationalist interests increasingly pressed upon the Labour Government the need for change in Northern Ireland. Harold Wilson himself represented a constituency (Liverpool Huyton) with a substantial Irish electorate.

In 1967 James Callaghan became Home Secretary. It was a critical moment in the career of this formidable and interesting politician. His term as Chancellor of the Exchequer had not been a distinguished or successful one, and he was keen to rehabilitate himself (though there was at that time little apparent prospect of his succeeding Harold Wilson, a younger man). For the first time in many years, he began to bring substantial indirect pressure to bear upon the Northern Ireland Government. Like all Home Secretaries since the early 1920s, he had a horror of assuming direct rule of a part of Ireland, thinking it much better to press the Northern Ireland Prime Minister and his colleagues behind the scenes. He had learned, no doubt, from his periodical exchanges with Terence O'Neill, that the Northern Ireland Prime Minister accepted the need for reform in Northern Ireland and would like to be able to bring it about.

The part played by O'Neill in the descent into tragedy will be more fully discussed in a later chapter. At this stage it was clear that the Home Secretary still lacked that 'feel' for the situation in Northern Ireland which would have allowed him to weigh O'Neill's readiness for change against the prospects of actually achieving it. He did not, himself, visit Northern Ireland during the O'Neill premiership, and it was only very late in the day that a meeting not with O'Neill only but with a delegation including the reactionary Bill Craig gave him a better measure of the difficulties and opposition facing the Northern Ireland Prime Minister. Under pressure in the House of Commons, the Prime Minister and Home Secretary expressed continuing confidence in O'Neill, while making it clear that they expected reformist action and would be deeply concerned about any reversal of policy.

The tragedy was that the really heavy guns of British governmental pressure were only brought to bear after the movement for civil rights in Northern Ireland, bringing together a mixed crew of genuine idealists, extreme radicals and proto-revolutionaries, began to run into serious trouble. This came to a head with a notorious police overreaction to the Londonderry march of 5 October 1968, with Gerry Fitt batoned and bleeding in the presence of the world media and a visiting delegation of MPs. Very late in the day, the British Government made it clear that the time for talking about change had run out; there must now be real action to achieve it. On the one hand, the possibility of dire constitutional consequences if the Northern Ireland Government failed to take decisive action gave O'Neill, for the first time, some real leverage to move his sceptical or even hostile Cabinet colleagues. Even so, a modest five-point package of reforms was only carried with difficulty through the Cabinet, with a most significant input from James Chichester-Clark, whose brother Robin, a Westminster MP, was close to the Conservative Leader Ted Heath. On the other hand, the process of convincing an unenthusiastic Unionist Party had involved an open admission by O'Neill, in his famous 'Ulster at the crossroads' speech on television on 9 December 1968, that external pressure rather than widespread enthusiasm for change had played a large part in the reform programme.

With the resignation of Terence O'Neill in April 1969, and the accession of James Chichester-Clark to the Ulster premiership, a comprehensive reform programme got under way, and there were brief hopes of a return to stability in Northern Ireland. As communal violence continued, and there was growing evidence of the inability of the RUC to contain the situation, the prospect grew of an appeal for military support in aid of the civil power. The RUC had developed in isolation from police services on the British mainland, and the geographical isolation of Northern Ireland ruled out the possibility – in a situation of widespread civil disorder – of reinforcement from neighbouring police forces. In England it had become a widely accepted tactic to flood an area anticipating civil disorder with very large numbers of police. At this time, the RUC establishment was of no more than three thousand officers, and since they could not all be on duty at the same time, the assembly of a deterrent 'mass of manoeuvre' was in reality almost impossible.

In cases of serious disorder in the United Kingdom, incapable of being contained by the civilian police, the Army is obliged to respond to requests from the competent civil authority for 'aid to the civil power'. It is my understanding that this well-established conventional route had been followed in coping with the Belfast sectarian riots of 1935. In 1969, however, the British Government made it very clear to Chichester-Clark that commitment of the Army would have to be a political decision, sought by the Northern Ireland Government and authorised by the United Kingdom Government. In a use of the kind of 'spin' which has since become more commonplace, a leading lobby correspondent was stimulated to speculate that it had been made clear to Stormont that commitment of the Army in Northern Ireland could have serious constitutional consequences. This could only be interpreted as a threat that, if the Northern Ireland Government had to seek military aid, it was likely to face a partial or complete withdrawal of its powers. The clear message was that the Northern Ireland Government should take every step open to it to contain the deteriorating situation, albeit with a hard-pressed and potentially overwhelmed RUC, unable (at the specific instruction of the United Kingdom Government) to use the stand-off weapon of CS gas or 'tear smoke' except in the most constrained conditions, and capable of urgent reinforcement (short of recourse to military intervention) only by the B Special Constabulary, who were wholly unsuited, both in terms of their training and their overwhelmingly unionist and Protestant background, to be introduced into situations of riot and communal conflict. It was one thing to use the 'Specials' to man Border roadblocks in defence against active terrorism, although even in that role they could cause friction and provoke resentment; it was quite another to contemplate interposing them, with any appearance of objectivity, between communities in heavily built-up areas in direct conflict with each other.

In the event the well-leaked hint of 'implications' proved to have been nothing more than bluff. In the aftermath of the inevitable call for military support, first in Londonderry and then in Belfast, it became clear that the preference of the United Kingdom Government was to retain the Stormont regime on a 'client' basis, preserving its powers in theory but using all its available means – which included a clear continuing need for army support – to influence and not infrequently dictate the exercise of those powers. The release of documents under the thirty-year rule now makes it very clear indeed that the Wilson Government remained averse to the introduction of direct rule. Long-headed and experienced Cabinet Ministers such as Denis Healey expressed a fear (proved all too realistic by later events) that it would be easier to get into Northern Ireland as the governing power than to get out of it again. But the Wilson Cabinet also demonstrated at that time the lack of real knowledge and 'feel' for Northern Ireland which arose from decades of detachment. Amongst other considerations weighing with Ministers was a fear that, in the event of the introduction of direct rule, the British Government might not be able to rely upon the loyalty of the Northern Ireland Civil Service, without which any administration inserted from London would be in great difficulty. Such a misconception could only have arisen out of profound ignorance. History will show that, through all the phases of the ultimate introduction of direct rule, the experiment of power-sharing, the operations of the Anglo Irish Agreement of 1985 and of the Belfast Agreement of Good Friday 1998, the Northern Ireland Civil Service continued to do its duty in serving whatever administration emerged from the laws made by the Crown in Parliament.

It is, however, my firm conviction that the delay in the introduction of direct rule following military intervention had some calamitous consequences. A Northern Ireland Cabinet, still notionally responsible under the Act of 1920 for the 'peace, order and good government' of Northern Ireland, found itself subjected to intolerable pressures, which permanently damaged the governing Ulster Unionist Party (UUP) and created ideal conditions for the rise of Ian Paisley and his adherents. In the discussions at 10 Downing Street on 19 August 1969, Chichester-Clark had been outmanoeuvred by the wily Wilson. He had readily agreed to the withdrawal of the B Special Constabulary from the immediate situation, whereas Wilson had in the event always intended that the force should be disbanded, with its role in armed support of the police assumed by a locally recruited regiment of the Army, to be known in time as the Ulster Defence Regiment. Thus the unfortunate Chichester-Clark found himself saddled with the reputation of one who had agreed to dismantle a bulwark of the unionist state. The Army itself, whose evident discipline and professional appearance initially gave confidence to the law-abiding and caused anxiety among the trouble-makers, was at first deployed in a 'separating the combatants' role; indeed, since some of the worst atrocities in the Belfast disorders had been perpetrated against Catholic communities, the Army enjoyed in such areas what the General Office Commanding (GOC), Lieutenant General Sir Ian Freeland, rightly foresaw as a brief honeymoon. More and more murky and violent factions began to emerge from the dust of civil commotion. This new challenge demanded a resolute and well-coordinated response. This was compromised by another consequence of the deferred onset of direct rule.

With two Governments now very directly involved, there was a clear division and a potential confusion of responsibility. The RUC continued to have a front-line role against civil disorder and terrorism, with a line of responsibility to the Northern Ireland Ministry of Home Affairs. Alongside them were deployed growing numbers of regular soldiers, responsible through the Chief of the General Staff and the Ministry of Defence to the Government in London. It was politically inconceivable and constitutionally *ultra vires* that the Army could be brought under Stormont control. Appreciating the need for some coherence in the struggles lying ahead, Chichester-Clark agreed with Wilson at the Downing Street meeting that, during the period of the current emergency, the GOC would act as director of all 'security operations', whether involving soldiers or policemen. But this decision, perhaps inevitable in the prevailing circumstances, nevertheless stood on its head all doctrine and precedent about military aid to the civil power. Nor did it take sufficient account of the enormous differences between the two 'security forces'. Soldiers are primarily prepared to confront their country's enemies, and to act as disciplined groups under orders. Policemen are supposed to be there as servants of their local community and all police training laid great emphasis upon the powers and responsibilities of the individual constable under the law. Thus two different cultures were to come together, and it says a great deal for the professionalism of both that in time they adjusted to the unusual situation. Yet many ironies were to lie ahead. The extraordinary controlling influence given to the Army was to be reversed in time by a return to 'police primacy'. It was expecting too much for senior military officers relatively new to Northern Ireland to be sensitive to every local nuance.

As a counterbalance to the directing role of the Army GOC, a Joint Security Committee, bringing together Northern Ireland Ministers, senior military, police and intelligence personnel and others, held regular meetings at Stormont. It would be a gross misrepresentation to present such meetings as taking executive decisions. The Committee was largely a forum for reports of what had happened, a trailer of upcoming events and occasionally the making of absurd and unrealistic suggestions by local politicians with large imaginations and limited military knowledge. If we could 'close the Border'; if we could monitor all crossings by detailed surveillance; if we could get stuck into dissident areas; if we could 'take out the enemy' – then, in the minds of certain optimistic fantasists, all would be well. Experienced police and military officers listened to such notions with as much polite tolerance as they could muster. Under growing pressure from his own party, notably on the notorious issue of 'no-go areas', the hapless Chichester-Clark found himself making more and more demands for higher troop levels without much personal conviction that they would do the trick, until – utterly weary of the whole business – he resigned on 20 March 1971, to be replaced by the brisk and energetic Brian Faulkner.

In practice, the Wilson Government had fallen spectacularly between two stools. On the one hand, it had failed to take into its own hands complete control of the situation, or to assert and exploit the authority of the Army before 'civil rights' had been overtaken by dissidence, a growing threat of terrorism and incipient civil war. On the other hand, the imposition of direct rule would merely be delayed rather than averted, if conditions were such as to expose the Northern Ireland Government to attack from many fronts. By the time of Faulkner's belated accession to the premiership, his unenviable legacy was a movement from 'civil rights' nationalism towards aggressive republicanism, an enhanced reputation for Paisley as a justified Cassandra, and growing pressure from his own ranks to find somehow, somewhere, a credible response to the mounting violence. We were soon to see the pernicious consequences of long-term British apathy, succeeded by belated intervention, an unhappy interregnum of divided authority, and the absolute abandonment of precedent in the involvement of the Army in aid of the civil power.

None of this is to take away from the personal energy and commitment shown by James Callaghan. Bullied, cajoled and charmed by him – as seemed most appropriate at the time – Northern Ireland Ministers found themselves committed to a range of reformist measures including comprehensive changes in local government, centralisation of the too-often abused local responsibilities for housing provision and management, the appointment of an Ombudsman, the creation of a Ministry of Community Relations and others. Brian Faulkner in particular, as Minister of Development in the Chichester-Clark Government, had carried this reform programme forward in a way which underlined his great executive capability. Unhappily none of this seemed to be having any constructive impact in persuading republican terrorism to scale down or abandon its activities.

I now turn to those two keynote events during the year-long Faulkner premiership which were to have such profound long-term consequences: the introduction of internment and the terrible events in Londonderry on 30

January 1972, since known the world over as 'Bloody Sunday'. To what extent did these events flow from grave errors of judgement, and to what extent was the British Government partly or wholly responsible for such errors?

In relation to internment, the lead responsibility clearly rested with the Northern Ireland Government, since the powers to intern were vested in it and conferred upon it by laws of the Northern Ireland Parliament. From my personal knowledge (since I was Deputy Secretary of the Northern Ireland Cabinet at the material time) I know that Faulkner entertained the possibility of internment without any enthusiasm. It was virtually certain to provoke, initially at least, an extremely violent reaction; it would be used in the United States and elsewhere as a stick with which to beat the British Government; and it clearly could not be carried out without the backing of the British Government and the involvement of the Army. Faulkner looked very carefully for evidence that any alternative measure could credibly curtail the escalating violence, and was not able to find it. It was becoming increasingly difficult to convince a critical party and community that everything possible was being done, since the instrument of internment had been used before, and to useful effect, both in Northern Ireland and in the Republic. With great reluctance, Faulkner concluded that he must seek the concurrence of the British Government, now led by the Conservative Prime Minister Edward Heath, with the introduction of internment, and for that purpose he travelled to Downing Street in great secrecy on 5 August 1971.

At that stage the British Government had a number of options open to it. It could absolutely rule out and, in the absence of military involvement, effectively veto any use of internment powers, but it had to face in that event a very real possibility that Faulkner would throw in his hand, saying in effect, 'I no longer want to preside over this mess. If you think you have a better answer, you had better get on with it.' Another option would have been not to dismiss the use of these powers out of hand, but to ask very searching questions about how they would be exercised. How confident were Northern Ireland Ministers that they had sufficiently accurate and reliable information about terrorist suspects? Was not loyalist terrorism a further (if at that time lesser) threat, and was it therefore envisaged that such action would be demonstrably bilateral rather than unilateral? Was there not a real risk that many of the leaders would seek and obtain sanctuary across the Border? Would it be worthwhile to seek to persuade the Irish Government that it should consider matching action? I do not recall any of these issues being pressed. Instead, Heath and his colleagues agreed to an internment strike, albeit with thinly veiled warnings that the internment exercise would be a 'last throw', and that its failure to achieve constructive results could bring forward more radical options for the future of Northern Ireland.

In the event, because police intelligence was proved to be in many instances faulty and unreliable, and because the exercise seemed to be aimed solely at one side of a divided community, it produced an even more adverse reaction than the greatest pessimists would have predicted. It proved to be a step change upwards in the widespread alienation of the Catholic and nationalist community from State power. These adverse consequences were, however, to be magnified by the outraged reaction to extraordinary methods of interrogation which surfaced at this time. It was well known that some of the key players caught up in the net of internment must have access to information which, if made known to the security forces, could be used to great effect in the battle against terrorism. With this justification, the security authorities brought into use, against a limited number of detainees, sophisticated techniques – such as 'wall-standing' and 'white noise' – developed and deployed previously outside the United Kingdom in the interrogation of terrorist suspects. The revelation of the use of such techniques was the cause of further outrage amongst the nationalist community, and exposed the United Kingdom to international odium and embarrassment in the context of accepted international standards for the protection of human rights. Semantic domestic explanations that these techniques had not crossed an ill-defined line between 'ill-treatment' and 'torture' were seen as deeply cynical and hypocritical.

If the primary responsibility for the introduction of internment must lie at the door of the Faulkner Government, the responsibility for the use of internationally unacceptable techniques must lie primarily with the United Kingdom Government. While the interrogation of suspects in custody by the RUC and other British police forces was not always of the nature of a 'friendly chat', and some degree of pressure upon steel-hardened terrorists was inevitable and amply justified by the danger they presented to the community, these novel techniques used in Northern Ireland had certainly not been perfected by the RUC.

Of course responsibility for the introduction of internment is not synonymous with responsibility for the failure of internment. With decent appeal procedures, and the progressive release of small fry, sustained use of internment could arguably, over time, have greatly reduced terrorist capability. But the British Government – soon to be wholly responsible for the matter after the introduction of direct rule – was too sensitive to Irish, American and world opinion to 'tough it out'. So far, at least, the Northern Ireland 'troubles' were having a limited effect upon life on the mainland. It could not be said, as an Israeli Government might argue in sustaining ruthless measures, that the whole life of the nation was at stake.

We were, however, soon to face an even more damaging episode than the introduction of internment and the massive adverse reaction to it. The Faulkner Government, with the full backing of London, had imposed a moratorium on all processions and parades, so often a source of friction in Northern Ireland and too often placing the security forces in the invidious position of being attacked from both sides, frustrated from coming to grips with each other. Various organisations then made it clear that they intended to march, regardless of any lawful prohibition imposed upon them. There could be no single sensible reaction to such breaches of the law. If a procession simply flouted the law but posed no danger to others in the process, the best course might well be to let the event proceed and consider afterwards the prosecution of any ringleaders who could be identified. In other cases, however, and in the interests of preserving public order, a procession might be stopped at source, re-routed or prevented from entering a particular area. Much would depend upon the numbers present on the day, and on the organisers' own ability to marshal and control the event with reasonable responsibility. The presence of large numbers of frustrated and bottled-up marchers, confronted by large contingents of soldiers and police, could easily build up a tense or even dangerous situation.

In commenting upon the events of 'Bloody Sunday', 30 January 1972, it is important to avoid judgements which now properly fall to the experienced jurists of the Bloody Sunday Tribunal. What is beyond doubt is that no fewer than thirteen civilians, all of them members of the majority Catholic community in the city, were shot dead by soldiers on duty there that day. Whether these killings, or any of them, were justified or wholly unjustified; whether they occurred as a consequence of individual judgements or misjudgements in the heat of the moment or were the fruits of a deliberate policy at Army or Government levels: these and other questions have been the stuff of controversy for many years, and it is greatly to be hoped that the painstaking work of the present Tribunal will put at least some of them to rest. What is indisputable is that soldiers of the British Army, ultimately responsible to the United Kingdom Government, were involved in action which could only intensify bitterness and prove a remarkably effective recruiting sergeant for militant republicanism. Internment followed by Bloody Sunday radicalised large elements of the nationalist community and persuaded all too many of their young men in particular that democratic means alone would never adequately protect their rights and interests.

Ever since the appointment of Reginald Maudling as Home Secretary in the Heath Government, it had been clear that there was no confidence in solving the intractable problems of Northern Ireland by security means alone. Initially a controversial curfew-and-search operation conducted in the Falls Road area of nationalist West Belfast – with minimal results in the discovery of materiel and maximum propaganda benefits to republicanism – had encouraged the hardliners in the Northern Ireland Government to believe that under the Conservatives the emphasis would shift towards an aggressive security stand. But Maudling, in spite of his idle and dilettante characteristics, was also an intelligent and sophisticated political operator, while his master Edward Heath's principal preoccupation was with cementing what he saw as Britain's destiny in Europe. A visit by Maudling to Northern Ireland had left him unimpressed by the fractious environment, the rampant sectarianism, and the obviously limited vision of too many of those in authority. Anecdotally he was credited with observing on his departing plane, 'What a bloody awful country. Bring me a large whiskey.' Another significant figure, Lord Carrington, who had struggled unsuccessfully to keep Chichester-Clark from resigning, shared this unfavourable view of Northern Ireland. 'I remember', he records in his memoir *Reflect on Things Past* (1988), 'that an early visit impressed me most unfavourably with the bigotry – and insobriety – of a lot of the fairly senior people in Ulster politics whom I met'. I must say that I fail to recognise in this the sort of unionist politicians I used to encounter, who were likely to be God-fearing Protestants who believed more in healthy rounds of golf and early nights than a life of wine, women and song. I recall, for instance, the judgement of an English journalist meeting Brian Faulkner for the first time: 'He struck me as the least dissipated man I had ever met.' Nevertheless, the distaste shines through.

Maudling had begun to repeat a mantra soon reduced to the acronym of PAG – the essence of which was that there should be developed within Northern Ireland 'a permanent, active and guaranteed role for majority and minority alike'. In the aftermath of Bloody Sunday, the Stormont Government was clearly drinking in the last chance saloon. This had been made pretty clear in the consultations about internment, and indeed Heath himself claims in his autobiography *The Course of My Life* (1998) that he had earlier made it clear to Faulkner that, if significant progress was not made in the next year or so, he would have to introduce direct rule. In Heath's view, Faulkner was aware, from the day he took office, that his premiership was Stormont's last chance. With the failure of internment, the Northern Ireland Government had exhausted its last opportunity to restore order and public confidence. If that Government could not credibly contain continuing mayhem, the sovereign Government of the United Kingdom would have to step into the breach.

The discussion of the belated development by the Northern Ireland Government of proposals which would, in their view, represent 'significant progress' more properly belongs in a later chapter where the motivation and actions of the Northern Ireland interests, including the Unionist Party and the Stormont Government, will be discussed in detail. What needs to be said here is that the Heath Government deemed these proposals inadequate to stave off a radical intervention. When Faulkner and his colleagues met Heath and other British Ministers at Downing Street on 22 March 1972, they did not find themselves faced with any real discussion or bargaining around their own proposals. Instead they were told of decisions already reached by the United Kingdom Government: that all the 'law and order' powers of the Northern Ireland Government should be transferred to Westminster; that internment should be phased out; that there should before too long be a plebiscite to determine whether the people of Northern Ireland wished to remain within the United Kingdom or join in a united Ireland; and that serious consideration should be given to power-sharing with the Catholic and nationalist minority.

It is easier to describe this démarche than to be sure what the Heath Government expected its outcome to be. We know now that Maudling in particular hoped to maintain a Northern Ireland Government in place as a useful buffer between the British Government and the daily problems of Northern Ireland. It is very difficult to believe, however, that a British Government now relatively well informed about the Province, notably through the United Kingdom Representative Howard Smith, could seriously have expected that Faulkner and his colleagues would accept such proposals. Indeed, Faulkner had been giving pretty clear signals that a further humiliation of the Northern Ireland Government would make his position wholly untenable. There had already, as I shall explain in a later chapter, been serious consideration of the steps which a British Government might take and of the Northern Ireland Government's ability to respond and react to them. In that context, too, one can examine the argument not infrequently advanced that, since Faulkner himself was willing in 1974 to lead a power-sharing administration without law and order powers, it was illogical and self-destructive to rule out such a prospect so completely in 1972. I myself, present as an official in support of Faulkner of the Downing Street meeting, was not in the least surprised by his reaction that, although he would discuss the outcome of that meeting with his Cabinet, there could be no doubt that their decisions would be to resign en bloc rather than accept the Heath démarche.

In the period running up to the encounter at 10 Downing Street, Howard Smith had frequently pressed me on the capacity and ability of the Northern Ireland Government to move further and faster with reform. In response I had made it clear to him that no one in my view had as good a chance or as much ability as Faulkner to move events in a constructive direction, but that the most he could realistically hope to achieve might still fall short of what was required to stabilise the situation and reverse the continuing boycott of

Stormont by elected nationalists. In this setting Smith began to speak openly of the need for – and I recall the phrase vividly – 'a discontinuity'.

It is not an unreasonable inference, then, that in spite of serious reservations on the part of a number of his colleagues, Heath by this time was convinced that the best outcome would be a limited and creative period of direct rule. The Northern Ireland politicians, under this concept, would be moved into sheltered housing while the political structures were reshaped, and would then move in again under a different tenancy agreement providing for co-ownership.

From close observation of the Northern Ireland political scene for nearly half a century, I have often noticed how skilful players can be in shifting the onus or the blame in controversial situations on to other interests. If, as I strongly suspect, Heath fully expected Faulkner to reject his proposals he could thereafter present direct rule as a 'cruel necessity' which would not have been needed if Faulkner and his colleagues had been prepared to accept perfectly reasonable proposals of his own. This ability to finesse a difficult and painful transition may have helped to hold the reaction in Northern Ireland largely at the level of rhetoric.

Of course the response of the outgoing Stormont Government was, very understandably, bitter. In spite of Heath's confidence that he had made the position clear to Faulkner early in the latter's premiership, Faulkner himself felt a real sense of personal and political betrayal. As rumours of imminent direct rule had begun to surface before the fateful Downing Street encounter, the word from Whitehall had been to characterise these rumours as 'pure speculation'. These, as every watcher of professional spin doctoring will know, are at best weasel words. What is speculated about can prove to be accurate or well-informed speculation. If Government really wishes to say 'This is an outright lie' or 'We will not take such a step in any circumstances', it can of course do so. There was a degree of innocence in Faulkner's confidence that the unthinkable would not occur. He had, perhaps, been lulled into a false sense of security by the close historic links hitherto prevailing between the Ulster Unionist and Conservative Parties. In a statement on 24 March, Brian Faulkner commented:

> This is a serious and sad situation, reached after three years of the most strenuous efforts to reform our society on a basis at once fair and realistic. I thought that by our actions and our attitude we had earned the right to the confidence and support of the United Kingdom Government. I fear, too, that many people will draw a sinister and depressing message from these events – that violence can pay; that violence does pay; that those who shout, lie, denigrate and even destroy earn for themselves attention that responsible conduct and honourable behaviour do not. They may ask – if

Belfast is to bow to violence today where will it be next year? Birmingham? Glasgow? London?

These, in the course of time, were to prove relevant rather than rhetorical questions. Yet I myself, close as I was at the time to the Faulkner Government and deeply involved in its efforts to avert intervention, would accept that by this stage direct rule had become inevitable and, if well handled, potentially useful. If, indeed, the British Government could meet its objective of a relatively quick in-and-out intervention, leaving behind it more widely acceptable political structures restored to local control, this would be a great achievement and a real contribution to peace. I have argued already that direct rule should have been undertaken alongside commitment of the Army, and that during the interregnum much time and opportunity were lost. But the position was certainly not beyond recovery.

CHAPTER THREE

The British dimension: direct rule to the UWC strike

Much now depended upon the personality and the capabilities of the new Secretary of State for Northern Ireland, William Whitelaw. Amongst the rather colourless products of the modern political machine, Whitelaw was an exotic. Behind a façade of booming affability there lurked one of the shrewdest minds in British politics. When encountered in person, he was a singularly difficult person to dislike, even in a community which had its share of sceptical and cynical people. He arrived at Stormont Castle accompanied by an exceptionally able group of junior Ministers, some of whom were later themselves to achieve Cabinet rank. He brought with him a very strong team of Whitehall officials led by the sardonic Permanent Under Secretary (PUS) Sir William Nield and including a later official head of the Northern Ireland Office in Philip Woodfield and a future First Civil Service Commissioner in Dennis Trevelyan. Very prudently, sensitive and considerate efforts were made to bind members of the Northern Ireland Civil Service into the new official team. The Head of the Civil Service, Sir David Holden, moved down the hill from Parliament Buildings to join the former Cabinet Secretary Sir Harold Black and myself as immediate advisers, with invaluable local knowledge and 'feel', to the new Ministers. It was indeed to fall to me, I remember, to draft a first 'submission' to the new Secretary of State on the subject of an approach from the Apprentice Boys of Derry, an organisation which had not so far been the subject of close study amongst the mandarins of Whitehall. 'The Secretary of State must appreciate', I wrote, 'that these are not apprentices, they are not boys and many of them do not come from Derry.' In writing this I had perhaps at the back of my mind some words used by Edward Heath on a visit to New York, where I was then serving in the British Industrial Development Office. Heath, explaining to Americans the rather esoteric title under which he then conducted important Foreign Office business relating to Europe, had assured them that he was 'neither a Lord nor a Privy, nor a Seal'. Outside the immediate team joining the Secretary of State at Stormont Castle, the Northern Ireland Permanent Secretaries were encouraged to form, under the rubric of the 'Future Policy Group', a think tank capable of developing various options for the future after direct rule. A great deal of my own time was spent preparing 'What if?' papers for this Group. What were the considerations bearing upon such options as power-sharing government, 'total integration' into the United Kingdom, more structured relationships with the Irish Republic, and so on? These reports were not only made available to the Secretary of State but were also discussed with him fully across the table.

All of this represented a sure-footed introduction to direct rule. A less happy initiative was the establishment of an appointed Advisory Commission of local worthies from 'across the community', with whom draft Northern Ireland legislation and other matters could be discussed. While it was understandable that Ministers parachuted into the local scene should wish to sound out local people beyond the Civil Service, and indeed wanted to demonstrate a willingness to take account of local advice, the rage and frustration of the former Stormont Ministers at being displaced were magnified by the position subsequently afforded to appointees. From the start, of course, Whitelaw and his ministerial subordinates sought regular encounters with the political parties, but arguably any need for wider consultation could have been met by ad hoc meetings with existing economic, social or cultural organisations. With the creation of an Advisory Commission, Brian Faulkner observed with some bitterness, Northern Ireland had been treated like a 'coconut colony'.

The question of legislation under direct rule presented real difficulty. Northern Ireland, using the powers transferred to its Parliament, had developed its own codes of law in many fields. In 1966, by way of example, no fewer than forty-three Northern Ireland Acts of Parliament had passed through all their stages (formal presentation or first reading; discussion of major principles or second reading; committee stage and report stage with opportunities for amendment; and third reading) in both the House of Commons and Senate before receiving the Royal Assent. There was, of course, no prospect whatever under direct rule of finding room in the crowded parliamentary timetable to take anything like this volume of legislation relating solely to Northern Ireland through the full formal procedures in both Houses of the United Kingdom Parliament. The options, then, were to impose some kind of legislative moratorium or self-denying ordinance; to cater in future for Northern Ireland's needs within wider United Kingdom legislation; or to provide truncated procedures for Northern Ireland during what it was hoped would be a relatively brief interregnum. The first of these options was rejected because the tone of the direct rule administration was to move things forward rather than hold them back; and the second was rejected because it could be seen as a significant step towards 'total integration'. While such a step could not be absolutely ruled out, it was likely to alienate nationalist opinion by seeming to foreclose the option of movement towards a united Ireland, and to reintroduce the virulent strain of Irish politics back into the bloodstream of the national political system. In these circumstances the third option was adopted. During what was hoped to be a brief period of direct rule most legislation for Northern Ireland alone would be enacted by Order in Council. Such Orders would come before Parliament in draft, and could be debated there using a relatively small amount of Parliamentary time, thereafter to be accepted or rejected by vote. These methods could be criticised, and not infrequently were, as treating the Northern Ireland people as 'second-class citizens'; the only people in the entire United Kingdom who could experience fundamental changes in the law affecting them without adequate debate or the possibility of amendment. A Government with a secure majority, albeit formed solely by Members with constituencies in Great Britain, could be confident of 'whipping' such Northern Ireland legislation as it chose through Parliament.

It is, however, difficult to see what else could have been done to safeguard the prospect of regular Northern Ireland legislation without clogging up the arteries of Parliament. Moreover, although the formal processes within Parliament itself offered merely an opportunity to debate and thereafter approve or reject, rather than an opportunity to consider in great detail and amend, there were other means to give some weight to local opinion. The legislative process could be preceded by the publication of a discussion paper, perhaps canvassing options. Except in situations of demonstrable urgency, Government could publish a pre-legislative document, a Proposal for a Draft Order in Council, allowing it to take on board local reactions either inside or outside Parliament.

There was, however, one very obvious drawback to the withdrawal, albeit in intention temporarily, of devolved powers. Alone amongst the citizens of the United Kingdom, the voters of Northern Ireland at that time had no opportunity to vote for or against any party which could potentially form a United Kingdom Government. Of course the Province was not unique in having political parties of its own; the Scottish National Party in Scotland and Plaid Cymru in Wales had built up substantial support in those jurisdictions. Nor was it unique to find a distinct area – even one which could without hyperbole be termed a 'nation' – wholly at odds with the political administration governing it at national level, as was certainly the case in predominantly Labour Scotland during the long years of Conservative Government in London. These potential tensions could only be ameliorated by devolution, and it is one of the many ironies of history that Scotland was eventually to achieve amelioration just when the huge gulf between Scottish sentiment and national sentiment had apparently narrowed.

It can be argued that an early decision by national political parties to organise and accept members in Northern Ireland would have had little practical effect; that party structures in any jurisdiction reflect the underlying divisions in its society, which in Northern Ireland were communitarian rather than social and economic. It was indeed to be the case that when, very belatedly, the Conservative Party, through a Conference revolt, decided to ignore the views of its Government and organise in Northern Ireland, Conservative candidates were to attract very little support there. There were, however, considerations of principle here. Across the Atlantic men had taken up arms under the slogan 'No taxation without representation'. Although the entity known as Northern Ireland could be said to be 'subsidised' by the British taxpayer, the individual citizen there paid the same national taxes as his fellows in Great Britain. The Brookes of Fermanagh, the Alexanders of Caledon, the Templars of Loughgall and many nameless sons and daughters of Northern Ireland had helped to fight Britain's wars, in the Crimea and at the Indian Mutiny, in the carnage of the Somme or the steamy battlefields of Burma. People registered to vote in Northern Ireland might well be first- or second-generation residents. They might, before moving from Great Britain for business, family or other reasons, have had deep loyalties to or even direct involvement in the Conservative or Labour Parties. In moving to Northern Ireland, an integral part of the United Kingdom, they forfeited the opportunity to preserve such loyalties or involvement. For an Ulsterman to have any prospect of sitting in a British Cabinet, he had to relocate himself to Great Britain.

In the absence of a mainline political presence, alliances of an unhelpful kind could develop. Prior to the onset of direct rule, the Unionist Party had placed a good deal of reliance upon its historic links with the Conservative Party. Their Westminster Members had on occasions reached the fringes of Government; their votes represented useful lobby-fodder. With the shock of direct rule, and the after-shock of the Anglo-Irish Agreement of 1985, these historic links were to be totally ruptured. On the other side of the House, the Labour Party has received with significant warmth, as a 'sister party', the nationalist Social Democratic Labour Party (SDLP). Anyone keen to support Labour in Northern Ireland has been steered to support this 'sister party'. This cosy relationship has made it very difficult for unionist sympathisers to accept the Labour Party as an impartial arbiter, and the relationship is all the more remarkable given the pronounced social conservatism of the SDLP. So we have had the anomaly of historic association between the Conservative Party and the Unionist members from solidly working-class areas and, on the other hand, between the Labour Party and an SDLP increasingly seen by Catholic voters from underprivileged areas as irremediably middle-class.

Of course, historic alliances and affiliations could bow very abruptly to the realities of power politics. Despite the expressed historic antipathy of Labour Governments to any increase in Northern Ireland representation at Westminster, it was to be a Government of this complexion which allowed such an increase when its own fate seemed to be in the balance. It is remarkable, but perhaps not surprising, that most Governments regard any other form of calamity facing the nation or a part of it as secondary to the greater calamity of their own loss of office.

These wider issues were to be of consequence throughout what turned out to be – except for a brief interregnum in 1974 under the power-sharing Executive – a very prolonged period of direct rule. Yet Whitelaw's objective was to move ahead quickly to pacify the community and restore devolved political institutions under cooperative management. In the process he made many genuine advances but also committed some serious errors, with long-term repercussions.

Under direct rule, pressure for restoration of the rule of law in all parts of Northern Ireland did not abate. In Londonderry in particular a large part of the city was effectively a 'no-go area', barricaded against entry by the security forces, and under the controlling influence of local activists, some though not all of whom had militant republican affiliations. In the early days of direct rule, it was a given that there could in no circumstances be any direct military intervention into such areas. Without reaching any useful conclusion, groups of officials toyed with all sorts of unrealistic schemes to restore normality through inducement and very indirect pressure. The atmosphere was to be utterly changed by the events of 'Bloody Friday', 21 July 1972 in Belfast, when the Irish Republican Army (IRA) set off twenty-six explosions in the city, killing eleven people and injuring a further 130. The most horrific incident was at the crowded Oxford Street Bus Station, where seven people were killed and where television – shedding for the occasion the reticence normally shown about too close a focus on blood and guts – carried appalling pictures of police literally shovelling up pieces of human beings. The utter public outrage was shared by the emotional and caring Whitelaw, and although Carrington as Defence Minister urged continuing caution the Secretary of State was persuaded that the extensive 'no-go areas' could no longer be tolerated as possible safe havens for people and organisations capable of planning and carrying out such atrocities. So only ten days later, in the early hours of 31 July, a reinforced Army launched Operation Motorman to clear away the barricades in Derry and Belfast. The forces involved were massive: some 21,000 members of the Regular Army, 9,000 of the Ulster Defence Regiment and 6,000 of the RUC being then available to take part in the operations or act as backup if required.

As the operation was prepared, Whitelaw agonised as to whether it should be a surprise or be signalled in advance. In theory a surprise swoop could have caught up in its net important wanted terrorists, but the movement into place of such large numbers of the security forces could hardly fail to alert the acute controllers of terrorism. There were real fears of a possible shooting war, with hundreds of casualties, and clearly if terrorist groups were to mount an armed resistance, the Army would have to respond to it. At least, though, an operation signalled in advance could reduce the risk to innocent civilians, who would be on alert to keep themselves out of harm's way. It hardly needs saying that the last thing needed by the new direct rule regime was any kind of a rerun of 'Bloody Sunday'. It may have been the case that, on the IRA side too, there was a reluctance to increase the odium falling upon them after 'Bloody Friday' earlier in the month. For whatever reasons, the security operations themselves met relatively little resistance, although not far from Derry the little village of Claudy lost six of its citizens when three car bombs exploded there. Many years later I was to have the poignant experience of joining two of the village children in unveiling a belated but moving monument to the dead of Claudy.

All of this had occurred at a most sensitive time. Following the onset of direct rule the Official IRA had declared a ceasefire on 29 May, and four weeks later the Provisional IRA (PIRA) had also entered upon a 'truce'. After contacts made at official level, Whitelaw took the momentous and perilous decision to meet leaders of PIRA in London. The truce had given rise to some hope that the PIRA campaign could be brought to an end under tolerable conditions. It might, then, be worth meeting the leadership if only to illustrate that Government had done its very best to bring the conflict to an end. Those who came on 7 July to parlay in great secrecy at the home of Paul Channon, a wealthy ministerial subordinate of Whitelaw's, included a young internee released for the purpose, and at that time quite unknown to a wider public, Gerry Adams.

Whitelaw conducted these tricky exchanges with the PIRA delegation with his usual innate courtesy, but was effectively presented with an ultimatum. PIRA's 'modest proposal' was that there should be a public declaration that the Irish people as a whole should decide the future of Ireland; that all British troops should be withdrawn from Irish soil by 1 January 1975; that, pending such a withdrawal, all troops should be withdrawn immediately from 'sensitive areas', and that there should be a general amnesty for all 'political prisoners', internees and persons on the wanted list.

This ultimatum, carrying with it the implicit threat of renewed violence, was wholly unacceptable, but it featured a number of the issues which were to arise in the later exchanges over the decades: political status, release of the convicted or detained, and the right of the Irish people alone to settle their destiny. With the refusal of Government to entertain such an ultimatum, an early breach of the 'truce' was to be expected, and two days later the return to violence was justified by a dispute over a housing issue.

Very prudently Whitelaw, having conducted the meeting in conditions of great secrecy (and indeed in the only conditions under which it could have taken place), was careful after the event to inform Parliament and the public of what had been taking place. His own obvious sincerity and goodwill sheltered him to some extent, even within Northern Ireland, from excessive criticism of his controversial initiative.

Yet this first acknowledged encounter between the British Government and the IRA raised the most important questions of principle and practice. Governments all over the world are quick to say 'We never negotiate with terrorists', and will explain with great vehemence how any particular encounter is designed to do no more and no less than convey a clear statement of the Government's position and enable a clear understanding of the position of the adversary. But this is often a very fine line. In later days, of course, the argument could be mounted that meetings with Sinn Fein, increasingly able as it was to point to a substantial electoral mandate, were quite different in kind from dealing directly with the IRA. There was, indeed, ample precedent for Whitelaw's initiative in Lloyd-George's shift from waging war to making peace. All over the world, yesterday's terrorists could be tomorrow's statesmen. In the latter role they could usually demonstrate overwhelming popular support; in the former they would take it upon themselves to embody a spirit yet to be implanted amongst the people as a whole.

It goes without saying that when the abortive talks were followed by the breakdown of the truce and the horrors of 'Bloody Friday', the idea of further parlaying with the IRA fell, for the time being at least, off the agenda. Far from leading to a calming of the situation, direct rule was now marked by a horrifying upsurge in violence. In July 1972 alone, there were 95 deaths (74 civilians), nearly 200 explosions and 2,800 shooting incidents. Many of these episodes could be laid at the door of the IRA, but in a mounting surge of sectarian assassinations, loyalist groups were also heavily involved.

Had Whitelaw's meeting with PIRA, then, been a grave error? It would be churlish to reach such a conclusion. To fail is not to negate the worthiness of an attempt. The real danger point would come in later repeated encounters, when the defence of 'never negotiating with terrorists' became a self-evident fiction.

Whitelaw was highly unusual as a very senior politician in his readiness to admit mistakes. This recourse can often be wise as well as generous. There is a splendid anecdote dating from the time when George Thomas, later to be Speaker of the House of Commons, answered Northern Ireland questions on his first appearance as a junior Minister at the Home Office. Northern Ireland has always been a semantic minefield in which there can be an explosive reaction to some mispronunciation or use of an unacceptable term. In the heat of the moment, Thomas innocently referred to Northern Ireland as 'the colony'. Predictable howls of indignation and outrage rose from the Unionist benches. 'My, my', said Thomas disarmingly, 'I wish I hadn't said that.' Such humble candour can be disarming in both senses of the word.

In June 1972 Whitelaw had indeed made what he later freely confessed to be a most serious error. It had arisen out of the well-practised technique in the republican repertoire, the hunger strike. By June 1972 one of the IRA's best-known leaders of the time, Billy McKee, was close to death in Belfast's prison. To avert such an outcome, Whitelaw decided to recognise within the prison system a 'special category' of prisoner. Under a specific regime, prisoners sentenced to more than nine months' imprisonment for offences related to the civil disturbances would in future not be required to work or to wear prison clothes. The creation of this category led to the construction at the old Long Kesh Airfield, later the Maze Prison, of a series of segregated 'compounds' within which prisoners with an expressed attachment to one proscribed organisation or another could mix freely with like-minded comrades.

The long-term malign effects of this decision were enormous. As we shall see, internment was shortly to be phased out under the incoming Labour Government, and henceforth sole reliance for the suppression and punishment of terror would rest upon the conviction of individuals by due process of law, for various criminal offences. Before the courts, then, members of terrorist groups were treated as criminals, but once convicted they were treated much more like prisoners of war. The inevitable failure to underline the criminal nature of shooting or bombing attacks was to be further reinforced by the need, in the face of the intimidation of witnesses and juries, to introduce special trial procedures for defined categories of activity. Needless to say the accumulation of like-minded activists alongside each other reinforced their morale and *esprit de corps*. With no obligation to work they were well placed to benefit from the 'university of terrorism' (although some, of course, sought to gain more benign knowledge and acquired new perspectives through a religious experience or otherwise). The concentration of so many skilful and dangerous people exposed prison officers at every level to threat, intimidation and actual danger. Over time, the 'special category' status became so well entrenched that any attempts to remove or dilute it were bound to face extreme resistance, as indeed they did.

The grant of 'special category' status gave respectability to terrorist arguments that they were fighting a 'war of liberation', or on the loyalist side resisting attempts to suppress their culture and identity. They were seeking, and indeed to some extent obtaining, the best of both worlds. In the guise of an army legitimated by the proclamation of 1916 (and in direct defiance of the assertion in the Irish Constitution that there could only be one national army maintained by the State), the IRA defended attacks upon soldiers or policemen as wholly legitimate acts of war, and shrugged their shoulders when innocent civilians died 'by unfortunate mistake' or 'as the regrettable consequences of legitimate attacks upon economic centres of imperialist power'. Had not the British incinerated German civilians at Dresden, and the Americans in Tokyo, Hiroshima and Nagasaki? Yes, war indeed was hell. The 'volunteers' themselves cheerfully endured great hardships to earn their country's freedom.

These arguments gloss over the reality that in a real war, involving real soldiers, people spying and carrying out acts of sabotage, and in no way identified as soldiers, expect short shrift. Nor, at the Nuremberg Trials and since, has it ever been an acceptable response to acts of blatant terrorism that they were justified in the national interest. Although, as we shall see, the formal special status was in time greatly modified, the distinction between 'political prisoners' and what the sardonic humorists of Ulster termed ODCs (ordinary decent criminals) remained. In time this unwholesome distinction was to have perverse consequences and to fall short of any decent standards of natural justice. As I write, some unfortunate who has killed a close relative in a fit of passion, and perhaps under great provocation, must serve out his prison term awarded by the Court, subject only to the usual rates of remission. Yet someone who has organised or even committed multiple murders of his fellow-citizens will not only be free to walk the streets but also may even have become a well-known face on television, presented as a wholly legitimate politician. When one has met as many of those who have suffered as I have been obliged to, this outcome truly turns the stomach.

The introduction of 'special category' status was a gross and grievous error, as Whitelaw himself would subsequently, and with characteristic candour, acknowledge.

In recent times, there has been an unthinking assumption that the so-called 'peace process' and the 'political process' are one and the same thing. They are inevitably interrelated, of course. Political agreement is particularly hard to reach when violence that is alienating the distinct communities continues; peace is very difficult to secure when there is no credible local democracy to which to rally, no continuing evidence that political measures can guarantee benefits in which all may share. Abandoning for the moment any real prospect of bringing about a multilateral ceasefire or a permanent and assured peace, Whitelaw and his officials turned to the demanding task of shaping a new polity in Northern Ireland to which the huge non-violent majority could turn for decent government and the protection of individual and common rights. Within this process, Whitelaw was in his element, showing great skill, patience and flexibility. Throughout he had to reckon with the propensity of Northern Ireland parties, if not confident of a favourable result from the game being played, to pick up their ball and head for home. Captain Boycott was to be the first of a very long line to experience this technique. The process opened with a three-day conference at Darlington to discuss broad options for the future. Of the seven invited Northern Ireland Parties only three (the UUP, the Alliance Party and the Northern Ireland Labour Party) agreed to take part, while the other four (SDLP, Nationalist, Democratic Unionist Party [DUP] and Republican Labour) rejected their invitations for various reasons. The resulting truncated gathering – particularly in the absence of any representation of nationalist opinion – could reach no useful or agreed conclusions.

In the absence of such agreement, Whitelaw had to bring his own proposals into play. Although the document *The Future of Northern Ireland* was published at the end of October 1972 as a discussion paper, it already embodied all the significant elements of a series of British Government proposals over a great many years: a reaffirmation of the determination to allow the people of Northern Ireland to decide whether or not they wish to remain within the United Kingdom; a warning that no future Government could be based upon a single community; and a significant recognition of an 'Irish dimension' to be taken into account. The British Government also moved ahead with preparations for a Border Poll to be held on 8 March 1973, and having as its outcome that almost 592,000 votes were cast for the proposition that Northern Ireland should remain in part of the United Kingdom, with fewer than 6,500 (in the context of nationalist advice to boycott the Poll) supporting the counter-proposition that Northern Ireland should be joined to the Republic of Ireland, outside the United Kingdom.

In the immediate aftermath of this result, Whitelaw moved rapidly to bring forward, in a White Paper published on 20 March 1973, his own more detailed proposals for the future. There would be a seventy-eight-Member Northern Ireland Assembly to be elected by proportional representation and a system of power-sharing in executive government. Westminster would retain, for the meantime at least, those law and order powers whose proposed removal had brought about the resignation of Faulkner's Government.

The return of proportional representation (PR) to the Northern Ireland scene, recalling the dramatic circumstances of its withdrawal in the 1920s, was a very significant decision. It was, perhaps, assumed that its outcome would not only be greater 'fairness' but an encouragement of moderation. It is certainly true that the 'first past the post' system, still prevailing at elections to Parliament from Northern Ireland as from other parts of the United Kingdom, embodies the risk of drawing the electoral map in the starkest black and white. Whole substantial areas, with significant pockets of 'the other sort', could seem to have gone over completely to the unionist or nationalist camp, with the ultimate outcome often liable to depend more upon the splitting of votes between candidates from the same broad faction than upon a genuine electoral swing from one 'bloc' to another of a kind almost unknown in Northern Ireland. Thus, today, a parliamentary constituency like Fermanagh and South Tyrone, now represented in Parliament (if this term can really be applied to a deliberate absentee) by a Sinn Fein MP, sends forward from the same area six members to the Northern Ireland Assembly, of whom two represent the DUP, two Sinn Fein, one the SDLP and one the UUP. On the other hand, the assurance given by the single transferable vote, in large multi-member constituencies, that all significant parties will win representation, can lead to growing factionalism both between and within parties and accord undue influence to small parties afforded the 'casting vote' by the electoral arithmetic, as seen not infrequently in such countries using PR as Israel or Germany. I myself had argued strongly within the Government for an alternative to the single transferable vote, in the form of a modified version of the German electoral system, which preserved a close link between most elected members and manageable constituencies, 'topped up' the constituency element with additional 'party list' members in the interest of overall proportionality, and required support above a well-chosen threshold to prevent excessive proliferation of small parties.

At that time, in 1972, many looked with some complacency to the break-up of the party monoliths which had dominated the political scene for so long. In practice, the complex pattern promoted by PR has proved more difficult to manage. At any time the search for political consensus in Northern Ireland has resembled the innocent game often discovered in my youth in Christmas stockings. The trick is to jiggle a lot of tiny steel balls into a series of minute holes. Almost invariably, an effort to tease into place some errant ball would displace another already in position. To concede to one faction is all too often to alienate another. Carried to extremes, one could argue (for example) that any police service wholly acceptable to nationalism is likely to be wholly unacceptable to unionism. Is there, then, some point in the middle which both sides can 'thole', albeit without enthusiasm? The jury is still out on that fundamental question.

At all events, the elections to District Councils on 30 May 1973 – the first conducted by PR since 1920 – were followed on 28 June by the crucial elections to the new seventy-eight-Member Assembly. These elections illustrated for the second time since 1969 – when the Stormont General Election had returned unionists both favourable to and opposed to Terence O'Neill – the difficulty of steering a united party in a reformist direction. The outcome was precarious for Faulkner as the party leader, and fell well short of giving him a clear mandate to enter a power-sharing administration, whose composition and relationships with the Republic of Ireland would still have to be negotiated. The crucial fact was that of fifty seats won by unionists of different hues, less than a half could be regarded as reliable supporters of Faulkner who were prepared to explore constructively the potential of the White Paper. Nevertheless on 5 October 1973 the Secretary of State convened at Stormont Castle an open-ended conference between Faulkner's Unionists, the SDLP led by Gerry Fitt and the Alliance Party led by Oliver Napier. Between them, these leaders led fifty-one representatives in the new Assembly, representing a very clear majority of all its members but with the other potential partners commanding more representatives – and more solidly reliable and supportive representatives – than Faulkner.

Over the course of the weeks which followed, Whitelaw conducted these difficult negotiations – frequently on the verge of total breakdown – with enormous skill. The electoral arithmetic presented a huge dilemma. If a coalition were to be formed, it would enjoy more support from Alliance and SDLP ranks when taken together than from the pro-Faulkner loyalists of the Unionist Party. Yet the overall sentiment expressed by the electorate was, in constitutional terms, unionist. A non-unionist majority in the potential Cabinet or Executive committee, or the designation of a non-unionist as its leading figure, would be certain to provoke widespread resentment or worse. On the other hand, the two potential coalition partners alongside Faulkner understandably looked for rewards of office proportional to their electoral success. Whitelaw finessed this situation with a piece of impressive legerdemain. There would be both an Executive, which Faulkner would lead, which would have a unionist majority and which would have the final word on overall policy, and a wider Administration, which would add to the Executive members holders of other governmental posts. Such situations were not, of course, without precedent in the wider British system. Enoch Powell, for example, had been Minister of Health in a British Government without having at that time a seat in the Cabinet.

It was, therefore, a massive triumph for Whitelaw to be able to announce on 21 November 1973 a successful outcome to the Stormont Castle talks, and in particular a conditional agreement to form an Executive. However, the coping stone of the new constitutional edifice would be a further conference in December in which the British Government would meet with the Irish Government and the three potential Executive partners to define the nature of an 'Irish dimension'. The SDLP would not settle on the basis of power-sharing alone. Only when satisfied about the nature and extent of the 'Irish dimension' would it be willing to take the final step of joining the Alliance and the Faulkner unionists in the new executive Government of Northern Ireland.

Yet behind this apparent triumph there lay worrying possibilities of ultimate failure. The voice of twenty-six unionist members (including eight from Faulkner's own party) had not been heard at the Castle talks. The unwillingness of these interests to participate constructively could not take away from the hard reality that one of the main pillars of the potential coalition was showing deep cracks. The principal responsibility for accepting the idea of executive functions for a new Council of Ireland must primarily rest with Faulkner and his colleagues, and in my later examination of unionist behaviour over the years I shall address this difficult question in detail. The SDLP was a vigorous *demandeur* and it could well have been the case that a refusal on the unionist side to contemplate executive functions would have prevented settlement. Nevertheless Whitelaw, as the active chairman of the Castle talks, should perhaps have been more conscious of the possible, even probable, reaction to such a far-reaching departure from previous unionist positions.

A further potentially grave mistake, which could well have torn open the new institutions if they had ever reached the open sea, was to allow the possible coalition partners to work out a programme for government which was little better than a self-indulgent wish-list, evidently incapable of being funded without Treasury generosity of unparalleled and unlikely proportions.

To this point, while of course reporting regularly to the relevant Cabinet committee, Whitelaw himself had been very much in the lead, although a visit by his chilly Prime Minister had shown him to be in 'holy awe' of Heath, a headstrong and excessively self-confident politician with many talents but few friends. At this crucial point in Northern Ireland's affairs, with what became known as the 'Sunningdale Conference' impending and with the final stages of the painstaking political process in sight, Heath took the extraordinary step of moving Whitelaw from the Northern Ireland Office to the Department of Employment. His translation was a compliment to his negotiating skills, deployed in succession as Chief Whip, Leader of the House of Commons and Northern Ireland Secretary. For Heath the principal problem on his agenda was now the deteriorating industrial situation and conflicts with the miners and other unions. It was very difficult to believe, though, that the politician who had gained a real insight into the attitudes of Northern Ireland politicians and parties could not have been spared to finish the task. Nor was this to be the last time that the excessively low priority accorded to progress in Northern Ireland was to be illustrated, in that at a later time Douglas Hurd was to be moved to the Home Office after only a year in Northern Ireland and only weeks away from the promulgation of the Anglo-Irish Agreement.

The consequence of Heath's ill-considered and deeply disadvantageous manoeuvre was to thrust into the forefront of the Sunningdale negotiations the Prime Minister himself, with a largely unprepared and uninformed new Secretary of State, Frances Pym, in attendance, and with the Rottweiler characteristics of the formidable PUS of the Northern Ireland Office, Frank Cooper, in support. Faulkner and his colleagues came under heavy pressure to agree from start to finish, and reluctantly signed up to a communiqué on 9 December riddled with ambiguities and exposing Faulkner to enormous danger of abandonment by his already limited support.

To have the faintest chance of selling the Sunningdale Agreement, Faulkner had to be able to claim some gains as well as admitting some concessions. He hoped to be able to claim de facto if not de jure recognition of Northern Ireland's constitutional position within the United Kingdom, and to point to the prospect of effective new cooperation between Northern Ireland and the Republic in combating terrorism. The alleged immunities of the IRA in using the Republic as a sanctuary, training ground and advanced base for operations within Northern Ireland were deeply resented within the unionist community. The notional gains claimed on these two crucial fronts soon proved to be worthless. So far apart had been the British and Irish positions on the status of Northern Ireland that it had been impossible to agree any form of words which would represent an agreed position; hence a quite extraordinary passage in the Sunningdale communiqué in which the separate positions were set out in parallel side by side. The problem of 'fugitive offenders' had presented such legal complexity that it had been kicked into touch by remission to a Joint Law Commission, which would take many months at best to reach any conclusion. The ambiguity of the 'constitutional reassurance' effectively devalued it as a weapon in Faulkner's political armoury, in the light in particular of a constitutional suit brought in the Republic by Kevin Boland (which is more fully discussed later), while the delay in addressing the complex issue of extradition left unresolved upon the table the emotive matter of fugitive offenders.

The next major impact of British Government decisions occurred with the calling of a General Election on the question of 'Who governs Britain', as industrial action by or in sympathy with the striking miners bit more deeply into the national economy. It would be expecting too much of any British Government to rate the possible impact upon Northern Ireland as a paramount factor in its electoral considerations. Nevertheless this election, held on 28 February 1974, could not have come at a worse time for a weakened power-sharing Executive. With the outright rejection by the Ulster Unionist Council of the proposed Council of Ireland, and the consequent resignation of Brian Faulkner from the leadership of the UUP on 7 January, the head of the new Executive and Administration had to rely upon the support of those of his followers ready to join him in a new Unionist Party of Northern Ireland. There was growing difficulty in convincing members of the unionist community that there had been a balanced agreement, with gains as well as losses or concessions. Meanwhile the opponents of the Faulkner line within unionism had got its act well and truly together, with the UUP (now led by Harry West as Faulkner's successor), the DUP (led by Ian Paisley) and the so-called Vanguard Unionists (led by Bill Craig) forming a coalition in opposition to the Sunningdale Agreement. The outcome was that, at the February General Election, supporters of the Faulkner line saw themselves opposed by a slate of agreed United Ulster Unionist Coalition (UUUC) candidates. Fears and suspicions of the proposed Council of Ireland as an all-Ireland Government in embryo were skilfully exploited, notably with its emotive posters claiming that Dublin was 'just a Sunningdale away'.

The outcome of the election was to be calamitous from the pro-Sunningdale point of view. Candidates representing the parties of the UUUC polled more than 50 per cent of all the votes cast, as against a 13.1 per cent share for the pro-agreement unionists. With the exception of West Belfast (where Gerry Fitt retained a seat for the SDLP), all the twelve Northern Ireland constituencies returned UUUC candidates. Many of the most prominent personalities in the UUP, who had remained loyal to Faulkner, were swept away in the electoral holocaust: Stanley McMaster, Rafton Pounder, Roy Bradford. The relatively 'smooth' men of the pre-1974 cadre were replaced by a more abrasive generation.

Not only had the General Election further (and some would say irretrievably) undermined the prospects for the new power-sharing Executive, but also it had also swept away the governing party at Westminster, with Harold Wilson and Merlyn Rees replacing Edward Heath and Frances Pym as Prime Minister and Secretary of State for Northern Ireland.

Wilson himself was regarded from the outset as better disposed to the nationalist than to the unionist community. The influence of the Irish vote, both nationally and in his own constituency, was widely known, and in November 1971 – in a speech to the House of Commons as Leader of the Opposition – he had at one and the same time accepted the need for agreement to change from the people of Northern Ireland, but nevertheless canvassed the possibility of a Constitutional Commission to work out arrangements for a united Ireland, to come into being fifteen years after agreement and the ending of political violence. Such a suggestion took little account of the certainty that any unionist leader agreeing to take part in such a Commission would inevitably be overthrown.

On the face of it the new British Government came into office fully supportive of the Sunningdale Agreement and of the power-sharing Executive. They must, though, have been deeply concerned by the evidence in the General Election results that support was crumbling to an extent which called into question, pragmatically if not legally, the validity of the Faulkner mandate. After all – and while there are problems in comparing elections held under different electoral systems – the support given to pro-Faulkner unionist candidates had fallen from 29.3 per cent of the first preference votes cast at the June 1973 Assembly Elections to 13.1 per cent of the votes cast at the February 1974 General Election.

Within the Northern Ireland Executive, Faulkner and his unionist colleagues had become increasingly persuaded that, unless some of the Sunningdale baggage could be thrown overboard, the Executive vessel would be swamped by a tidal wave of resistance. He sought to persuade his coalition partners – particularly in the SDLP – that a Council of Ireland should not assume executive functions or responsibilities without a further 'test of opinion', by General Election or otherwise. This was a very bitter pill for the SDLP to swallow, but its Executive members included enough realists to persuade them that this deferment option should be put to the wider membership of their Assembly party. On first consideration, the Assembly Party were disposed to reject the proposition, but were persuaded to change their minds through a critical intervention by Merlyn Rees's deputy, Stanley Orme, whose impeccable pro-nationalist credentials well equipped him for this tricky role. His was a brave, constructive and realistic effort in the very difficult circumstances.

However, while all this agonising was going on, the opponents of Sunningdale were getting into place for a final push against the Agreement. Introduced by the anti-Agreement unionist, John Laird, the Assembly began an acrimonious and prolonged debate on a motion to renegotiate the Sunningdale Agreement. It was, of course, obvious from the start that this motion would be defeated, since the Faulkner loyalists together with the SDLP and Alliance Party members of the Assembly still constituted a secure overall majority in the chamber; and on 14 May, the Executive duly won the Assembly vote on Sunningdale by forty-four votes to twenty-eight.

The following day, however, opened a new and dangerous phase of events. In the immediate aftermath of the vote a previously shadowy body calling itself the Ulster Workers' Council (UWC) had threatened power cuts as a form of protest. On the following day, 15 May, this protest began to take effect. There were extensive power cuts, imposed by loyalist elements in key generating installations, and a widespread withdrawal of labour from other enterprises, either because they had no power to operate, their workers or some of them unreservedly supported the protest action or, if still willing to work, they were prevented or dissuaded from doing so by 'picketing' or intimidation, whether at the exits to housing estates or at the entrance to places of work.

It is important to appreciate the nature of the central direction of what soon came to be called 'the UWC Strike'. A coordinating committee was chaired by Vanguard Unionist Assemblyman Glenn Barr, alongside other politicians in Bill Craig, Ian Paisley and Harry West, the leaders of Vanguard, the DUP and the UUP respectively. They were joined, however, by a number of representatives of loyalist paramilitary organisations, including the Ulster Defence Association (UDA) and Ulster Volunteer Force (UVF). There can be little doubt that paramilitary elements decided upon direct action, and that the mainline opposition politicians had come on board to simulate some impression of being in control.

What we are concerned with here is the reaction of the British Government to these developments. It had assumed the 'law and order' powers of the old Northern Ireland Government, leaving its successors incapable of sustaining their own position through forces under their control or influence. The Executive might well fall at any time, through divisions or defections within its own ranks; indeed, the great difficulty in persuading the SDLP to go slow on a Council of Ireland had strikingly illustrated its fragility. Within the unionist camp remaining loyal to Faulkner, there was some growing concern about the credibility of its mandate, because of course Faulkner had gained support in the 1973 Assembly elections without the electorate having the chance to express a judgement on a settlement still to come, with its precise power-sharing arrangements and 'Irish dimension'. The much more recent test of opinion represented by the General Election had shown a conclusive rejection of the Sunningdale terms within the unionist community. There had been those, even in 1973, who, while sympathetic to reform, had argued that it would be prudent to put any comprehensive agreement to the people by referendum. That, of course, would in itself have raised complex questions. Should the settlement require the ratification of a simple majority or predetermined percentage of those actually voting, or those eligible to vote? The Border Poll, after all, had demonstrated vulnerability to boycott in the interests of undermining a result. Should the settlement require ratification in each 'community', as well as overall majority support? If so, how would a 'community' be defined, and would such a device require separate electoral rolls? It might be observed here that there is national and international precedent for polling within a community which distinguishes itself, for example in the United States through registering as a Democrat or Republican, or indeed in the British Conservative Party through formal party membership. There is, however, plenty of current evidence, in the context of the Belfast Agreement, that a favourable vote at a referendum is not in every case a shield against later withdrawal of support. Voters may feel they have been led to support a particular proposition on the basis of ambiguities subsequently clarified in a sense antipathetic to their interests, or against the background of unfulfilled promises or expectations of future developments.

There were, therefore, solid reasons for scepticism as to whether the Executive could long survive. On the other hand, despite its all-too-evident weaknesses and deficiencies, it was the lawful Government of Northern Ireland within the ambit of its own powers. Although, under the Northern Ireland Constitution Act 1973, no Administration failing to cross the line of communal division could have been appointed, the member parties had entered of their own free will and on the basis of agreements reached between them. No new Government anywhere could be expected to produce positive results, encouraging to those who had supported it, within a few short months of appointment; and the Executive represented not just the test of a new Government but the test of a new system. True, there was evidence of widespread opposition amongst the electorate; but a Westminster Government does not resign if, early in its life, local government or other elections show a marked swing of the pendulum away from its policies. Above all, what was at issue here was not whether the Executive would necessarily survive in the longer term. It was rather whether a democratically elected Government in a part of the United Kingdom, constructed with great care and effort by the previous Conservative Government, could be seen to be brought down by demi-constitutional means or worse. Faulkner, on resigning office as Northern Ireland's last Prime Minister, had expressed anxiety that violent means could be seen to pay. A collapse of the Executive in the face of intimidation and extra-parliamentary pressures was likely to have at least two extremely unfortunate consequences: all across the community the 'hard men', the men with paramilitary muscle, would learn the message that the British Government could be made to bow the knee; in the nationalist community in particular, it would become easier for republican militants to spread the message that political negotiations, concessions and agreements could be a waste of time – that any useful movement would ultimately be blocked by unionist intransigence and British indifference.

Of course at the outset of the strike, and under strong pressure from employers and trade unions not to give ground, the Northern Ireland Office mouthed appropriate phrases of condemnation of the unacceptable methods of the UWC, and of determination to support and uphold the lawfully constituted Executive. Little was done, and that little far too late, to back up such words. There can be little doubt that the forceful Lieutenant General Sir Frank King, who had been GOC (Northern Ireland) since February 1973, was both anxious about a potential war on two fronts, and extremely dubious about the use of military power against widely supported civilian action. He was indeed to say later, after leaving Northern Ireland, that 'if you get a large section of the population which is bent on a particular course then it is a difficult thing to stop them taking that course'. King's view is certainly not to be lightly dismissed; he was no soft touch but a tough and resolute commander. Yet the security forces – obliged at that time to take their lead from the Army – would certainly have responded to a clear Government direction to take no nonsense. Here, questions of personality and attitude are important. Merlyn Rees, the most likeable and honest of men, was inhibited by humanitarian instincts and an inbuilt irresolution. Few such inhibitions were to deter Roy Mason as Secretary of State in 1977 when faced with an attempt to rerun the 1974 strike. While this was certainly mounted by a weaker coalition and in much less promising circumstances, its early collapse resulted in no small degree from firm and resolute action from the outset against those preventing law-abiding citizens from going about their legitimate business. A damning indictment of Government inaction is implied in Glenn Barr's later admission of astonishment at the lack of opposition offered to the strike in its earliest days. It is by no means the case that it enjoyed overwhelming support at the outset. But when people see that no credible effort is made to protect their travel to work, and that de facto authority to provide fuel and other vital services and supplies has passed into hands outside Government, support for lawful authority can rapidly ebb away. A critical compact, under which citizens bow to the authority of Government but in turn expect its protection, is then dangerously fractured.

The gross error of flaccid inaction was soon to be magnified by another. The Executive leaders, who had taken grave personal as well as political risks in the attempt to find a way forward, appealed directly to Prime Minister Harold Wilson for maximum support in restoring vital services. His reaction was to proceed with the notorious television address of 25 May, in which he used emotive language about people in Northern Ireland 'sponging on Westminster'. It is, perhaps, sufficient commentary upon this ill-timed diatribe to note that subsequently every one of those known to be Wilson's regular speech writers denied having any part in it. Apparently vigorous words were used to cover the fact that Wilson and his Government had done pitifully little to sustain the Executive. Thus the only bridge so far thrown across the communal abyss in Northern Ireland – a fragile and ramshackle structure admittedly – was allowed to fall into the torrent with the collapse of the Executive on 28 May.

CHAPTER FOUR

The British dimension: from the collapse of power-sharing to the Anglo-Irish Agreement of 1985

From that point in 1974 the story of the British Government's role must take account of a number of further developments: the nature of successive efforts made to restore devolved Governments to Northern Ireland; the methods used to combat ongoing violence resulting from both republican and loyalist terrorists; and the nature of the dialogue – whether one terms it 'exchange of information' or 'negotiation' – conducted at first covertly and then overtly between the British Government or its representatives and the mouthpieces of terrorism.

Successive British Governments were to seek by a variety of means to move the local political parties towards a new agreement on future political structures, but also considered at times 'unboycottable' measures which could move the political process forward. Here some basic realities must be spelled out. Any machinery of government requiring for its operation a direct participation of locally elected people must, to succeed initially and prove stable thereafter, enjoy the willing support of local parties on terms with which their electorate can live, either enthusiastically or with a degree of reluctance. By 1974 it was quite clear to me that nationalist opinion would never again accept a system under which unionists alone exercised executive power, even if inhibited by extensive safeguards and protections against abuse. Anything resembling a Cabinet in Northern Ireland would have to embody both nationalist and unionist elements, and it followed from this that any route blocked by either interest would prove a cul-de-sac. Faced by the propensity of one party or another not merely to veto progress but to withhold participation from negotiations to achieve it, one could expect from time to time a strong desire to present the local parties with a fait accompli achieved behind their backs or over their heads, if need be in direct negotiations between the British and Irish Governments. As we shall see, the Anglo-Irish Agreement of 1985 was the product of just such impatience, and of the quest for an 'unboycottable' way to make progress. But in truth such steps were likely to prove at worst harmful and at best palliative; real and enduring progress in a divided Northern Ireland could only be obtained by the willingness of local parties to work together. This necessarily raised the question whether all parties would have to be involved. This would bring some very strange bedfellows together, well beyond the compass of any voluntary coalition around the world. How much support, though, did a faction need if it was ready to paralyse an unacceptable system rather than serve within it or accept a role as 'loyal opposition'?

Successive Secretaries of State were to use subtly different mechanisms to promote the political progress they sought. In the aftermath of the Executive's collapse Merlyn Rees, influenced by what he saw as a growing 'Ulster nationalism', decided that the best framework would be provided by a political convention bringing together locally elected people under a local chairman. The chairman chosen for this sensitive and difficult task was to be the widely respected Lord Chief Justice of Northern Ireland, Sir Robert (later Lord) Lowry, who stepped aside from his duties at the head of the local judiciary while the work of the Convention proceeded in 1975–76.

In spite of Lowry's admirable qualities, his selection may have been a mistake. The widely divided parties were, on all past form, unlikely to come together without some vigorous pushing. Lowry, who had come from the Bench and fully intended to return to it (as indeed he did) must have had to be careful about taking on too vigorously political a role as Convention chairman. He could more readily be chairman and facilitator than *animateur*. Fortunately he had available two thoughtful and ingenious civil servants in the persons of Dr John Oliver and Maurice Hayes, but they too had to be careful about the nature of their involvement.

The great surprise of the Convention was the stance adopted by Bill Craig. A hard-line opponent to O'Neill, Chichester-Clark and Faulkner, the founder of Vanguard and a key figure in the UUUC, he had headed the poll in East Belfast at the Convention election of 1 May 1975. Here the parties of the UUUC commanded more than 54 per cent of the first preference votes (as against 7.7 per cent for Faulkner's Unionist Party of Northern Ireland (UPNI). It was, then, a wholly unexpected development when Craig floated the idea of a voluntary coalition, including the SDLP, to hold office for a limited period in countering the current emergency. In making this suggestion, he drew a clear distinction between institutionalised or imposed 'power-sharing' and the option open to democratic parties in any country to come together voluntarily to confront a national crisis. However, Craig's bold and unexpected démarche failed to gain support not only from the UUUC partners, the UUP and the DUP, but also from the Vanguard members elected to the Convention. In these circumstances, any hope of an early accommodation between unionism and nationalism as represented by the SDLP faded, leading to the failure of the Convention, which was wound up in 1976.

Craig, it has to be said, had always been one of the most interesting if enigmatic figures within unionism. He had been a crucial player in securing the premiership for O'Neill in 1963 and a forward-looking Minister of Development, but his later transition to Home Affairs had brought out his more authoritarian and unyielding qualities, while the Vanguard movement at full flood had taken on a militaristic and threatening posture. Yet Craig's appeal had been shown by his ability to attract into Vanguard people like David Trimble or Reg Empey, who were later to seek to lead unionism in a new direction.

Although Roy Mason, who was to become Secretary of State in September 1976, was to undertake some exploratory discussions with the local parties, he was not persuaded that any push for devolution could succeed in the existing atmosphere, and therefore concentrated primarily upon security measures and the strengthening of the Northern Ireland economy. In the latter field the major apparent breakthrough achieved by the Mason regime was the attraction to West Belfast of the De Lorean motor project, which was seen as likely to build confidence amongst the small Catholic community in the wish and ability of Government to serve their interests. Unhappily this saga was to end in ultimate disillusionment.

As the prospects of a General Election approached once again, the leading influence in developing Conservative policy for Northern Ireland was Airey Neave, barrister, Colditz escapee and close confidant of Margaret Thatcher. He had begun to dismiss any revival of the power-sharing formula as outside the realm of practical politics, and to favour in its place the transfer of substantial powers to elected local government bodies in the form of new 'regional councils'. It is certainly the case that any attempt to introduce this scheme would have met outright opposition from the SDLP. Many of the past injustices from which their adherents had suffered had been laid at the door of local rather than regional (or Stormont) Governments. Even if they were to win control of one or more of the hypothetical new councils, they foresaw the possibility of submitting a great many of their supporters to unionist dominance at local level. Whether they would have carried their antipathy to the point of boycotting Council elections must be a matter of speculation, but it certainly could not be ruled out. However, on 30 March 1979, little more than a month before the impending General Election, Neave himself was killed by a car bomb as he drove his vehicle out of the House of Commons car park. Subsequently the Irish National Liberation Army (INLA), a militant republican group distinct from PIRA, was to claim responsibility for this assassination. In these painful circumstances the office of Secretary of State went not to Airey Neave but to a former Chief Whip, Humphrey

Atkins (later Lord Colnbrook). Atkins was one of those physically attractive figures, reminding one in his case of a former juvenile lead in the West End, who were from time to time shown partiality by Margaret Thatcher. His arrival was greeted with general surprise in Northern Ireland and he never quite recovered from an early designation as 'Humphrey Who?'. In the event he did not rush to introduce the Neave plan or to launch any high-profile political initiative. Between January and March 1980 he summoned the local parties to attend a constitutional conference, but in a familiar ploy one of the main parties – on this occasion the UUP – refused to play ball, sensing no doubt a shelving of the Neave plan to which they had been sympathetic. For many unionists, an extension of local powers under the overall umbrella of direct rule was to remain more attractive than a restoration of devolved government on terms antipathetic to their electorate. The subsequent meetings of the DUP, SDLP and Alliance in Conference produced no useful result. As a fall-back position Atkins canvassed the idea of an appointed advisory council, formed from Members of Parliament, MEPs and other elected representatives, but this idea too came to nothing in a deteriorating security situation.

In any event, much of Atkins' time as Secretary of State was preoccupied by the enormous problems in the so-called 'H Blocks' at the Maze Prison. Although the 'special category' status unwisely created by William Whitelaw in 1972 had been progressively phased out in terms of the newly convicted, by mid-1978 the number still enjoying that status was around 800, and a crunch came with a decision to move prisoners from the compounds to the new cell blocks. A protest which began with a refusal to wear prison clothing (the 'blanket protest') escalated into a refusal to wash or use toilets (the 'dirty protest') and finally into a refusal to take food (the 'hunger strike'). A first phase of this ultimate form of protest, begun on 27 October, came to an end on 18 December 1980 without the death of any prisoner and after efforts to persuade the involved prisoners to accept that they would be treated reasonably.

However, the 'hunger strike' broke out again on 1 March 1981, amidst accusations of bad faith, and led between then and 20 August to the slow deaths by self-inflicted starvation of ten republican prisoners, beginning with Bobby Sands. Throughout the strike, great domestic and international pressures were brought to bear upon the British Government – by the SDLP, by the Irish Government, by the Catholic Church and by various international organisations – to make concessions sufficient to bring the protest to an end. Such arguments carried little weight with Margaret Thatcher, who saw the concession of anything resembling political status as utterly unacceptable. This rigorous defence of principle in defiance of pragmatic common sense was to have the most profoundly damaging consequences. An April 1981 by-election to Parliament, won by the 'hunger strike' leader Bobby Sands, was followed by a further by-election in August after the death of Sands, with a return of his former election agent Owen Carron. These developments illustrated the huge boost given to the political fortunes of Provisional Sinn Fein (PSF). Now the martyrs of the hunger strike had won their places alongside the heroes of the Easter Rising in Irish martyrology. Significantly it was only after the strike was brought to an end, largely by the pressure of prisoners' relatives, that James Prior as Humphrey Atkins' successor felt able to announce that all prisoners would be allowed to wear their own clothing at all times. Thereafter, no one could doubt the formidable resolution and commitment of a movement where members would rather die than accept defeat on what they believed to be a point of principle. This willingness to die was matched by an utterly ruthless willingness to kill – often indiscriminately – for 'the cause'.

James Prior had succeeded Atkins as Secretary of State in September 1981. By this appointment, Northern Ireland was plunged into the maelstrom of the Conservative Party's internal politics. Although Margaret Thatcher had spoken quite openly of her determination to have in her Cabinet colleagues who would accept her lead and avoid arguments around the Cabinet table, she did not yet feel quite sure enough to put the leading personalities amongst the socio-economic 'wets' to the sword. Prior was a heavy hitter, a 'big beast of the jungle' and a potential handful if pushed out on to the back-benches. One cannot help recalling President Lyndon Johnson's celebrated adage that it was better to have an awkward customer 'inside the tent pissing out, than outside the tent pissing in'. Prior came to Northern Ireland reluctantly (and was unwise enough, in terms of his credibility there, not to conceal it), and resenting his obvious exclusion, in spite of continuing membership of important Cabinet committees, from the centre of economic decision-making, where hitherto he had been making a contribution as Employment Secretary. Not only had Prior accepted his 'exile' with ill grace, but he had struck a hard bargain for going moderately quietly, including an unusual degree of choice in his own subordinate Ministers at the Northern Ireland Office, and a relatively free hand to govern Northern Ireland as he thought best, whether from the constitutional, economic or social point of view. Thus Prior was able to build up an exceptionally able team at the Northern Ireland Office, including in Lord (Gray) Gowrie and in John Patten two future Cabinet Ministers, as well as Nicholas Scott, who would certainly have reached that level in a political environment more welcoming of his liberal views. It was, however, an observable phenomenon of the Thatcher era that the Prime Minister herself could, without apparent discomfort, detach herself from the activities of her own Ministers and subvert their efforts by ill-disguised snorts of disapproval behind the scenes. However, a leading political figure like Prior, still at that stage a conceivable candidate for his party's leadership in other circumstances, was not willing to be characterised as a mere caretaker in Northern Ireland. By temperament and by conviction he wished to move things forward. After initial soundings had warned him off the notion of an appointed local administration, he embraced an idea initially propounded by Brian Mawhinney, the Conservative MP for Peterborough. The point has already been made that an Ulsterman could arrive in the House of Commons as a member of a governing party only if he had been selected by a constituency in Great Britain. Mawhinney was just such a rare bird. A son of the Royal Belfast Academical Institution (the alma mater of Sir Robert Lowry and many others in positions of prominence in Northern Ireland) – and a graduate of Queen's University, Belfast, Mawhinney's subsequent studies and work had taken him first to the United States and then on to England, where he had become active in Conservative politics.

It was Mawhinney, who had played an active role in his party's back-bench Northern Ireland Committee, who had first formulated an idea which came to be called 'rolling devolution'. Under proposals now brought forward by Prior, there would be elections to yet another Northern Ireland Assembly. This Assembly would have a dual capability. In the first place, it would have a consultative and scrutinising role, with the ability to call before it representatives of Northern Ireland Departments for examination as witnesses. While carrying on in this mode, the Assembly would also have the potential to act as a constitutional convention, seeking 'cross-community' support to return to local control some or all, in a single phase or in successive phases, of the powers and functions exercised by a Secretary of State under direct rule. Unhappily the absence of adequate cross-community support for the initiative itself diminished the prospects of making progress within it. For the first time in Northern Ireland's history, members of PSF put themselves forward for election to a Northern Ireland body, in a move designed to test and demonstrate the extent of their support, but both they and the SDLP made it clear in advance that members elected would not take their seats in the new Assembly. Nor had Prior found it easy to drive the enabling legislation through the Commons. The Secretary of State had faced a filibuster from a group of right-wing Conservative members, and the Prime Minister herself could not be said to have rushed enthusiastically to Prior's aid. In the election itself, on 20 October 1982, PSF polled 10.1 per cent of the first preference votes. Largely as a consequence of this, the SDLP won five fewer seats than it had held in the 1973 Assembly and three fewer than in the 1975 Convention.

How cross-community support could be won within a framework from which the SDLP and PSF would both be absent was indeed a conundrum. Heartened by Margaret Thatcher's agreement with Taoiseach Charles Haughey to set up an Anglo-Irish Intergovernmental Council, reached at Downing Street in November 1981, the SDLP was more keen than ever to resist a purely 'internal solution', without a substantial 'Irish dimension', and after the elections was further stimulated by the hot breath of PSF at the back of its neck. Thus only fifty-nine members out of the seventy-eight elected attended the first meeting of the 1982 Assembly, and as it proceeded the UUP also took extended periods of absence from its work in protest against this or that, either within the Assembly or the wider world outside. Only the DUP and Alliance members both took their seats and were present throughout. Between its first sitting and its eventual dissolution in June 1986 the Assembly, given its evident handicaps and disadvantages, produced some useful and responsible work on issues of ongoing Government business, but proved wholly incapable of producing any scheme for movement to or towards devolution likely to gain real cross-community support.

We must now pause to consider the developments of the so-called 'Irish dimension', which has loomed so large alongside 'power-sharing' since the then Government's discussion paper of 1972.

Largely at the behest of John Hume, who had become an articulate exponent of the need for an agreed nationalist strategy, the Irish Government had established a New Ireland Forum, first meeting in May 1983, to examine the possibility of an agreed approach to a Northern Ireland settlement, although in inviting views from any quarter, the Forum and its architects must have known perfectly well that no unionist party would take part. Historically, unionism had always rejected interference by the Irish Government in the domestic affairs of Northern Ireland, and had regarded the constitutional position of Northern Ireland within the United Kingdom, guaranteed by successive United Kingdom legislation and declarations by British Governments, as not open to any negotiation. The parties of unionism had not yet come to grips with the corollary of 'no change without consent', which was, of course, 'change in the event of consent'.

Thus it was that the Forum brought together only parties of nationalist Ireland: Fianna Fail, Fine Gael, the Irish Labour Party and the SDLP. From the outset this initiative was viewed with disfavour by the British Government. Not only Mrs Thatcher herself, whose basic instincts were fundamentally unionist and British nationalist, but also James Prior, who did not warm greatly to many of the unionist politicians, saw the Forum initiative as a distraction from efforts to promote a home-grown solution. Thus one had running in parallel an all-Ireland search for a solution in the absence of unionists, and an Assembly search for a solution in the absence of nationalists.

In its ultimate report the New Ireland Forum discussed four options for a new all-Ireland Constitution. At the strong insistence of Charles Haughey, now out of office but still the powerful leader of Fianna Fail, the report expressed a clear preference for a unitary thirty-two county state, but also canvassed the further options of a federal arrangement and joint authority over Northern Ireland to be exercised by the British and Irish Governments together. Although the report went on to express an openness to 'other views which may contribute to political development', unionist reaction was understandably focused on the preference for a unitary state and the prospect of alternative options as mere staging posts en route to that objective. Moreover, in its analysis of the underlying political, historical, cultural and socio-economic background, the Forum had signally failed to take adequate cognisance of strong arguments advanced by economists that it would be financially impossible for a unitary Irish state to maintain existing standards of public services in Northern Ireland. And although the report was charged with concern to preserve the rights and distinctive ethos of the Protestant and unionist majority in Northern Ireland (and prospective minority in a united Ireland), it appeared to characterise that ethos as 'Protestant' rather than British.

It is true that the unionists' sense of their own identity has at times been confused and ambiguous. Certainly there are some who see the British connection as 'a means to an end' – that end being the maintenance of a Protestant hegemony – rather than an end in itself. But for many others the connection with 'Britain' had a wider significance, as illustrated by loyal and willing service to the British state both in peace and in war. Increasingly the case was to be argued, even by those who accepted the principle of consent, that the strong links between nationalists in Northern Ireland and fellow Irishmen in the Republic must receive adequate institutional recognition. One did not often hear the corollary which was that, in a different electoral situation affecting ultimate sovereignty, the links of Ulster unionists with fellow-citizens of Great Britain could not just be dismissed and erased from memory.

Of course the nationalist parties were failing to recognise or acknowledge another characteristic of unionism. Perhaps only the South African Afrikaaner had a comparable sense of God-given mission. Of all communities, they were amongst the least likely to yield to duress. The New Ireland Forum was inevitably seen as nationalist Ireland 'ganging up' against them. The inevitable reaction fostered an inbuilt laager mentality.

We are, however, concerned here primarily with the British Government's reaction to the work of the Forum. Thatcher had initially got on surprisingly well with Haughey, whose feline skills, accompanied by the gift of a silver teapot, had been used to good effect. It was, after all, with him that she had agreed in December 1980 to review 'the totality of relationships between the two countries', leading to the setting up of the Intergovernmental Council already referred to.

Yet her attitude was inconsistent to the brink of schizophrenia, given her robust declaration in July 1982 that 'no commitment exists for HM Government to consult the Irish Government on matters affecting Northern Ireland'. With the Irish reaction to the occupation of the Falklands and the subsequent war to recover the islands, which was deemed deeply 'wet' and unhelpful by Mrs Thatcher, Haughey totally lost his charms for her. In the event it was to be his successor as Taoiseach, Garret FitzGerald of Fine Gael, who undertook the task of moving forward from the report of the New Ireland Forum. A meeting for that purpose held at Chequers in November 1984, was, on the face of it, wholly unproductive. At a news conference which followed it, Margaret Thatcher characterised the three options (in the process showing some confusion about what they actually were) as 'out, out, out'. The courteous and affable FitzGerald reacted to this brusque dismissal with some bitterness.

We were, however, about to witness a strange phenomenon: the conversion of a triple negative into an affirmative. What occurred between the apparent outright rejection of November 1984 and the conclusion of the Anglo-Irish Agreement in 1985, clearly reversing the policy of 'no commitment to consultation with the Irish Government on matters affecting Northern Ireland' enunciated as recently as July 1982?

Since the 1985 Agreement is widely (and rightly) regarded as a most significant turning point in the relationship between Britain and Ireland, and between north and south in Ireland, it is important to analyse how that turning point was reached, before examining the question of whether (as its negotiators certainly claimed) it represented a huge step forward, or on the other hand was likely to be counter-productive in the longer run.

So what, then, were the influences bearing upon Britain's formidable and strong-minded Prime Minister? Until the day of his death Enoch Powell, who had a weighty and some would say malign influence upon the Ulster Unionist leadership, saw the hand of the United States behind every move detrimental to the unionist cause, linking it to a supposed American plan to bring Ireland fully into the NATO ambit. These fanciful notions greatly exaggerated the potential strategic importance of Ireland in the modern world. What was true, however, was that no American President could wholly ignore the persistent drumbeat of the Irish-American lobby. While this lobby was stronger and more influential within the Democratic Party, the Republican

President Ronald Reagan was nevertheless himself the great-grandson of an Irish famine immigrant. For her part, Margaret Thatcher, deeply suspicious of European federalists and their machinations, and endlessly in conflict with her European community 'partners', saw the core of Britain's foreign policy interests as lying within the political, military and intelligence alliance with America. Ideologically, Thatcher and Ronald Reagan were soulmates.

On his visit to Ireland in 1984, Reagan spoke favourably of the New Ireland Forum initiative, while in the House of Representatives the influential Speaker, 'Tip' O'Neill, was a strong advocate of a forward line by the United States on Irish issues. At a meeting in Washington in December 1984, Thatcher became conscious for the first time of real American pressure to achieve a breakthrough, coupled with a readiness to be involved constructively in the economic regeneration of Northern Ireland in a more favourable situation.

Alongside this, important elements within the Whitehall bureaucracy had become convinced of the need for a new approach to the Northern Ireland problem, which was proving so costly in so many senses. There were no realistic hopes that the all-unionist Assembly would now come forward with any constitutional proposals likely to command widespread acceptance. Much of the momentum came from the Cabinet Secretary, Sir Robert Armstrong, the ultimate 'insider's insider', and a skilled and experienced diplomat, David Goodall. Armstrong succeeded in persuading the Prime Minister that exploratory talks should be opened with the Irish at official level, with the Irish team led by the honourable and straightforward Dermot Nally, Secretary to the Irish Government. Any negotiating team could not, of course, exclude the Northern Ireland Office under its PUS, Sir Robert Andrew. But the negotiations were in no sense driven by the Northern Ireland Office, although its collective memory enabled it to judge possible reactions in Northern Ireland rather better than any other Department. The hard fact of the matter was that the Northern Ireland Office was a very modest player on the wider field of Whitehall, compared for instance with the Cabinet and Foreign Offices, which were understandably more concerned with wider issues. This disproportion in departmental 'weight' might have been rectified by the 'Get your tanks off my lawn' approach of a Frank Cooper. Sir Robert Andrew was swept along with the tide, albeit with very considerable reservations.

I would have little doubt that initially the Prime Minister's pretty unenthusiastic backing was secured by arguments that terrorism could not be defeated without more whole-hearted cooperation from the Irish Government, that such cooperation could only be secured by a willingness to contemplate certain 'concessions' to the Irish side, and that a wide-ranging political accommodation would be the best bulwark against further electoral successes by Sinn Fein.

It is my opinion, however, that the entire process was deeply flawed. Although it was perfectly clear to everyone that the Irish Government at every stage would be careful to keep in step with John Hume and the SDLP, the British Government accepted no matching obligation to keep unionist parties in touch. Not only were these politicians distanced from the process (at least until a stage when they could only have compromised themselves by involvement), but also non-political members of the Northern Ireland Civil Service who might, if consulted, have been able at least to point out some obvious pitfalls, were also kept at a distance. There could be some rationale for this exclusion, in that a senior member of the Northern Ireland Civil Service could be disadvantaged in relating to any future devolved government by implication in controversial negotiations. I am not, though, myself convinced that such considerateness was the real rationale. The involvement in the crucial discussions about the future of Northern Ireland, both of the Northern Ireland Office PUS and its Deputy Secretary, threw into rather stark relief the exclusion of the Second PUS (a position held by the Head of the Northern Ireland Civil Service). There was, one felt, an inference that one could not wholly be trusted to be objective; coupled, perhaps, with the fear that one might offer inconvenient advice if afforded the opportunity to give it.

There was a wider significance to this imbalance. The Irish Government very clearly entered into the talks process as the champion of nationalist Ireland. The British Government was not, and could not be, the champion of the unionist interest in Northern Ireland. The consequences of this disparity were to be quite apparent on the face of the ultimate Agreement, which entrenched the Irish Government as the accepted guarantor of nationalist interests, without any balancing reassurance to unionists.

Moreover, one key element soon dropped off the table as the talks proceeded. These discussions were taking place in the context of the existing provisions of the Irish Constitution, Articles 2 and 3 of which could be regarded as representing a real claim to Northern Ireland and as affording some dangerous respectability to forceful methods of fulfilling this national aspiration. I have already pointed out how this issue was sidestepped in the wording of the Sunningdale declaration of September 1973; and it had been amply established in subsequent legal proceedings that well-meaning but ambiguous phrases in a communiqué could not override or replace a constitutional provision. In later exchanges, leading to the Good Friday Agreement, and with the unionist interest directly represented at the table, it was made perfectly clear that the quid pro quo for radical concessions to the nationalist interests must be a clear agreement to seek constitutional amendment. No doubt the British Government pressed this argument on the earlier occasion, but seems to have dropped the matter in the face of an argument by FitzGerald that he could not guarantee a favourable outcome to any referendum to remove the Articles, and that nothing could be more damaging to the wider relationship than a failed attempt to secure amendment through rejection by the people. In this, of course, he may well have been right. Issues of this sort are much more likely to be 'sold' by Fianna Fail, with its republican 'protective colouring', than by someone like 'Garret the Good'.

At all events Margaret Thatcher – I suspect with grave continuing inner reservations – was persuaded to sign the Anglo-Irish Agreement alongside Garret FitzGerald at Hillsborough Castle on 15 November 1985. Then, and subsequently, the negotiators were smugly satisfied that they had accomplished an historic leap forward. With quiet pride some of them were to sport thereafter on occasions an 'AN' (that is to say, Armstrong/Nally) tie, as if they were members of some very prestigious club. And to this day, of course, it is a commonplace to accept the view that the 1985 Agreement was the most significant breakthrough on the road to progress, demonstrating in particular a new and entirely helpful understanding between the British and Irish Governments.

So let us examine more closely the extent to which the Agreement delivered its own known objectives. The negotiators on both sides clearly recognised that any settlement dealing with the Irish dimension alone would be incomplete; that another primary objective must be to foster, encourage or stimulate the creation of domestic political structures within Northern Ireland which could command widespread cross-community support. Those parties which had failed to agree on a home-grown solution through the consultative Assembly were now, it was hoped, to be persuaded by the ingenious drafting of the Anglo-Irish Agreement. At its heart and core was the creation of an Anglo-Irish Intergovernmental Conference, jointly chaired by the Secretary of State for Northern Ireland and the Irish Foreign Minister. Under continuing direct rule it would leave open for discussion within the Conference all aspects of Northern Ireland's affairs; constitutional, political, security-related, social and cultural. If, on the other hand, a devolved Government could be established on a widely acceptable basis, any negotiations with the Republic under the devolved powers would be conducted on the northern side by Ministers in the devolved Administration, with the British Government withdrawing from the process. Unionists detested the Anglo-Irish Agreement, and their detestation was entirely foreseeable (although its extent greatly underestimated by the immediate negotiators). It was the hope that this very detestation would persuade unionists to make concessions to achieve acceptable devolution, since this would withdraw from the hated Conference many of the topics which would otherwise feature on its agenda.

If this was one important objective, it was certainly not realised. The outrage of the unionist parties at the inside track accorded in the negotiating stage to their political opponents was certainly not diminished by the inherently unilateral character of the Agreement's processes. The degree of influence which the Irish Government would henceforth exercise over Northern Ireland business was ambiguous and mysterious. To avoid frightening the horses of unionism, the British Government stressed the essentially consultative nature of the Conference and denied that it had any of the characteristics of 'joint authority'. It would, indeed, be embarrassing to concede that an approach dismissed as 'out' by the Prime Minister comparatively recently was in fact now 'in'. Yet the Agreement entitled the Irish side not only to bring forward views and proposals on a wide range of issues, including the 'modalities' of devolution, the role and composition of important public bodies, security and legal matters and practical economic and social affairs, but also included a pledge that 'determined efforts shall be made ... to resolve any differences'. Did this formula describe consultation plus or joint authority minus? Further mystery was provoked by the establishment at Maryfield near Belfast of a joint Anglo-Irish Secretariat, within which able Irish civil servants could play a shadowy role. Some of these, indeed, had been regular 'travellers' into Northern Ireland well before any right to Irish involvement had been conceded by Government. The British authorities must have been aware of these activities, but had done nothing to check them.

I have earlier made the point that, throughout the negotiations, the Irish Government could and did present itself as the champion of the nationalist interests while the British Government had to adopt an even-handed stance. This unhappy imbalance became all too manifest on the face of the Agreement itself. In considering 'modalities' for devolution, it would be the role of the Irish to propose schemes on behalf of the interests of the minority community. On political matters, the Irish Government put forward proposals on behalf of the minority where major legislation or policy was involved. Thus the Irish Government was to become, in effect, the specific guarantor and champion of the nationalist community in Northern Ireland. It could of course be argued, and was indeed argued by some, that 'there is nothing wrong about the British Government having a special concern for the rights and interests of those who consider themselves British, with the Irish Government having a like concern for those who consider themselves Irish'. Albeit verging upon joint authority, such a balance would have had at least the appearance of equity. As I pointed out in my memoir *Stormont in Crisis* (1994), I felt that 'in a perverse way the Irish adherence to such an agreement would be the antithesis of all that a principled nationalist like Wolfe Tone had stood for: an Ireland in which equal value would be attached to Catholic, Protestant and Dissenter'.

Unlike the Council of Ireland envisaged in the Act of 1920, the later version envisaged at Sunningdale in 1973 or the cross-Border arrangements established under the Good Friday Agreement, the consultative or more than consultative processes of the Anglo-Irish Agreement represented a one-way street. There was an implication that Northern Ireland, unless restrained by Irish Government influence, would be a sink of iniquity and discrimination, whereas the Irish Republic was a sweet-smelling bed of political roses. In the fullness of time, processes of investigation and enquiry were to raise intriguing questions about the political and personal behaviour of some of those afforded an opportunity to pontificate about the supposed iniquities of Northern Ireland.

Far from persuading the unionist parties to resume discussions about devolution, the Agreement had the immediate consequence of totally rupturing all contact between United Kingdom Ministers and the leadership of the unionist parties. As this unhappy breach – reinforced by mass demonstrations and protests – continued, it was perhaps an irony that some of those excluded from the negotiating process were drafted into the frontline trenches when it came to coping with the aftermath. The first faint signs of a thaw were the willingness of Harry West (who had now been succeeded as UUP leader by James Molyneaux) and David McNarry to meet me for some preliminary discussions; thereafter we moved on, with agonising slowness, to exploratory talks between James Molyneaux and Ian Paisley, on the one hand, and senior officials on the other, about the possibility of modifying or replacing the 1985 Agreement. These led in the fullness of time to direct discussions with the Secretary of State, Tom King, who from the start had seen the potential downside of an Agreement already on the brink of completion by his arrival in office.

Two other considerations became impediments to any movement towards devolution by the unionists. At the time of the Agreement's signing, the Northern Ireland Assembly, which was a potential though not realistic vehicle for new constitutional proposals, was still operating, but after the Agreement it turned aside from its moderately useful work of scrutiny to become the vehicle for ever more strident protests against the Agreement. This led to its inevitable dissolution in June 1986. The second consideration was that once again the question of the status of Northern Ireland had been fudged. Article 1 of the Agreement recognised that any change could only occur with the consent of a majority in Northern Ireland; and it further recognised that there was no present wish for change. If, however, a wish for change were to be expressed in the future, this would be given legislative effect. Thus, for the first time, a British Government made explicit the previously implicit corollary of the long-standing affirmation that there would be no change without the consent of the people of Northern Ireland, whether expressed through its Parliament (while that existed) or by the people themselves through referendum. Now, explicitly, if a majority were in the future to indicate a wish for Irish unity, legislation would be introduced to give effect to that wish. Unionists could perhaps accept this if the Irish Government was truly committing itself to the 'consent principle'. Thoughtful unionists, however, had long memories about the consequences of the 'Boland' case in 1974, and suspected that the consent apparently given by the Irish Government had no validity in its own constitutional law. The brothers Christopher and Michael McGimpsey, leading members of the UUP, sought to resolve the confusion by taking this issue to the Irish courts in 1988. Such legal processes are liable to be protracted in any jurisdiction, particularly in one such as Ireland with a written Constitution. However, the ultimate judgement, given in the Supreme Court of Ireland in March 1990, could hardly have been more embarrassing to those who presented Article 1 of the Agreement as embodying a useful Irish endorsement of the principle of majority consent. While the Court concluded that it could not overturn the Anglo-Irish Agreement as such, it must rule that Article 2 of the Irish Constitution represented not simply an aspiration to ultimate unity but a 'constitutional imperative'. Against this background, any influence the Agreement may have had in moving the unionist parties towards devolution was, if it existed at all, very slow-acting.

A second objective of the Agreement was to inhibit the alarming growth in support for Sinn Fein. The onset of republican hunger strikes within the Maze Prison in 1980, followed by the deaths of Bobby Sands and nine other prisoners, had caused a huge upsurge of sympathy and support for republicanism within the nationalist and Catholic community. On 9 April 1981 Bobby Sands himself had been elected MP for Fermanagh/South Tyrone, to be succeeded on his death by his former election agent Owen Carron. By the 1982 election to the Northern Ireland Assembly PSF was winning 10.1 per cent of first preference votes, as against 18.8 per cent for the moderate and constitutional SDLP. At the 1983 United Kingdom General Election the PSF share of votes cast had risen to 13.4 per cent, albeit with the SDLP well ahead at 17.9 per cent. By the 1985 District Council Elections the PSF share had, however, fallen back to 11.8 per cent of the first preference votes cast, with the SDLP at 17.8 per cent. So, between the election of Bobby Sands and the conclusion of the Anglo-Irish Agreement, the PSF share of the single or first preference votes cast in widely contested elections had fluctuated between 10.1 per cent and 13.4 per cent of the popular vote. At the first post-Agreement test of electability, the 1987 General Election, the PSF vote registered another slight fall to 11.4 per cent of the total poll as against 21.1 per cent for the SDLP. Thus, there were some initial grounds for modest confidence that the Agreement would strengthen the hand of the SDLP against its rivals for the nationalist vote, with further encouragement at the 1992 General Election, where the PSF share fell again to 10.0 per cent, and the SDLP position further improved to 23.5 per cent. However, the decade of slow decline in support for PSF came to an end at the 1993 District Council Elections, as the gap closed again between PSF at 12.4 per cent and the SDLP at 22.0 per cent. Any real prospect of containing an inexorable rise by Sinn Fein was, however, to be extinguished as John Hume pursued a controversial and politically hazardous encounter with Gerry Adams and Sinn Fein. I shall discuss more fully in a later chapter the consequences of this Hume policy, not just for Northern Ireland but for the SDLP itself. I would simply note here the repercussions in the constituency of West Belfast, the heartland of the nationalist and republican community in Northern Ireland's principal city. At the 1983 General Election, Gerry Adams had succeeded in unseating the experienced sitting member Gerry Fitt, at one time leader of the SDLP but now standing as an Independent. Fitt had in fact come third at the polls, with Adams achieving a majority of 5,445 over the SDLP's Dr Joe Hendron. With this defeat, however, the SDLP began to fight back against the abstensionist Adams, who refused to attend the United Kingdom Parliament, and at the 1987 General Election had reduced his majority to 2,221 votes. Finally, at the next General Election in 1992, Hendron managed to unseat Gerry Adams in his turn, albeit with a modest majority of 589 votes. All this laborious effort was prejudiced by the ever-growing cosiness of the Hume–Adams relationship. Hendron, the quintessence of decency and moderation, was dispossessed at the following General Election in 1997, and showed exceptional loyalty to his party in not pointing out the obvious fact that the blurring of the edge between constitutional and militant nationalism was bound to work to the disadvantage of the SDLP. Hume himself clearly judged the pursuit of the 'peace process' to be more important than the protection of his own party's interests, including its interests in achieving progress towards Irish unity solely by unambiguously peaceful means.

A third benefit anticipated from the Anglo-Irish Agreement was a marked improvement in security cooperation between the British and Irish Governments. It was, perhaps, difficult to reconcile this thrust to do better with the vehement declarations by successive Irish Governments that they had been doing their best in the campaign against terrorism all along. Certainly police-to-police contacts across the Border had been close and friendly for some considerable time. Although the Garda inevitably included some republican sympathisers, the disposition of police chiefs in Dublin was to regard the IRA in no less unfavourable a light than their opposite numbers in Belfast. If the Irish police contribution to the common cause was inhibited, it was more through lack of resources than lack of will. There were, however, difficult and touchy areas where the armed forces were involved. With so much activity in Border areas, in response to high threat levels there, it was hardly surprising that planes occasionally overflew Irish sovereign territory, or that members of the British Army strayed over a largely unmarked frontier. It would be naïve to suppose that all such incursions were accidental. Some degree of covert activity across the Border was an inevitable response to the use of the Republic's territory as a training ground, arms dump, forward base or place of safe haven. But most of the incursions detected by the Republic's authorities were wholly accidental.

There was, too, a real reticence about direct communications between the British and Irish armies. In the eyes of the unchanged Irish Constitution, Britain in Northern Ireland represented an occupying or colonial power, the presence of whose Army on Irish soil was an affront to national sovereignty. It goes without saying that the continuing existence of republican armed forces, whether PIRA or INLA, represented at least as great an affront to the Irish Constitution, under which the only legitimate army to be maintained in Ireland was that army answerable to the Irish State.

The institutions of the Anglo-Irish Agreement did, at least, reduce the recourse to megaphone diplomacy. A controversial incident or development could be discussed around the table at the Intergovernmental Conference or explored in the joint Secretariat at Maryfield. Things were not always as they seemed at first blush. The British Government itself had, in the past, been exposed to embarrassment (as in the case of the controversial Gibraltar shootings) through premature and factually inaccurate reaction to events. There was, of course, a great temptation to present the version of Government as early as possible, since in any incident involving paramilitary groups one could be sure of early attempts to give a 'spin' favourable to themselves, regardless of truth or balance. Nevertheless, ever-improving security cooperation could equally well have been achieved through the growing mutual confidence between police chiefs. The strong-minded RUC Chief Constable, Sir John Hermon, was fiercely protective of his force's operational autonomy, whether from British, Irish or Anglo-Irish pressure.

In practice a great deal of the time of Conference was to be taken up by endless discussions about 'accompaniment'. Although the RUC had been regularly demonised as a 'sectarian' force (not least by those prepared to take extreme measures to discourage Catholics from joining it), it suddenly became a prime cause on the Irish side to secure police accompaniment of every Army patrol (and of course the Army would include at times members of its locally recruited Regiment) which might come into contact with the civilian population. The diversion of invaluable police manpower into a kind of human seal of approval for an Army patrol which might or might not encounter civilians was not regarded by successive Chief Constables as a constructive contribution to the security effort.

If this analysis of the 1985 Agreement seems basically critical, it should not be assumed that a development somewhat on these lines was avoidable. In discussing the attitude of Faulkner to internment, I have sought to argue that Governments are sometimes drawn into radical action in spite of their own misgivings by a realisation that public opinion will not indefinitely accept things as they are. The British Government had given the local parties, whether under its own direction, under independent chairmanship or at an elected conference table, successive opportunities to frame their own acceptable devolution proposals. They had not succeeded, nor did there seem to be promising prospects of future success. Meanwhile the cost to the entire United Kingdom steadily mounted. No British Government could accept that this state of affairs should prevail indefinitely. If the Northern Ireland parties could not agree of their own volition, they might require a push. Moreover, institutions not dependent upon the immediate participation of the local parties could not be boycotted.

Some initiative, then, was to be expected, but I would remain deeply critical both of the processes of negotiation and the thrust of the Anglo-Irish Agreement itself. With an Irish Government acting at the negotiating table as a surrogate for the SDLP, unionist parties were certain to be resentful of patently unfair treatment. The notion of a unilateral process, allowing deep intervention into Northern Ireland affairs by the Irish Government, but with no reciprocal role in relation to the Republic, extended to members elected by constituencies in the twenty-six counties of the Republic formal consultative rights not available to members elected within the six counties of Northern Ireland. Above all the specific role of guarantor of nationalist interests given to the Irish Government was bound to reinforce the unionist sense of inexorable pressure from 'pan-nationalism', as already illustrated clearly in the New Ireland Forum, and subsequently to be heightened by the developing relationship between Hume and Adams.

CHAPTER FIVE

The British dimension:
the Anglo-Irish Agreement of 1985
to the Good Friday Agreement

A further phase of the British Government's role opened with the arrival of Peter Brooke as Secretary of State in July 1989. The son of a former Conservative Home Secretary (Henry Brooke) at a time when the Home Office still handled Government relations in Northern Ireland, and with substantial family links with Ireland, Brooke was one of those unusual figures thrown up by the Conservative Party from time to time (and probably now obsolete). Scholarly, courteous and honourable, with a manner vaguely suggestive of the Bench of Bishops, Peter Brooke concealed an ingenious and analytical mind behind an avuncular exterior. His manners and methods were in the Whitelaw mode. So far, in my view, history has not done him justice. A long shadow was cast over his reputation by an absurd episode during the Gay Byrne television show in Dublin, when his innate courtesy, allied to discomfort about a previous line of questioning, led him to break into song on the day of a notorious PIRA multiple murder. It was, as he readily admitted, a real error of judgement, but it was peculiarly unlovely to witness those local politicians who had hitherto found him consistently courteous and helpful elbowing each other out of the way to cast the first stone.

His major contribution to political development was to make it absolutely clear that the British Government regarded the pursuit of the republican objective of Irish unity, if undertaken by peaceful and constitutional means alone, to be as legitimate as the defence of unionist views. In a particularly controversial and significant statement (later to be re-echoed both in the Downing Street declaration and in the Good Friday Agreement itself), Brooke affirmed that the British Government had 'no selfish strategic or economic role in Northern Ireland'. These few words were to be construed and misconstrued as if they were the Dead Sea scrolls. Irish commentators were sometimes prone to insert a non-existent comma between the words 'selfish' and 'strategic', with the implication that the British Government had no interest whatever in Northern Ireland's destiny. Like many high-profile statements too often interpreted out of context, the controversial phrase needs to be viewed against the wider argument of the whole 'Whitbread' speech (as it came to be called). This was concerned in the wider sense with what it termed the 'British presence' in Northern Ireland and its objective was to focus the minds of nationalists and republicans, Irish politicians, Irish-Americans and others on the real nature of that presence. For too long the myth had been propagated, without sustained or convincing challenge, that partition had been the consequence of a British determination to retain a foothold in Ireland, and that if they could be persuaded or forced to withdraw that presence, Irishmen of all denominations and affiliations would soon acknowledge their common nationality. In the 'Whitbread' speech, Brooke sought to examine analytically the several apparent aspects of the 'British presence'. Yes, the British Army was present in Northern Ireland in large numbers. Far from being a benefit to Britain, the scale of this commitment – made necessary only by the threat of terrorism – represented a major diversion from other priorities, in NATO and elsewhere. With a normalisation of the situation, any military presence would gladly be reduced to normal garrison levels.

Was there not, though, a strategic British interest in maintaining bases in this part of Ireland? After all, the greater cover of 'western approaches' made possible by forward bases in Northern Ireland had been of real strategic importance, as acknowledged by Winston Churchill himself at the end of the Second World War. Yet Britain had demonstrated as early as 1938 that it had no determination to maintain its bases in an environment which could be antipathetic to them. Neville Chamberlain was to receive some subsequent criticism for agreeing, in negotiations with de Valera, to cede control of the 'treaty ports' in the Irish Free State. Certainly such facilities would have been of real benefit to Britain and its allies in the course of the war, but it is easy to imagine the complications which would have arisen if belligerents had been operating from enclaves within an otherwise neutral country. In any case, the strategic and technological realities had so changed since the end of the Second World War as to make ludicrous the strategic fantasies of Enoch Powell and his disciples.

If this 'British presence', supposedly maintained as a matter of national policy and in the overall national interest, was not about strategic benefit, perhaps the aim was to exploit in some way the wealth of the Province? This, after all, had been the underlying motive for much colonial activity in the nineteenth century and before it. Yet the most perfunctory study would reveal that the financial and economic support inherent in the 'British presence' allowed its citizens in Northern Ireland to enjoy a standard of living and of public services well beyond the domestic means of the region.

In reality, then, the ultimate 'British presence' was represented by that substantial part of the population, still in a clear majority, who had lived under the British Crown for centuries and under the ultimate jurisdiction of Parliament since 1800 and were fervent in their wish to remain so. It was not the case that Britain had no interest in Northern Ireland; it had the very great interest of ensuring that the wishes of the majority would not be overridden.

This speech, and in particular its controversial phrase, was to give rise to much unionist criticism, both at the time and later. Such critics would often focus on the fact that no comparable statement had been made, or was likely to be made, about any other part of the United Kingdom. They complained that they were being regarded as 'second-class citizens', mere associate members of the British polity. Complaints of this kind were stimulated from time to time by the overweening manners of some (though certainly not all) English politicians or officials imported into the Province. Certain Ministers failed to appreciate the resentment aroused by references to 'out here', or were unwise to make it clear that they had accepted appointment in the Northern Ireland Office under sufferance. Local touchiness was not reduced by media skits (as in *Yes, Minister*), suggesting that a posting to the Northern Ireland Office was the political equivalent of involuntary exile to Siberia. The poet Norman Dugdale, English-born member of the Northern Ireland Civil Service, captured the atmosphere in the opening lines of his poem 'Provincia deserta' (1983):

> Well, here it is: not Botany Bay
> But a penal settlement all the same.
> The sentence life without remission – saving,
> Of course, Sir, such as yourself, gentlemen newly come
> To live here at the Governor's Lodge. Two years from now
> You will be safely home again and dining out
> On your bizarre experiences, which cannot fail
> To please your hostess and amuse the company.

Pace Margaret Thatcher, Northern Ireland was not 'as British as Finchley'. The Act of 1920 establishing its institutions had clearly envisaged, and provided for, the ultimate coming together of the two parts of Ireland, albeit of course within the United Kingdom. From the first there had been embodied in statute law the assertion that there could be no change without consent, with the necessary implication that there could or might be change with consent. And now, well before the Brooke speech, it had been made perfectly clear that, in the event of a majority decision favourable to unity, the wishes of that hypothetical majority would prevail. I would add that, although it would be the strong wish of most Englishmen to retain Scotland within the United Kingdom, and any statutory reference to possible independence is very unlikely in foreseeable circumstances, it would be extremely difficult to contemplate how that part of the Union could be sustained if a clear majority of Scots were no longer willing to do so.

Above all, Brooke's speech was intended to be a message to Irish nationalism. Britain would not negotiate to end partition over the heads of the people who lived there. Nor would it act as a 'persuader'. The real British presence with which nationalists had to reckon was that large unionist community in Northern Ireland. Their trust, their compliance, their willingness to move towards if not directly to a united Ireland could not conceivably be gained by murdering or threatening them, or by imagining that they could be delivered unwillingly, wrapped up like a gift parcel, into the hands of those who had shown so little sympathy or understanding for their culture, traditions or aspirations.

It was during Peter Brooke's tenure, from July 1989 to April 1992, that the search for a domestic settlement again picked up momentum. There was a prolonged period of 'talks about talks' with – and this needs to be stressed – only those parties committed to purely constitutional means, that is to say, the UUP, the DUP, the SDLP and the Alliance Party. On the SDLP side it was very clear that this party, under Hume's dominating influence, would wish to see any form of talks process covering that 'totality of relationships' referred to in the Haughey–Thatcher exchanges. There were, as Hume saw it, three 'strands' or dimensions: internal relationships within Northern Ireland; relationships between north and south in Ireland; and relationships between Britain and Ireland.

In April 1991 (as it happens the very month of my retirement from the Northern Ireland Civil Service) the process moved forward from the exploratory discussions to more formal talks, on the basis that a 'new, more broadly-based agreement' would be considered during a specified gap between meetings of the Anglo-Irish Intergovernmental Conference. These talks would adopt the 'three-stranded' approach, with talks bearing on the separate strands proceeding in parallel. After some difficulty in identifying an independent chairman for the north–south talks, Sir Ninian Stephen, a former Governor General of Australia, was appointed to that position. However, the talks process had made little progress before going into recess on 3 July 1991, with a further meeting of the Intergovernmental Conference impending. Increasingly the existence of arrangements with which unionist parties could not agree was proving an obstacle to discussion about alternative arrangements which might be more acceptable to them. However, the Prime Minister John Major was able to secure an agreement to a formal resumption in March 1992, with the understanding that strenuous efforts would be made to press ahead after the General Election call for 9 April 1992.

The Labour Party led by Neil Kinnock had entered the election campaign with a demonstrable and excessive degree of self-confidence, and the British media generally gave the low-key Major, whose approach was such a contrast with the self-confident and aggressive stridency of Margaret Thatcher, little chance of electoral success. In the event the electorate preferred his modest demeanour to the show-business puffery of a grotesquely mishandled Labour campaign, and once again returned a Conservative Government. It was, unfortunately for the Conservative Party and the nation at large, to prove a weak and divided Government. The party was hopelessly split on Europe and the Maastricht Treaty, and the fiasco of precipitate withdrawal from the Exchange Rate Mechanism (ERM) created an air of financial incompetence and near panic. The weakness of the Government meant that in certain crucial votes the support of the UUP would be needed to assure a majority, and it is generally good neither for Northern Ireland nor for the wider United Kingdom if the unionist tail is seen, or believed, to wag the national dog.

It has to be said, though, that Major deserves recognition and enormous credit for placing the Northern Ireland issue very high on his governmental agenda. Predecessors had sometimes made brief forays into the Northern Ireland camp but had failed to demonstrate deep, continuing and conscientious personal involvement. Some British Prime Ministers, indeed, had never visited Northern Ireland at all. Major, on the other hand, in the midst of myriad party and governmental problems, was to show firm commitment to seeking progress in Northern Ireland from the beginning to the end of his premiership. If it was to be Tony Blair who had the glory of planting the flag on the summit of agreement, it was John Major who had carried heavy loads far up the mountain. In these efforts his principal instrument was to be a new Secretary of State, in the person of Sir Patrick Mayhew, formerly the Attorney General. I had myself first glimpsed him many years before in the debating chamber of the Oxford Union Society when 'Mr P.B.B. Mayhew (Balliol)', had spoken confidently from the Dispatch Box as to the manner born. Mayhew had some useful credentials. Like Brooke, he had family links with Ireland, and had already as Attorney General grappled with some of the more knotty aspects of Anglo-Irish relations, such as extradition. If he had disadvantages, they were in terms of his personal appearance and manner. As I had by then left the Civil Service, I was never to have the chance to work closely with him, as I had done with all his predecessors – Whitelaw, Pym, Rees, Mason, Atkins, Prior, Hurd, King and Brooke. However, all of my old colleagues who remained to serve him were to characterise him as wise, kind, clever and considerate. Unhappily this was not the generally received public image. A tall, imposing man with an advocate's booming manner, one somehow expected him to appear one day in the plumed hat which he would have worn so comfortably. He would come across at interviews on occasions as patrician and condescending; a figure from Norman Dugdale's telling poem.

An important change on the wider scene had been the replacement of Charles Haughey as Taoiseach and leader of Fianna Fail by Albert Reynolds, a successful businessman and shrewd 'gut politician', with deal-making a significant element in his inner nature. I have already observed that Fianna Fail has always been the party best placed to be a party to a settlement, in view of its pronounced nationalist and republican credentials. It will always be easier for Fianna Fail in opposition to attack Fine Gael and its partners as 'soft on the Brits'.

As talking resumed after the election, the issue of constitutional status rose again out of the mists like the 'dreary steeples of Tyrone and Fermanagh' in Winston Churchill's telling phrase. Negotiations on the Irish side were initially led by the then Tanaiste John Wilson, with whom I was to work so many years later in the attempt to recover the bodies of the 'disappeared'. The Irish did not rule out the possibility of a referendum to modify Articles 2 and 3 of their Constitution in the context of a wider settlement acceptable to them. But in the discussions themselves the precise future status of Northern Ireland must be an open question; if the 'constitutional claim' was to be on the table, so also must be the Government of Ireland Act 1920 (although much of the constitutional machinery now rested on the Northern Ireland Constitution Act 1973, which had significantly varied the 1920 provisions). As to the prospects for the internal dimension of a settlement, there seemed to be little chance of finding common ground at this stage. The UUP had nailed its colours to the mast of opposition to Cabinet-style power-sharing on the 1973–74 model and were running instead with the idea of wide powers for Assembly Committees, and while the DUP and Alliance did not rule this pattern out entirely, John Hume had by then decided not only that majority rule would be unacceptable but also that any power-sharing model could prove unstable. However, his counter-proposal for a complex model which might be described as 'joint authority plus', with local politicians, alongside representatives of the British and Irish Governments and the European Community forming a commission to run Northern Ireland, was not favourable to the making of progress. The floating of such a controversial proposition, with not a shred of a chance of acceptance by the unionist parties, cast real doubt upon Hume's seriousness in the search for agreement at this time. The huge gulf evidently still dividing the political factions in Northern Ireland illuminated the unwisdom of one of the conditions attaching to the talks process. This was that 'nothing is agreed until everything is agreed'. This mantra recognised some of the inevitable characteristics of any complex negotiation. There will be a temptation to play it very much like a game of cards, keeping one's cards close to the chest until obliged to 'show'. Many discussions would take place on a 'What if?' basis. Positions will be tested and explored. Non-papers will be circulated, carrying no authority or commitment.

On the other hand, what the gulf between the opening bids of the several parties revealed all too clearly was a devastating lack of trust and mutual confidence. It could be better to look for modest progress in the right general direction than to remain stuck in the trenches. The all-singing, all-dancing settlement might prove unachievable, at least for now. The situation cried out for confidence-building measures, for some imaginative effort to allay the fears of others without fundamental prejudice to one's own position or objectives. As it was, the Brooke–Mayhew talks came to an end in November 1992, without making any substantial headway.

But the Prime Minister, John Major, had by no means given up hope of making progress in Northern Ireland, drawing in part upon an excellent relationship with Albert Reynolds, with whom he had done business under an EEC umbrella before either had reached the highest office. He also had to reckon with the election to the American presidency of Bill Clinton, who was soon to show an unprecedented appetite for involvement in Northern Ireland affairs.

Against this background, the 'political process' began to merge with the 'peace process'. It was by no means certain that, even if the constitutional parties in Northern Ireland, the British Government and the Irish Government were able to agree to new structures, this would of itself deliver Northern Ireland from the burden of political violence which it had borne for so many years. There had been no evidence whatever during the brief 'power-sharing' interregnum of 1974 that republican violence would be moderated or even abandoned because of the inclusion of nationalists in Government. Indeed, during the Executive's brief life, Harold Wilson had made much of captured documentation which seemed to point, if anything, to an intensification of the IRA campaign.

To this point, the attitude of the British Government to PSF had, over the years, been confused and ambiguous. The delegation received by Whitelaw at Paul Channon's home in London had been clearly speaking for the IRA. However, up to 1974 PSF had been proscribed alongside PIRA, and Merlyn Rees's decision to lift the proscription was based upon a hope that the political wing of republicanism would flourish while the military wing withered away. Nevertheless the distinction between the two arms of republicanism was to be seen as risible not only by non-republicans in Northern Ireland but also by not a few mainline Irish politicians from 'republican' parties like Fianna Fail. Not only were some of the party's leading figures involved, or formerly involved, in the 'military' operations of the IRA, but it also became a regular feature of the annual PSF Ard Fheis (or conference) for one or more 'volunteers' to be presented from the platform and received with acclamation. The concession of democratic respectability to Sinn Fein was compounded in the British reaction to the brief ceasefire declared in February 1975, under which British officials found themselves dealing with representatives of PSF in seven 'incident centres' set up to monitor the ceasefire and provide a means of easy contact.

Despite the resumption of the PIRA campaign, PSF had remained a lawful organisation, although revealing again and again its exceptionally close links to PIRA terrorism. Indeed, the 1982 Ard Fheis instructed all future candidates to give unambivalent support to the 'armed struggle', reflecting on the question posed by Danny Morrison: 'But will anyone here object if, with a ballot paper in this hand and a Armalite in this hand, we take power in Ireland?' This statement illustrated with brutal clarity the essential unity of a single republican movement prepared to support any means – peaceful or not – likely to advance its ends.

Nevertheless, the British Government, or at least those purporting to speak in its name, continued highly covert contact with the republican movement. In his fascinating book *Brits: The War against the IRA* (2001), the distinguished television journalist Peter Taylor describes in detail the determination of a named intelligence officer to keep open channels of communication. In this book Taylor quotes the officer in question, Michael Oatley, as referring to 'an engaging group of amateurs led by a marvellously charismatic figure, "Willy" Whitelaw, trying to grapple with a maze of problems which they didn't understand at all'. Oatley himself presumably arrived in Northern Ireland endowed with a God-given understanding wholly withheld from those of us who had lived and worked and struggled there for a great many years. The statement attributed to him smacks of the dangerous elitism of an intelligence apparatus better able to secure the nation's safety than its elected Government. It was striking that successive Governments in the Irish Republic, supposedly sympathetic to the ends, though of course not the means, of the IRA, were for many years determined to keep Sinn Fein/IRA at arm's length, and retain a ban on broadcasting by illegal organisations and PSF. Yet on the British side we had Michael Oatley opening up a 'bamboo pipe' for communication with the IRA.

It is against this background that one must consider the developing relationship between John Hume and Gerry Adams. As early as February

1985 Hume had held a brief and unfruitful meeting with PIRA, to the great irritation of Garret FitzGerald, who was keeping militant republicanism at a distance. However, in January 1988 John Hume reopened discussions with Adams. There could be no serious criticism of Hume's motives; he genuinely believed that all other considerations must be secondary to achieving an end to the violence which had divided and disfigured Northern Ireland for so long. Appreciating that arguments based on morality or high democratic principle were unlikely to enjoy a sympathetic hearing, he stressed instead that the 'armed struggle' was proving counter-productive in terms of the ultimate Irish unity supported by both. There was, he believed, incontestable evidence that British attitudes or interests were no longer a barrier, and if the Irish Government, the SDLP and PSF could present a united but wholly peaceful democratic front, their negotiating position would be extremely strong. While there was no evidence of the security forces' ability to crush the IRA, there were equally no grounds for believing that PIRA could 'win the war' against the British Government and the formidable forces available to it. Continued bloodshed would not only be futile and useless, but would also inevitably deepen the gulf between nationalists and those unionists who they hoped would become one day citizens of a united Ireland. However, in spite of extensive discussions between Hume and PSF leaders these initial talks petered out in September 1988.

But Hume had not abandoned the idea of persuading PSF that its objectives would be better served if PIRA were to bring its campaign of violence to an end. Further talks began in April 1993, initially on a confidential basis, but leading to a statement on 25 April confirming the dialogue. A further joint statement issued on 25 September reported considerable progress towards the realisation of a 'peace process', which would be appropriate for consideration by the two sovereign Governments.

All of this was to give rise to a number of difficult and important questions. Was unionist support for any agreement, without which it could have no useful long-term effect, likely to be encouraged by an impression that the terms had been 'pre-cooked' by Hume and Adams? Was it truly in the public interest for Hume to endorse so openly the political credentials of a party so clearly and inextricably linked with an horrendous campaign of violence? There had been signs, after the Remembrance Day massacre at Enniskillen in November 1987, of widespread public revulsion against the activities of PIRA / PSF. Was it right, was it seemly for Hume, as early as January 1988, to bring them in from the cold? Was he, through these ever-closer relationships, fatally blurring the line of distinction between the SDLP as a fully constitutional party and PSF as the mouthpiece of republican terrorism? What would this association mean in the longer term for the electoral prospects of the SDLP? These are questions to be considered more fully in assessing later the role and responsibilities of the local political parties.

We are, however, concerned here with the activities of the British Government. There was considerable obscurity about the nature, indeed the very existence, of any formal document embodying the products of the Hume/ Adams exchanges. Whatever these were, they appear never to have been communicated directly to the British Government, but John Major was effectively briefed by Albert Reynolds, with whom Hume had maintained close contact. Major is now on the record as having persuaded his Irish opposite number that the Hume–Adams approach was excessively 'green' in hue. It was, in any case, a matter for the two Governments, rather than for Hume and Adams in private conclave, to set out the parameters for political progress. In intensive discussions the two Governments now hammered out the Joint Declaration of 15 December 1993 (the 'Downing Street Declaration').

The essence of the Declaration is well conveyed by a letter addressed at the time by the Secretary of State, Sir Patrick Mayhew, to a number of interested parties: He wrote:

> The 'declaration' sets out constitutional principles and political realities which safeguard the vital interests of both sides of the community in Northern Ireland. The text both reiterates Northern Ireland's statutory constitutional guarantee and re-affirms that the British Government will uphold the democratic wish of a greater number of the people of Northern Ireland on the issue of whether they prefer to support the Union or a sovereign united Ireland. On this basis the British Government reiterates that they have no selfish strategic or economic interest in Northern Ireland and that were a majority in Northern Ireland to wish it, the Government would introduce legislation to bring about a united Ireland. For their part, the Irish Government accept that it would be wrong to attempt to impose a united Ireland in the absence of the freely given consent of a majority of the people of Northern Ireland. The British Government undertake to encourage the achievement of the objective of the Talks process begun in 1991, namely an overall agreement based on full respect for the rights and identities of both traditions in Northern Ireland. The text does not envisage, nor advocate, any particular outcome. It states that:
>
> > the British Government agree that it is for the people of Ireland alone, by agreement between the two parts respectively, to exercise their right to self-determination on the basis of consent, freely and concurrently given, North and South to bring about a united Ireland, if that is their wish
>
> The Irish Government accept:
>
> > that the democratic right of self-determination by the people of Ireland as a whole must be achieved and exercised with and subject to

the agreement and consent of a majority of the people of Northern Ireland.

So it is clear that the consent of a majority of the people in Northern Ireland is required before any constitutional change could come about.

The Irish Government also confirm that, in the event of an overall settlement, they will as part of a balanced constitutional accommodation put forward and support proposals for change in the Irish constitution, which would fully reflect the principle of consent in Northern Ireland.

The Declaration reinforces the firm foundation for future political development, on the same three-stranded basis that the main constitutional parties in Northern Ireland and the two Governments have already accepted. Both Governments reiterate that, following a cessation of violence, democratically mandated parties which establish a commitment to exclusively peaceful methods, and which have shown that they will abide permanently by the democratic processes, are free to participate fully in democratic politics and to join in dialogue in due course between the Governments and the political parties on the way ahead.

I would regard this Joint Declaration as the most convincing and well-balanced document to be produced by either or both Governments throughout the period beginning with the onset of violence. It is of the utmost importance to appreciate the significance and subtlety of some of the words and phrases used.

The use of the words 'the democratic wish of a greater number of the people of Northern Ireland' rather than 'a majority of the people' was a subtle nod in the direction of unionist leader James Molyneaux, who had for some time been using the expression 'a greater number' to convey his conviction that the Union could and did enjoy the support of people who were not members of what was commonly called 'the Northern Ireland majority'. It will be seen that the Brooke phrase concerning 'no selfish strategic or economic interest', with all its implications earlier explained was picked up and reiterated. Equally significant was the acceptance on the Irish side of the need for 'freely given' consent, since there had been frequent arguments from nationalist quarters that Britain should act as 'persuaders' for unity, with its implication of subtle pressure of one sort or another upon the unionist community. By these words of the Declaration, the Irish Government was accepting that the British Government would continue to play a neutral role. Many unionists, of course, regarded neutrality itself as a breach of duty by the British Government. They would have liked to see a statement that all parts of the United Kingdom would be retained under the Crown and Parliament, come what may. They had forgotten, perhaps, that as long ago as 1800 the Act of Union had appeared to give this assured status to the whole of

Ireland. In any case, this particular 'as British as Finchley' argument had been lost long ago.

Of greatest significance were the formulations of the 'consent' principle. Here it has to be appreciated that the 'old' Sinn Fein/IRA and its ideological successors had rested their claim to act for the Irish people upon the outcome of the last all-Ireland elections in 1918, when Sinn Fein had won an overwhelming majority of the Irish seats in Parliament. The Governments and Parliaments in both parts of Ireland resulting from later developments did not, in their view, represent or reflect the electoral decisions of the whole people of Ireland. From this flowed the long-standing policy of refusing to participate in 'partitionist' institutions (including the Oireachtas in Dublin) and their assumed right to bear and use arms in the nationalist interest, notwithstanding provisions to the contrary in the Irish Constitution. John Hume, in particular, had puzzled over this conundrum. Republican ultras, as he knew from his direct dialogue with them, would never accept the right of the British Parliament or a mechanism established under its laws to overrule the wishes of the whole Irish people (who were assumed to be, by a huge majority, fervent for Irish unity). On the other hand, Hume knew very well that no British Government could renege with any credibility from repeated statutory and other assurances that Northern Ireland would not be removed from the United Kingdom without the consent of the majority of its people. And so there fructified in his mind an interesting and potentially productive idea. What if the Irish people alone, and the whole of the Irish people, were to have an opportunity to vote on a series of propositions including the reaction to the present status of Northern Ireland (de jure in British and indeed international law; de facto in Irish reality)? Might it not be the outcome – the package as a whole being balanced and acceptable – that a majority of voters in the Republic would accept the reality and validity of the present status of Northern Ireland within the United Kingdom (albeit reluctantly and with the hope and aspiration for further change), while alongside them a majority of voters in Northern Ireland could be expected to endorse that same stance with enthusiasm? In that event it could be argued that for the first time since 1918 the whole people of Ireland, and no one but the people of Ireland, would have made a judgement about its constitutional configuration. These ideas could readily be detected behind the wording on self-determination now used by the two Governments.

Another crucial area concerned possible amendment of the Irish Constitution. Realities accepted by the two Governments had never been fully embodied in the statute and constitutional law of the two states. On the British side, it was now clear that there was a commitment to legislate for Irish unity if a local majority were to express that wish, yet the existing law still embodied the negative statement that Northern Ireland would not quit the United Kingdom without the consent of its people. On the Irish side, reassuring statements by successive Governments had not altered the fact that their Constitution included an implicit constitutional claim to Northern Ireland judged by their own Supreme Court to be an 'imperative'. Garret FitzGerald had argued in 1985 that the search for constitutional amendment could be counter-productive unless accompanied by striking advances both on the north–south axis and within Northern Ireland. Now, for the first time, an Irish Taoiseach was to give a conditional promise of constitutional amendment. It was a brave and useful step on his part.

Finally, the words used about parties associated with violence deserve and demand the most searching examination. As already explained, PSF was by this time able to demonstrate a substantial electoral mandate. It had, for example, at the District Council Elections of May 1993, won 12.4 per cent of the first preference votes cast. On this basis it could legitimately claim, in the language used by the Declaration, to be a 'democratically mandated' party. It is, of course, questionable whether its overall weight within the political process would have been anything like as compelling if it had not been regarded as able to turn on or turn off the most serious violence. Nevertheless, any party commanding the support of something like one in eight of the electorate had clearly established itself as a substantial political force, whether one liked it or not. It was very understandable, then, that the two Governments should have considered in what circumstances PSF (or indeed parties of a 'loyalist' hue associated closely with Protestant paramilitary bodies, albeit so far enjoying minimal electoral support or political influence) might be admitted to the talks process.

Here, though, I would repeat my previously used analogy of the childhood toy, intended to locate several tiny steel balls in various holes, in face of the tendency, while manoeuvring one ball into place, to displace another. It would not be a question simply of the two Governments deciding to invite PSF (perhaps with others) to talks; such a move would be fruitless if other vital interests were to leave the table in reaction.

On this issue the Downing Street Declaration, so admirably forthright on so many other crucial issues, degenerates into vagueness. One condition would be 'a cessation of violence'. Did this mean a complete cessation, a permanent cessation, or merely an armistice or ceasefire? And what, in this context, would be regarded as 'violence'? Clearly, shooting attacks on soldiers or policemen, or car bombs placed in cities, towns or villages would constitute 'violence'. But what about the underlying pattern of small-time thuggery used to discourage or punish dissent; the beating up in a dark alley, the intimidatory threat, the exposure of unpopular individuals to involuntary exile? Whatever such a 'cessation' might be, it was to be followed by other evidences of a sincere and permanent turning away from undemocratic and violent methods. These evidences would have to include establishing 'a commitment to exclusively peaceful methods' and showing that 'they will abide permanently by the democratic process'. How, in practice, could the sincerity and permanence of such commitments be established?

The two Governments were in danger here of falling into an elephant trap first dug for them by Merlyn Rees in removing PSF from the category of proscribed organisations. So who, precisely, were the 'they' who would be expected to furnish credible evidence of an abandonment of violence? It has been a favourite expression of local politicians in recent years to claim that 'even the dogs in the street' know this, that or the other. Even these legendary dogs knew very well of the intimate and even inextricable links between PSF and PIRA, and between various emerging loyalist parties and their paramilitary allies. The British Government was certainly well informed about these links, both through the activities of its intelligence services and through direct unacknowledged contacts with PIRA itself. Yet, in the years which followed, Adams and his colleagues, when under pressure about this or that, would argue that PSF as a party was doing all that it had committed itself to do. The answer to embarrassing questions was often to be in the form: 'That is absolutely nothing to do with us. We can't answer for the IRA, although you can be confident that we are using our benign influence with them; but of course we are in no position, you understand, to give directions to them.' The latter statement may well, to some extent at least, have been true. There had been considerable earlier evidence that it was the Army Council who gave directions to the elected representatives of PSF, rather than the reverse. Danny Morrison had spoken with brutal frankness of a single strategy pursued by the deployment of two parallel methods, characterised as 'the ballot box and the Armalite'. Since PIRA was a secret (and secretive) organisation, it never gave any information about the composition of its Army Council or its command structures. This was hardly surprising, given that membership of a proscribed organisation could itself constitute a criminal offence. When released from detention in 1972 to accompany a PIRA delegation to the London meeting with Whitelaw, it is naïve to assume that Adams was present as some kind of uninvolved lay adviser. Martin McGuinness, in a submission to the Bloody Sunday Tribunal, has been prepared to acknowledge his position in the PIRA hierarchy at the time of the controversial parade and shootings, but has been notably reticent about any role he may have played in PIRA before or after these events. Gerry Kelly, a prominent figure in PSF circles, and as hard-faced a character as one is likely to meet, had served a prison sentence for terrorist offences.

The subsequent evasions of PSF were as if, at the conclusion of the Second World War, leading members of the Nazi party accused of war crimes and crimes against humanity were to say, 'We were only politicians, joining Adolf Hitler after his lawful appointment as Chancellor. As for these awful things alleged about the SS, you had better ask them.' When Lloyd-George had met the Irish delegation to negotiate the Treaty, he had been well aware that people like Michael Collins had been directly involved in violent military activities against the British State and was capable of bringing those activities to a permanent end.

By this time, however, the so-called 'back channels' of communication between PIRA and a representative of the British Government, initially set in place without specific governmental authority, were in regular and authorised use. In his own autobiography John Major records the receipt in February 1993 of a message purporting to come from PIRA leadership in terms which included the following:

> The conflict is over but we need your advice on how to bring it to a close. We wish to have an unannounced ceasefire in order to hold a dialogue leading to peace ... We cannot meet the Secretary of State's public renunciation of violence, but it would be given privately as long as we were sure we were not being tricked.

Whether PIRA leaders had drafted or even authorised the use of these precise words is still a matter of considerable doubt. It seems rather more likely to have been an optimistic gloss placed by an intermediary on his own contacts and exchanges. In its eventual response, passed to PIRA through the 'back channel', the Government welcomed the opportunity to open an exploratory dialogue without a precise predetermined outcome, but reiterating that the British Government would uphold the Union for as long as (but no longer than) the majority of the people of Northern Ireland wished to retain it.

Between October 1990 and November 1993 periodic communication between the British Government and Sinn Fein was maintained, from April 1993 onwards alongside the Hume–Adams talks, leading eventually to a PIRA 'ceasefire' in 1994.

The next major overt move on the governmental front was the joint launch by John Major and the Taoiseach John Bruton, on 22 February 1995, of a thirty-seven page publication entitled *Frameworks for the Future*. The use of the plural rather than the singular form underlined the fact that this publication embodied two separate documents: on the one hand a 'Framework for Accountable Government in Northern Ireland', promulgated with the sole authority of the United Kingdom Government; on the other hand an 'Outline of a Comprehensive Settlement' recording a joint understanding between the British and Irish Governments. It would be naïve, though, to suppose that the Irish Government had no input into, or influence upon, the purely internal 'Framework'.

The formal separation of authority was consistent with the concept of 'three strands' (arrangements for government and administration in Northern Ireland; arrangements for relations between north and south in Ireland; and arrangements for relations between the two islands), which had underlain the inconclusive talks process begun in March 1991. Within that concept it was always clear that it was to be the United Kingdom Government and the domestic political parties in Northern Ireland who would discuss internal arrangements for government there (although it should not be overlooked that under Article 4 of the Anglo-Irish Agreement of 1985, which was still in effect, the Irish Government might 'put forward views and proposals on the modalities of bringing about devolution in Northern Ireland, in so far as they related to the interests of the minority community in Northern Ireland' within the framework of the Intergovernmental Conference established by that Agreement). Within this phrase the United Kingdom Government had effectively abandoned any effort to exclude the Irish Government entirely from arrangements purely domestic to Northern Ireland.

It is also interesting to note that the so-called 'east–west' strand was to be concerned, in the terms of the Prime Minister's foreword to the Frameworks document, not with the relations between the United Kingdom of Great Britain and Northern Ireland, on the one hand, and the Irish Republic, on the other, but 'between these islands', thereby in a sense implicitly promoting the 'Irishness' of geography above the 'Britishness' of sovereignty.

The publication of the Frameworks, and indeed some earlier (and clearly far from inaccurate) leaking of key elements and their drafting, had been made the occasion for a substantial furore by various unionist parties in Northern Ireland. Subsequent reactions showed them not only to perceive themselves as isolated, but also to be in reality isolated. Indeed some eminent political correspondents commented colourfully upon that isolation, on occasions coupling it with an admonition or implication that the unionist community and its political leadership should 'pull itself together' or run a serious risk of being blamed as the main obstinate procrastinator standing in the way of the so-called 'peace process'.

In discussing the Frameworks document, a detailed examination of its wording is a matter of substance rather than pedantry. It did matter whether the Framework was one document or two; whether east–west meant United Kingdom–Republic or Britain–Ireland; whether Britain was declaring no real interests at all in the Union or rather defining its motives for upholding it in existing and foreseeable circumstances.

Part of the uproar created in unionist circles arose from a lack of congruence between the title of the document and its detailed contents. A 'framework', in common parlance, is a very broad outline or indication of parameters; it draws the lines on the pitch rather than dictating the course of play. The word 'consultative' was also bandied about by the co-sponsors. That, again, is a term more comfortably applied to a range of options for future discussion by all affected parties rather than to a single coherent set of ideas evidently hammered out, no doubt with some difficulty and at numerous meetings, by the 'sovereign Governments' in the absence of crucially interested parties.

While the document certainly recognised the desirability of restoring more locally accountable government to Northern Ireland, I regarded the precise model of internal government tabled by the British Government as being in many respects unworkable, unacceptable and incapable of winning that support from a majority of the people of Northern Ireland without which it could not prosper.

The joint 'Outline of a Comprehensive Settlement' embodied proposals for Northern Ireland institutions, which smacked of institutional dirigisme rather than practical common sense, and retained the idea of a standing Intergovernmental Conference which many would construe as able to oversee and shape any north–south body. The use of the word 'harmonising' was significant. From the unionist standpoint, it might be acceptable to take sensible steps, justified by mutual benefit, to move Northern Ireland in some respects closer to the Republic; it would be quite unacceptable, however, if those very steps were progressively to detach Northern Ireland from Great Britain. It had been Margaret Thatcher, albeit at an earlier time and in a different context, who had warned where one might end up if subject to a ratchet which would permit movement in only one direction.

It was, by this time, quite clear that some relatively strong north–south institutions would be essential if any Irish Government were to feel able to submit to its electorate with confidence a referendum to amend the terms of Articles 2 and 3 of the Irish Constitution. Many unionists found extraordinarily unattractive the idea of paying a price for the removal of a territorial claim which they viewed as basically immoral and wholly incompatible with the common membership of the two countries in the European Union. Yet the written Irish Constitution and the mechanisms required to amend it could not simply be wished away.

How, then, to move forward from the Frameworks document? In particular, how to make progress in restoring devolved government in Northern Ireland? Did the mantra 'Nothing is agreed until everything is agreed' hold good, and if it did, was the inference that any elected body could only emerge as the product of a successful talks process, or might such a body offer the best means to carry the process itself forward? Above all, who would have a seat at the table (or perhaps, given the concept of 'strands', at several tables)?

Looming ever larger was the sensitive issue of 'decommissioning' or 'putting arms beyond use'. When PIRA announced its 'cessation of violence' on 31 August 1994, it was very careful to avoid any use of the word 'permanent'. Here one must return to the wording of the Downing Street Declaration of December 1993. There had been, in the terms used by the Declaration, a 'cessation of violence' on the part of PIRA, followed by similar 'cessations' declared by loyalist paramilitaries. It soon became apparent, though, that violence had not in practice totally vanished from the Northern Ireland scene. Certainly the volume of violent incidents fell to much lower levels than had prevailed before the ceasefire, but it became clear that a lower level of killing and maiming would persist, as paramilitaries paid off old scores within their own communities, took 'disciplinary' action within their own organisations, maintained a grip of fear in localities they dominated, and defended lucrative rackets or criminal activities. There had essentially been a pause in 'military' activities – in particular attacks on members of the security forces or inter-paramilitary open warfare across the interfaces. No one had proved willing to describe the ceasefire as 'permanent' or to declare openly that 'the war is over'. This was not necessarily sinister. Paramilitary groups themselves were all too likely to split between the 'ultras' and the pragmatists, rather as old Sinn Fein had done under the stress of the Treaty. Moreover the British Government had earlier received back-channel indications that the war was in fact coming to an end, even if this could not openly be acknowledged. (I have, however, already expressed doubts about the reliability of these supposed indications.) The balance of probability is that the PSF leadership had persuaded the republican movement that a pause would be valuable to test the temperature of the water as had been done more or less briefly on previous occasions. There had, after all, been signals regularly since Peter Brooke's time of a more open attitude towards movement in the direction of Irish unity.

However, the Downing Street Declaration had made it clear that, following a cessation of violence, democratically mandated parties seeking to participate in the political process would be expected to 'establish a commitment to exclusively peaceful methods' and to demonstrate they would 'abide permanently by the democratic process'. Clearly PSF, now enjoying substantial electoral support, could credibly claim to be a democratically mandated party. James Molyneaux (who remained leader of the UUP until September 1995) openly called for a substantial period of delay before making any judgement about the permanence and stability of the ceasefire. In his mind, PSF, with the strong whiff of Semtex about it, would need to be decontaminated. Major, on the other hand, did not wish the process to stall, and initiated a series of exchanges with PSF beginning at official level. The British Government was very anxious indeed not to be criticised on the grounds of premature negotiation behind closed doors. What took place, then, was supposedly a process purely of 'clarification'. The British Government set out its well-established and publicly known position. PSF sought clarification on a range of points, including the vital question of how the British Government would define a renunciation of violence; the reply continued to rest on the vague and woolly wording of the Downing Street Declaration on this issue.

It is to be noted, however, that the relevant part of the Declaration had not made any specific reference to the decommissioning, surrender, destruction or disposal of weapons or the materiel of warfare. While the United Kingdom Government had entered upon direct rule in 1972 with profound ignorance of many historical and other realities, by the mid-1990s its able Ministers and officials had had every opportunity to inform themselves of the nuances of Irish history and politics, not least through exposure to Irish interlocutors who were steeped in it. They ought to have known that the mindset of historical republicanism was strongly averse to any implication of surrender. An organisation commanding the loyalty of members prepared to starve themselves to death was not ready to accept humiliation. While increasingly recognising that it could not 'win the war' by military means, or certainly by military means alone, it nevertheless did not accept that it had been defeated. It had indeed shown over a long campaign an ability to replace and even augment lost weaponry, and to recruit zealous new volunteers to replace those brought to trial and imprisonment.

So strong was this aversion to 'surrender and disarmament' that the argument was sometimes advanced that no 'liberation army' anywhere in the modern world had agreed to hand over its weapons.

By pure chance, I discovered that to be untrue. In 1990 I found myself briefly in Bangladesh, acting as a consultant in modernising the local Civil Service. At a meeting with the Speaker, Humayun Rasheed Choudhury, in Dacca, he had casually mentioned to me the recent steps to bring to a conclusion the long-running insurgency in a part of his country known as the 'Chittagong Hill Tracts'. There, in the context of a wide-ranging political settlement, the local paramilitary organisation known as Shanti Bahini (the broad equivalent of ETA or the IRA) was bringing weapons to designated points and handing them over with some ceremony. I was enabled to visit this relatively remote area near the border with India, and see the situation for myself and meet some of those involved.

However, the thought of Gerry Adams handing over a collection of Armalites while accepting a garland of flowers from John Major, although not displeasing in itself, had little contact with reality. In practice, the British Government moved, after the evasive process of mutual 'clarification', to harden its stance. In March 1995 the Secretary of State, Sir Patrick Mayhew, used the occasion of a visit to Washington DC to define three 'tests' required to validate any purported renunciation of violence. These were: acceptance of the principle of disarmament; progress in defining the 'modalities' by which disarmament would be achieved; and the requirement of a demonstrable act of good faith before entry to the talks, in terms of some gesture of actual decommissioning. PIRA chose, and not without some degree of justification, to regard these 'necessary steps' as quite new hurdles, previously undisclosed to them, and coming close to the posture of surrender they found wholly unacceptable. On the British side, though, it has to be said that they could not forever fudge the issue of how 'commitment to exclusively peaceful methods' could be demonstrated.

Mention has already been made of the inherent instability of John Major's Conservative Government, now riven by terrible divisions on the issue of Europe, compounded by growing personal animosities. It has been widely suggested, both at the time and subsequently, that Major always had to keep in the back of his mind the possibility that UUP votes could be vital in a crucial Commons division. He himself has vehemently denied allowing this consideration to affect his conduct of Northern Ireland affairs, and he deserves, I believe, the benefit of the doubt by reason of the very high priority he always accorded to Northern Ireland amidst a host of other problems. However, he and his Secretary of State were bound to be much influenced by another consideration. The object of this exercise was not simply to bring PSF to the negotiating table, but to bring it there under circumstances which would not drive other essential elements away from that table. And the end game, moreover, was not just to persuade all the vital interests to come to the table, but to assist them to rise from it, somewhere down the line, with agreement on a broadly acceptable general settlement.

However, any prospect of progress was set aside for the time being when the ceasefire came to a spectacular and costly end in the Canary Wharf bombing of February 1996. The decommissioning impasse remained the main impediment to progress. A major part in moving out of this impasse was now to be played by the former Majority Leader of the United States Senate, George Mitchell of Maine. In the course of seeking election to the presidency, Bill Clinton had made it clear that he foresaw a more active involvement in the affairs of Northern Ireland, including the possible appointment of an 'envoy'. With the precedent of Henry Kissinger's involvement in the Middle East before them, Clinton's potential initiative gave rise both to exaggerated expectations and to equally exaggerated apprehensions. To the more militant members of the Irish-American lobby the idea of an 'envoy' held out the prospect of a tough activist banging heads together to produce a solution 'made in America'. To the apprehensive unionists, the idea smacked of an unwarrantable intrusion by the United States into the domestic affairs of another country which had consistently proved to be America's most loyal ally. In the event, while Clinton undoubtedly carried into office some degree of personal sympathy for the nationalist cause generated during his brief term at Oxford as a Rhodes scholar, and could be expected to listen with respect to Senator Edward Kennedy and others, he moved cautiously in terms of an 'envoy', although willing to risk the wrath of the British and the disapproval of his own State Department on the issue of relations with Sinn Fein.

So it was that George Mitchell's introduction to Northern Ireland in December 1994 was as an 'economic envoy' to seek trade and investment developments which could buttress and facilitate the wider political process. By late November 1995, however, in discussion with the Irish Government, Major had decided on a further effort to break out of the decommissioning impasse, through a 'twin-track' process which would seek to make progress on the decommissioning issue alongside, rather than before entry into, wider political talks. The decommissioning issue was to be remitted to an international panel, chaired by George Mitchell, supported by the retired Canadian General (and former ambassador in Washington) John de Chastelain, and former Prime Minister of Finland, Harri Holkeri. The panel's report, published in January 1996, made the point that success in the wider process would involve other issues than the disposal of arms but did accept the need for 'confidence building measures' during (but not before) all-party negotiations.

The six principles enunciated at that time by the panel are of cardinal importance. Participants in the talks process should be expected to commit themselves:

(a) to democratic and exclusively peaceful means of resolving political issues;

(b) to the total disarmament of all paramilitary organisations;

(c) to agree that such disarmament must be verifiable to the satisfaction of an independent commission;

(d) to renounce for themselves, and to oppose any efforts by others, to use force, or threaten to use force, to influence the course or the outcome of all-party negotiations;

(e) to agree to abide by the terms of any agreement reached in all-party negotiations and to resort to peaceful and democratic methods in trying to alter any aspect of that outcome with which they may disagree; and

(f) to urge that 'punishment' killings and beatings stop and take effective steps to stop such actions.

We must now analyse rigorously these several propositions. They did not solve the very basic problem that, in form at least, the parties seeking to join in political negotiations would not be the same as those organisations which possessed, and had hitherto ruthlessly used, arms. True, more than one of the parties in question clearly numbered amongst their leading figures people who had served terms of imprisonment for terrorist crimes. In at least one of the Province's District Councils a sitting councillor at an earlier period had sought to destroy the historic building in which that Council met. It was, of course, the case that many countries in the modern world had witnessed a transition from armed 'freedom fighter' or 'terrorist' (from one perspective or another) to active democratic politician, Government Minister or even international statesman. In some cases, although by no means all, the earlier violent attacks had been undertaken with the full approval of a disenfranchised majority oppressed by a governing minority. Merlyn Rees's de-proscription of PSF had been clearly intended to ease that transition. But had it truly taken place? The paramilitary organisations themselves hid their organisation, funding and links with active politicians under a veil of secrecy. No one could doubt that, at the very least, politicians in PSF and the loyalist parties continued to have very considerable influence with the secret armies in the shadows. But these were not, in themselves, armies in the same sense as the conventional armed forces of a nation-state. PIRA had very consciously developed, from fear of penetration, a cellular structure within which few people knew the whole wider picture. Loyalist organisations were regionalised and deeply factional. In some cases, there were real grounds for suspicion that the party in question merely had influence. In the case of PIRA, both open admissions and covert information gave an impression of a single organisation, under a single ultimate higher command, and prepared to use a variety of means. Yet the Curragh Incident had illustrated many years before that, even within a regular army, there can be problems in keeping all one's forces onside, and in Northern Ireland both sides have shown themselves prone to fragmentation in paramilitary organisations; indeed PIRA itself had been a product of just such a split. In a curious way, both the paramilitary-linked parties and more conventional parties faced similar problems: the conventional parties needed to seek agreement on terms that their supporters would accept; and the paramilitary-linked parties needed to seek agreement on terms that their supporters and 'soldiers' would accept.

The 'principles' envisaged the total disarmament of all paramilitary organisations. This begged the question as to whether a party seeking entry to negotiations could satisfy the principle by agreeing to it while disclaiming any direct responsibility for its accomplishment in practice.

The recommendation to remit the responsibility for verification to an independent commission also raised difficult questions. Would Government, parties or people be satisfied with the evidence regarded as providing verification, if made available (as it surely would be) in secret?

The principle relating to the renunciation of the use or threat of force went to the heart of the matter. It was the presence of such a threat which gave the greatest anxiety to some of those expected to sit down with paramilitary-linked parties before any significant disarmament had taken place. The 'twin-track' approach envisaged progress in parallel. What did this mean? Could a perfunctory gesture, confined perhaps to an insignificant amount of materiel, secure a ticket of entry to the talks, leaving purely constitutional politicians to negotiate under the implicit duress of the substantial remaining arsenal? There was, of course, the third difficulty that – in spite of the best effort of intelligence professionals on both sides of the Border – no one could be sure of the total inventory of weapons held by an individual organisation, or the number or location of places at which they were held.

We were, moreover, living in a world where large quantities of weapons were freely available to those with the resources to acquire them; and PIRA in particular, with much American and other financial backing and a lucrative income from rackets, had no shortage of resources. The greater problem would be to bring such weapons into Ireland, but past experience had shown how difficult it would be to monitor imports around an island of very extensive coastline and with a high volume of incoming trade, which would grind to a halt if every load or container were to be meticulously inspected. Weapons surrendered or destroyed (if any eventually were) could easily be replenished or replaced.

Since 'punishment' killings and beatings were set to continue for further years, the principle relating to this matter is also significant. It was open to circumvention by parties which uttered routine words of condemnation and restraint but, when these brutalities nevertheless continued, fell back upon the argument that they had no responsibility beyond using their best endeavours.

In an interview with Peter Taylor, recorded in his book *Brits* (2001), George Mitchell was later to be very frank about the stance taken by himself and his colleagues:

> The Unionists quite rightly wanted some reassurance. They did not want
> to have talks occur in a setting in which the threat of violence or the use of

violence influenced the negotiations. That's the reason for the request for prior decommissioning. It soon became obvious to us, very soon into our consultation, that prior decommissioning, however desirable, was simply not a practical approach. It wasn't going to happen. The British Government wanted prior decommissioning and they wanted inclusive negotiations and it became clear that they could not have both.

Thus the Mitchell body rejected insistence upon prior decommissioning as unrealistic, but equally stated: '... there is a clear commitment on the part of those in possession of such arms to work constructively to achieve full and verifiable decommissioning as part of the process of all-party negotiations...'

It has to be noted, though, that even this degree of reassurance was itself full of ambiguities. The commitment was attached to 'those in possession of arms'. PSF and its loyalist party equivalents could be expected to repeat that they were not themselves in possession of any arms at all. In any case the obligation was simply to 'work constructively'; unhappily one could sometimes work constructively without effect. It is not at all clear whether, in expressing such commitment, the Mitchell body felt it had received encouraging signals from PIRA. Assuming that some individuals wore two hats – the political and the military – what hat were they wearing when face to face with Mitchell? All of this work related to the conditions under which parties could enter the talks process. Republicans sitting at it would certainly claim to be speaking only for Sinn Fein, not the IRA. But Adams in particular was not to be slow in reminding the community at a critical time that the men in the shadows 'had not gone away'. If that was not an attempt to 'threaten to use force to influence the course or outcome' of ongoing political negotiations, I do not know what it was.

The Major Government was now caught upon the horns of a dilemma. It had grave continuing reservations about the influence of armed paramilitaries on the political process, but did not wish to accept a state of deadlock. Not for the first or the last time, PSF scored by playing hardball. On the basis of Sinn Fein's frankly cynical 'acceptance' of the Mitchell principles, Major turned to the problem of bringing unionists to an all-inclusive table. The vehicle was to be a concession to unionist opinion that negotiations must rest upon a contemporary electoral mandate. As an initial step they decided to provide for elections in May 1996 to a 110–member deliberative forum, as a rudimentary foundation for subsequent negotiations. But the SDLP was still deeply committed to the mantra that 'nothing is agreed until everything is agreed'. Indeed John Hume was by now so wedded to endlessly repetitive formulae as to resemble some Tibetan Lama spinning his prayer wheel. Any new Assembly should be the product of successful negotiations, weaving together all three 'strands', rather than a precursor to such negotiations. PSF reacted even more adversely to what it regarded as 'putting Stormont back into place' (although in fact the Forum when elected was to meet elsewhere, in the sterile surroundings of the downtown Interpoint Centre).

As it happens, I myself was due on the evening of Friday 9 February 1996 to attend at the Europa Hotel the annual 'Superbowl Ball' of the Flax Trust, an organisation led by a charismatic priest, Father Myles Kavanagh, and involved in various benevolent cross-community exercises, with much support from Irish America. I had, however, started the evening at the Belfast offices of the Independent Television Authority (ITA) where – as the Northern Ireland Governor of the BBC – I had joined a farewell party for David Glencross, outgoing Chief Executive of the ITA. It was there that I heard the literally explosive news that the PIRA ceasefire had been brought to a dramatic end, with a massive bomb at Canary Wharf in London. Shortly before the bomb went off, PIRA had issued a bitter statement accusing the Major Government of bad faith and collusion with the unionist leadership. The ceasefire had lasted just over seventeen months.

The choice of that prestigious target in London was transparently deliberate. Although from time to time national politicians have made resolute Churchillian noises about never yielding to violence and republican failure to appreciate the mettle of the British people, the reality was that spectacular violence on the British mainland had an enhanced impact. It was not the first or the last time that PIRA had underlined its capacity to endanger institutions and individuals at the heart of the British state. A mortar bomb lobbed into the garden at 10 Downing Street, or the close call for Margaret Thatcher at Brighton won column inches, radio and television airtime and political attention well beyond the norm for attacks in Northern Ireland. There it was to take a truly massive 'spectacular' – a Bloody Friday or Bloody Sunday, a Warrenpoint or Enniskillen or Omagh – to engage the attention of the nation. Otherwise the steady repetition of murder in Northern Ireland could seem at times like a distant, monotonous drumbeat.

Moreover, the economic and financial impact of a massive explosion amidst expensive and closely packed properties was bound to be enormous. The ultimate directors of the republican movement – people of subtle intelligence and great experience – appreciated that any British Government would consider the wider issue of whether a settlement on balance served the national interest. This is not to say that it felt no care or concern for the suffering people of Northern Ireland. Major himself clearly had their interests very much at heart. But the British people as a whole were now in the firing line. The next 'spectacular', in the centre of Manchester, fortunately led to no fatalities but injured some 200 people and caused damage amounting to hundreds of millions of pounds.

Meanwhile the election of a Forum rolled ahead, under elaborate and unusual electoral arrangements designed to secure at least a minimum representation of two seats for each of the top ten parties contesting election. By this means parties with relatively modest support, such as the paramilitary-linked 'loyalist' Progressive Unionist Party (PUP) and United Democratic Party (UDP), as well as the moderate Women's Coalition, would be able to take part in the deliberative process. Perversely, the party making most ground at the Forum elections was the party which could not not be admitted to its deliberations, PSF with a 15.5 per cent share. The SDLP also refused to take seats in the Forum, thus enormously reducing its capabilities to make any real progress towards substantive negotiations. The Forum was to prove a talking shop.

Thus a fundamentally weak Conservative Government, albeit led by a Prime Minister who had demonstrated a real commitment to Northern Ireland, had failed to make a truly significant breakthrough. But it had greatly improved relationships with the Irish Republic, and created the first real prospect of ultimate agreement about constitutional status and the 'consent principle'. On the downside, the Major Government could be criticised for putting up a bold front which, under pressure from the single-minded 'hard men' of republican terrorism, it was unable or unwilling to defend. Unionist confidence in the straightforwardness of the British Government had certainly been damaged by the revelation in November 1993 of previously secret talks between Government and PIRA. Hitherto Government had flatly denied any suggestion that it had been negotiating with PIRA, and although Sir Patrick Mayhew's subsequent explanation to the House of Commons, stressing the distinction between negotiations and the willingness of Government to clarify its well-known position, was accepted with remarkably little demur by the great majority of Members; it did nothing to reduce unionist paranoia. The truth of the matter was that for a number of years, while Irish Governments were by and large holding the line of 'not talking to terrorists', the British Government or its agents had been doing just that. While, with the 'broadcasting ban' in place, the ordinary citizen was not even permitted to hear the actual speaking voice of republican leaders on radio or television, those same voices were being heard directly by the Government or its authorised representatives.

We are in muddy waters here. Governments cannot always be fully candid with the House of Commons if they are to serve the public interest. Many questions, such as 'Is the Government still considering a devaluation of sterling?' have to be met with a straight bat. To use Robert Armstrong's most celebrated phrase, it may sometimes be necessary to be 'economical with the truth'. Even on more mundane issues, Ministers at the Dispatch

Box do not go out of their way to saw off the branches on which they sit. But what has to be avoided in all of this is an outright lie. I would not wish to argue that this crucial line was crossed in exchanges about discussions with PIRA, but certainly the sudden exposure of these previously unacknowledged contacts was hardly a 'confidence-building' measure in the eyes of the unionist community. Moreover, the relatively tough line on decommissioning expressed by Mayhew in Washington had been much blurred by subsequent events. One could argue convincingly that decommissioning should never have become such a shibboleth in the first place. But it was not only British but also Irish Ministers who had introduced it as a key issue. There was now a growing willingness to fudge that issue.

The paramount reason for the priority given to drawing PSF into the talks was its links with PIRA. Although it had by now gained a significant electoral position, this had not in the past prevented British Governments from moving ahead without the participation of a significant party, such as the DUP. Nor would such ingenious efforts have been made to ensure the presence at the Forum of loyalist parties with very modest electoral support, if they had not been viewed as closely linked to, and capable of influencing, the principal loyalist paramilitary organisations. Violence never pays? Cant.

Perhaps the most significant step taken by the Major Government was the acceptance of a growing role for George Mitchell. In many respects, Major had been disappointed and even appalled by what was perceived as the cosy relationship between the Clinton administration and militant republicanism. The appointment as American Ambassador in Dublin of the late President's sister, Jean Kennedy Smith, was a significant indicator of a change of stance. In Washington Senator Edward Kennedy had been at the centre of Irish-American political pressures, while 'young Joe' as a brash Congressman, with other children of the late Robert Kennedy, had shown marked sympathy with the republican cause. There was early evidence that in relation to Northern Ireland, the advice of Jean Kennedy Smith would receive a more favourable reception than that of the highly experienced London Ambassador, Raymond Seitz, accredited as he was to the Government of the United Kingdom of Great Britain and Northern Ireland. Clinton clearly believed the reversal of previous policy to withhold an entry visa for Gerry Adams would serve to reinforce the message that republicanism could expect better returns from the political route than from its alternative. Major was known to be furious about the grant of a visa to Adams, and the subsequent spectacle of a republican leader being widely lionised did little to alleviate his concern. The first Adams visit led on to a series of further visits by himself and others, to the opening of a representative office in the United States and to a huge boost in the fund-raising capability of Sinn Fein. It was to dawn rather belatedly upon those involved in the democratic politics of the Irish Republic that it might not be healthy for the Irish polity to face growing penetration by the richest party in Ireland, and that a party still closely associated with paramilitarism. It was also fascinating to observe that the reputation as 'the greatest living Irishman' assiduously built up by John Hume over many years of persistent lobbying, began to dim in the fierce light of competition from the persuasive Adams, who had increasingly, in his dress and overall presentation, taken on the protective colouring of some liberal arts professor. Provo-chic became the latest thing.

Yet Major was a realist. He welcomed Mitchell's initial introduction to the scene as a special 'economic envoy'. Mitchell himself no doubt assumed that his would be a relatively brief in-and-out involvement. But in fact one thing led to another. Advice on tricky issues had to be remitted to a 'neutral'. In spite of the involvement at one stage of a former Australian Governor-General, nationalists and republicans were inclined to regard anyone from a Commonwealth country as pro-British. Many able American citizens disqualified themselves from playing a useful role (even if they had wished to do so) by previous more or less partisan declarations on related issues. Mitchell did not have, in that sense, a 'record'. He was circumspect, well respected across party lines in the United States, and enjoyed a close relationship with President Clinton. On moving from the role of economic envoy to the chairmanship of the decommissioning panel he had faced – and later frankly acknowledged – his inability to square the circle. Yet he had gained the confidence and respect of all parties.

Although neither the SDLP nor PSF were willing to take part in what they saw as the pure talking shop of the Forum, the elections in May 1996 had produced an electoral mandate for teams who might be involved in a talks process. All the ten parties elected to the Forum were willing to take part in such talks, but with the decommissioning impasse still unresolved, PSF was initially excluded. Nevertheless 'all-party' (or in reality nearly all-party) talks opened on 10 June 1996 under the chairmanship of George Mitchell, now moving on to yet another demanding role. But little initial progress could be made. The Major Government was running out of time and increasingly some of the Northern Ireland parties (whether included or excluded at that stage) were holding fire to wait for what they now expected to be a Labour victory at the approaching General Election. It can be assumed that the unionist parties, on the other hand, would have been keen to make as much progress as possible while a Government less likely to favour Irish unity remained in office. There were some dangerous misconceptions here about the stance of both the major political parties. True, the UUP had at one time been an acknowledged 'sister party' of the Conservatives, with the occasional unionist even holding office. There also continued to be, towards the right wing of a party, a strongly pro-union element, as exemplified before his murder by the late Ian Gow. Yet it was, after all, this party which, when in Government, had first of all swept away the old Stormont Parliament and later been a party to the Agreement conceding to the Republic its substantial continuing role in Northern Ireland's affairs. Within the Labour Party, on the other hand, the accession to leadership of Tony Blair after the untimely death of John Smith had seen the removal from the post of Shadow Secretary of State of the long-serving Kevin McNamara, who had never made any secret of his sympathy with nationalism and antipathy to unionism. Others in the Labour Party, such as Clare Short, with her family links with Crossmaglen, still had a deeply rooted sympathy for nationalist objectives, and the general thrust of Labour opinion in Parliament and the country continued to favour Irish unity as the best ultimate outcome. But if the 'consent principle' remained paramount, what would matter in the end would be the wishes of the Northern Ireland people themselves. Unionists, of course, were likely to remain deeply suspicious that the practical links with Britain would be progressively weakened and those with the Republic progressively reinforced, to the point where British sovereignty would become a mere shell.

A new dawn broke, both for Great Britain and for Northern Ireland, as Blair's Labour Party swept to power in the May 1997 General Election, with a massive majority. In spite of the earnest, honest and decent leadership of John Major, the country as a whole had become thoroughly sick of the Conservative Government, with its seemingly endless divisions, backbiting and 'sleaze'. The Tories had by then been in office for a dangerously long time. As we shall see later in discussing the role of unionism, prolonged tenure of office by any party in any jurisdiction is all too likely to lead to complacency, arrogance, insensitivity and intellectual exhaustion. Some of the workhorses of the Conservative Party had been drawing the plough for a very long time. The people might well have dismissed the Conservative Government at the previous General Election, but for the adverse reaction of the country to the garrulous personality of Neil Kinnock and evidence of premature and presumptuous triumphalism.

The arrival on the scene of a new British Government with a secure majority led to a fracture of the log-jam. The continuing influence and interest of President Clinton began to exert their effect. So far George Mitchell, appointed as 'Talks Chairman' more than a year before, had been able to make very little headway; in the new situation Sinn Fein felt confident to proceed with discussions under his chairmanship. He was known to be very close to President Clinton, whose visa decisions and wider attitudes had represented 'confidence-building measures' for Sinn Fein. It was also the case that, from the earliest days of the Blair premiership, Clinton had emphasised the urgent White House interest in the Northern Ireland settlement. For his part Blair, coming into office without the usual background of senior ministerial experience, was anxious to hit the ground running. He decided that the talks would be expedited by setting a time deadline. There would be a 'make or break' year of negotiations.

The actual admission of PSF into the talks was preceded by some careful choreography. Blair had made it clear that, if the IRA instituted a new ceasefire, there could be immediate talks between Government officials and Sinn Fein, but this was coupled with the warning that the process could not be held up indefinitely. The 'settlement train', as he termed it, would leave the station with or without PSF. For its part, PSF had its confidence reinforced by the outcome of the District Council May elections, in which it won 16.9 per cent of the votes and was clearly closing the gap with the SDLP (at 20.6 per cent).

Blair's crucial decision at this time was to make it clear to PSF that it would be admitted to the talks process after a ceasefire on the basis of its acceptance of the 'Mitchell principles' but without any actual prior decommissioning. Previous declarations of principle, both by British and Irish Ministers, were therefore overridden. It was a decision of the purest pragmatism. Britain wanted a ceasefire at the earliest possible moment to avert further Canary Wharf or Manchester incidents. Britain also wanted to explore progress towards a comprehensive settlement. Neither the intermediate nor the ultimate objective seemed capable of achievement without giving ground to the obduracy and steel-hardened determination of PSF.

I had read many years before how the great Turkish nationalist Kemal Ataturk had prevailed in negotiations by an ability to go on saying 'no' indefinitely. I would reflect here that an infrequently recognised factor in the Northern Ireland associations was a real cultural difference. Behind a mask of ideology, most British politicians are in reality inclined to compromise, to be reasonable, to be ready to give ground in order to make progress. The hard men and women of PSF were of an utterly different cast of mind. In their ruthless and undeviating pursuit of their objectives, they exhibited a coolly calculating pattern of mind and behaviour. The Blairite Labour Party was, over time, to be accused of being 'control freaks' who demanded that all adherents should stay 'on message'. Compared with the postgraduates of PSF, most Labour Ministers were still in the nursery school of single-mindedness.

As so often, this evident and major concession to the obduracy of PSF ran a risk of creating a conference table on one side of which nationalists and republicans would confront empty seats. Unionists of all descriptions were outraged by the decision to admit PSF to talks solely on the basis of its formal adherence to the Mitchell principles, but without the slightest shred of any binding commitment to decommissioning in the future, let alone any actual decommissioning even at the most symbolic level.

Ian Paisley and the DUP, who lived in a world of absolutes, made it very clear that they would take no further part in political negotiations under conditions they deemed wholly unacceptable. The position of David Trimble as leader of the UUP was more complex. His party's consistent line hitherto had been one of no negotiation with PSF without decommissioning. On the other hand, he was faced with a full term of Labour Government and could see that, in the absence of some settlement 'made at home', the British Government might move in directions wholly contrary to the unionist interest. His predecessor had argued for years for an alternative to, or replacement of, the 1985 Anglo-Irish Agreement, focusing his criticism in particular upon the Intergovernmental Conference and Anglo-Irish Secretariat as mechanisms to transact Northern Ireland business over the heads of their elected representatives. There was no reason to believe that sabotaging the prospects of a devolution system would impede the growth of cooperation with the Republic; the outcome might well be an Intergovernmental Conference Mark II with the British side of the table occupied by members of a party more sympathetic to ultimate Irish unity than their Conservative predecessors.

In this wholly unenviable situation Trimble, a subtle academic lawyer, was able – not without difficulty – to persuade the UUP to remain within the process, on the basis of an assurance by both the British and Irish Governments that the decommissioning issue would be pursued in tandem with the talks. The vehicle for this parallel activity was to be an Independent International Commission on Decommissioning, chaired by General John de Chastelain.

The story of the fraught negotiations leading to the conclusion of the Belfast Agreement on Good Friday 1998 is too well known to require repetition here. Undoubtedly the achievement of an apparently successful outcome owed a very great deal to the extraordinary patience and skill of George Mitchell. Yet, amidst the immediate euphoria and the general astonishment that such disparate parties should have been capable of reaching any agreement, two malign developments were given inadequate weight. Trimble had not been able to commit to the Agreement all of that small group of supposedly close supporters who had constituted the UUP delegation to the talks. The late defection of Jeffrey Donaldson has been attributed to a variety of motives, but it was a warning signal that the DUP would find within the UUP elements supportive of its resistance to the deal. The even more serious reality was that the key issue of decommissioning remained unresolved. In the face of the assurances of the British and Irish Governments that the decommissioning issue would be pursued in tandem with the talks, and indeed a joint declaration when they opened in September 1997 that they viewed 'the resolution of the decommissioning issue as an indispensable part of the process of negotiations', Trimble and his colleagues were entitled to expect some real and demonstrable progress. Total decommissioning was the ideal, perhaps unachievable; it seemed reasonable, on the other hand, to expect as a minimum some initial gesture or symbolic action, accompanied by agreement on a reasonable timetable and modalities for future action. There were even some who suggested that there might be an alternative to decommissioning as a credible demonstration that 'the war was over'. Nothing of the kind was available.

We must examine here a crucial question of how to conduct complex negotiations between conflicting parties who have good reasons to distrust each other. In such negotiations there will be secondary issues on which, perhaps under pressure from an outside mediator, compromises can be made. But inevitably, at some stage, the negotiators will come close to the heart and core of their long-standing dispute.

Some years ago I had the opportunity to hear at first hand something of the conduct of Israeli–Palestinian negotiations conducted secretly through the 'Norway Channel'. Inevitably these negotiations had reached the central and highly controversial issue of the future status of Jerusalem, on which the objectives of the negotiating parties were apparently quite irreconcilable. What is one to do for the best when one is confronted by such an impasse? Does one accept that, unless the crucial issue can be solved, any apparent agreement on other matters will prove to have shallow foundations and ultimately collapse under the weight of its own contradictions? Or does one press ahead with an incomplete agreement representing some progress albeit on less emotive issues, in the hope that somewhere down the line, in a calmer atmosphere and after a slow building of mutual trust, the final coping stone can be put into place? In the case of the Middle East, a partial agreement with central issues still unresolved led over time to an increase rather than a reduction in mutual animosity.

Even the most amateur of political observers could sense at the outset how vulnerable the Belfast Agreement might prove in the absence of unexpected definitive progress on the issue of decommissioning. But was the Agreement in itself likely to promote that build-up of mutual confidence which might open possibilities of movement on the weapons front?

To answer this question, it is necessary to examine in some detail the provisions of the Agreement itself. I emphasise again that, while the Agreement was of course the product of negotiations as between what John Hume, in one of his wonderfully repetitive mantras, called 'both Governments and all the parties' (but excluding, of course, the DUP), the British Government remained the sovereign power responsible for the welfare of all of its citizens who lived in Northern Ireland. It had, therefore, an ultimate and incontestable obligation not to sign off on any Agreement likely to move the problems 'to the right' rather than actually solve them.

An inherent weakness in the entire process was that the local negotiators of the Agreement could not bind all the parties to the ongoing conflict. Frequent reference had been made to a 'peace process', but a true 'peace process' binds armed forces as well as governments or political parties. Neither PIRA nor INLA nor the UVF nor the UDA were party to, or conclusively committed by, the negotiations. PSF, for example, was in some broad sense regarded as speaking for the wider republican movement, but there were no grounds for believing that PIRA had committed itself to the declaration made in the Agreement. The 'political process' might, hopefully, contribute to a 'peace process', but it was not synonymous with it.

Secondly, it should be realised that Trimble and his team were negotiating on a most unequal basis. On one side were the Irish Government, the SDLP and PSF, all nationalist in sentiment and ultimate aspiration, however divided about previous methods of pursuing it. On the other side Trimble negotiated from a precarious position within the UUP, and with the DUP characteristically absent from the battlefield. It was a luxuriously comfortable position to leave Trimble alone to defend the broad unionist position and subsequently criticise him for failing to gain enough ground.

Thirdly, there lurked in the background the unresolved question of whether the Agreement reached was a stable destination or a mere staging post. Unionists were entitled to expect that, having conceded the possibility of unity if a majority supported it, they would receive reciprocal respect for Northern Ireland's position within the United Kingdom as long as this enjoyed the support of a majority of the people. Would the Agreement bring assurance of at least interim stability, or simply another ratchet to move Northern Ireland inexorably away from the United Kingdom and into the Irish orbit?

Apparently trivial matters can have a profound symbolic impact in the semantic minefield that is Northern Ireland. And in that context it was striking that, although the Agreement itself referred throughout to 'Northern Ireland', such a prominent SDLP figure as Seamus Mallon seemed unable to bring himself to abandon the terminology 'the North of Ireland'. It was to be a bizarre feature of Northern Ireland's future government that its second-ranking figure was reluctant to describe the jurisdiction within which he governed by its proper name.

Fourthly, it has to be emphasised that the Agreement itself, rather than solving some crucial problems, remitted them for resolution by others. There would be a new Northern Ireland Human Rights Commission, a new statutory Equality Commission, and above all a commission on policing (subsequently to be chaired by Chris Patten).

So let us examine, then, whether the Agreement was a balanced settlement, inevitably reflecting compromises and sacrifices made by every party to it, but overall equitable as a political settlement and likely to be a constructive contribution to the 'peace process'.

There were certainly some real gains for unionism, going far beyond those ephemeral gains claimed by Faulkner in 1973, which had disappeared in the midst of the 'Boland' case and the tedious arguments by jurists about fugitive offenders. For the first time an Irish Government committed itself, subject to overall approval of the Agreement in both parts of Ireland, to recommend the Irish people to remove from their Constitution by referendum the wording regarded by unionists as asserting a 'territorial claim' to Northern Ireland. The very unsatisfactory law-making procedures under direct rule would be replaced by a power to enact new laws locally. The executive Government of the Province would pass again into the hands of locally elected people, with important ministerial offices, including the office of Chief Minister, held by unionists. There would be the establishment of a British–Irish Council in which for the first time representatives of the Irish Government would be drawn into close encounter with the other Governments of the British Isles. Along the north–south axis, future dealing would be bilateral, rather than unilateral as it had been under the Anglo-Irish Agreement of 1985.

There were also, of course, gains for constitutional nationalism in the shape of the SDLP. For the first time since the brief power-sharing experiment of 1974, some of its ablest and best people would be able to take on executive responsibilities. Important protections for the rights, culture and sense of 'Irishness' of their electorate would be in-built. Very significantly, the process had taken on board John Hume's sophisticated arguments about self-determination. For the first time in decades the people of Ireland as a whole, and the people of Ireland alone, would be able to express their democratic judgement on a set of constitutional and governmental principles and arrangements. Inevitably the vote would be taken in the two separate jurisdictions, but on the same day. There was, of course, an inherent risk that a majority in one jurisdiction or the other would withhold consent. But if, on the other hand, the outcome would be a clear majority in each jurisdiction, the people of Ireland as a whole would have exercised their right to self-determination in support of the principles and provisions of the Agreement.

The position of PSF was characteristically ambiguous. The outside world could regard it as a striking gain for its members that they had broken through from the status of political agitators to that of potential Ministers, who would not only share in the Government of Northern Ireland but sit as full members at the new north–south table. Yet it became clear to me subsequently that, in terms of the republican mindset, it was regarded as a concession by Sinn Fein rather than as a concession to them to sit in an Executive still under United Kingdom sovereignty and take seats at Stormont, for years the hated symbol of unionist and Protestant hegemony.

My own first direct encounter with a leading member of PSF had occurred in March 1996, when I accepted an invitation to be speaker in a series of talks given in the Clonard Monastery in west Belfast. Accepting this invitation, I was conscious of the striking role played in the development of events by Father Alec Reid and others. It was the Redemptorist Father Reid who in 1988 had administered the last rites to two army corporals who had blundered into the path of a funeral procession for one of the victims of Michael Stone's murderous assault at Milltown Cemetery, and who had themselves become victims in an appalling episode of hysterical savagery. It was Father Reid, too, who had done much – for better or worse – to bring Adams and Hume together that same year. At a well-attended event in the monastery church on 3 March, 1996 I had found myself under the chairmanship of the suave and able Caoimhgin O'Caolain, the first member of PSF to take up a seat in the Dail in Dublin. In the aftermath of the Agreement I was to extend my personal knowledge of some leading PSF personalities, as fellow-guests encountered at the dinner tables of Northern Ireland Office Ministers. These encounters left me in no doubt about the consummate political skills and steely abilities of such people, but also persuaded me that they saw the 'process' as essentially a step on the road towards 'getting the Brits out of Ireland'.

On one memorable occasion I found myself briefly face to face with Gerry Adams himself. It was a sunny day and I was standing with a colleague at the top of the steps leading up to the Stormont Parliament Buildings when I was aware of this tall, striking and wholly unmistakable figure approaching me. He eyed me – or as an RUC protective officer who had worked with me might have said – he eyeballed me. 'You're Ken Bloomfield,' he said, in a declaratory rather than interrogatory way. In the midst of this sudden encounter with the leader of an organisation that had used my attempted assassination in 1988 to discourage Civil Service colleagues from continuing to do their duty, I was not quick enough to utter any reaction before he passed through the swing doors. Only in retrospect did it occur to me that I should have replied, 'Yes, but tell me, who are you?'

If the republican movement wanted 'Brits' out in the long run or sooner if possible, it wanted its 'political prisoners' out in the short run. Although the 'special category' initially accorded by William Whitelaw had been formally abandoned, large numbers of prisoners – both on the republican and loyalist sides – continued to be distinguished from the prison population at large, not least by the special court procedures leading to their conviction and imprisonment. The parties associated with paramilitaries were bound to argue strongly that the quid pro quo of ceasefires declared by republican and loyalist paramilitary organisations must be the release of 'prisoners of war'. It was, of course, conveniently overlooked here that in the wider international community a body of law was developing which did not allow even soldiers in an army acting under orders from a lawfully constituted Government to evade moral and legal responsibilities for war crimes and crimes against humanity. The self-styled 'political prisoners' covered a wide spectrum, reaching from idealistic young men convicted for membership and low-level activity to case-hardened terrorists responsible for multiple murders and acts coming close to classic definitions of genocide.

It had long been clear to me, as to many others, that some degree of early release or amnesty was likely to feature in any comprehensive settlement. And it has to be remembered that outside his own delegation Trimble could look for support on wider unionist concerns only to the representatives of the loyalist political fringe, including people who had themselves committed heinous crimes for which they had served terms of imprisonment.

Yet any such scheme was bound to be deeply painful to many people. The security forces who had run extreme risks to bring these offenders to justice, the prison officers who had tried to keep a credible prison regime in place under appalling difficulties, and above all the many relatives of the murdered I had met face-to-face as Victims Commissioner – all of these had found a mass release of prisoners hard to stomach. Yet I had found a willingness, even amongst many whose personal lives had been blighted, to swallow a very bitter pill if it was really to help cure the community, resolve the conflict and set Northern Ireland on a better course.

What, in reality, was to be the return for the agreement that all prisoners affiliated to organisations maintaining the ceasefire would be released within a maximum of two years from the commencement of the scheme of accelerated release? Could people say, 'Let the prisoners be released. The war is over'?

The section of the Agreement on decommissioning gave little grounds for optimism. Yes, the participants in the Agreement confirmed their intention 'to continue to work constructively and in good faith with the Independent Commission and use any influence they may have to achieve the decommissioning of all paramilitary arms within two years following endorsement at referendums North and South of the Agreement, and in the context of the implementation of the overall settlement'. Yet again I would point out that the armed organisations were not themselves party to the Agreement, nor did the parties linked to them offer or promise any ability to deliver their compliance on this or indeed any other issue. Political parties could claim to be following the letter of the Agreement by keeping the Independent Commission in play and declaring that they were of course using such influence as they had to move things forward. Moreover, the use of the phrase 'in the context of the implementation of the overall agreement' offered to relevant parties an escape clause. On the pretext that no progress, or insufficient progress, was being made on some other front, they could claim that the conditions favourable to actual decommissioning had not been created. Most objectionable of all was the prospect that opened for paramilitary-linked parties to lever demands for progress on other fronts. In the face of repeated declarations that the possession of weaponry could not be allowed to influence political development, the abject decommissioning section of the Agreement afforded precisely that opportunity.

All this has subsequently been justified by the argument that, if PSF had been pressed harder on the decommissioning front, no Agreement would have been achievable. Certainly by this time, with the gap between the SDLP and PSF rapidly closing, the SDLP had no appetite for a deal excluding PSF. The Agreement must be 'all inclusive', although no one seems to have regarded the absence of the DUP as an impediment.

I had myself sought to address the question of arms in an article I wrote for the *Northern Ireland Monitor* in June 1996:

> Why ... should any interest wish to hold on to illegal weaponry other than as an implicit threat to renew violence if its full political expectations cannot be satisfied? As against this, it is perfectly clear that paramilitary organisations on all sides are unwilling to contemplate actions which could be construed as an admission of their defeat. I suggest that we think in wider terms. Progress was made in East/West relations not on the basis of unilateral disarmament but on the basis of a phased multilateral de-escalation. Thus the risk of open conflict between the great powers has been reduced if not entirely eliminated, and mutual fear and suspicion greatly diluted. Here in Northern Ireland Government has frequently made it clear that the armed profile of security forces can and will be reduced as the circumstances allow. A mutually agreed de-escalation with all parties and interest participating could not be characterised as a surrender by any of them.

At the time of the Agreement all the elements necessary for a balanced deal were present: release of prisoners; police and criminal justice reform; and steps of a specific kind towards normal peacetime security arrangements. Although these were multi-party negotiations, it must be remembered that all the key issues – police and criminal justice reform, the level of security arrangements and the treatment of prisoners – were under the control of the British Government and not envisaged for early devolution to domestic institutions. The British Government had all the pieces; why did it not play the game?

I regard the complete and unconditional (save for the preservation of a rickety ceasefire) release of paramilitary prisoners, without any correlation with reciprocal movement towards a real end to hostilities, as an appalling mistake and dereliction of duty. Whatever the views of other negotiating parties, the British Government should have insisted that a continuation of prisoner releases – after an initial gesture of goodwill by the release of a first tranche unconditionally – would be dependent upon measurable progress towards that 'resolution' of the decommissioning issue, which participants to the Agreement had recognised as 'an indispensable part of the process of negotiation'.

The fact of the matter is that the British Government was pledged to move – and did move – towards 'normal security arrangements' in a situation which remained profoundly abnormal, and through the Patten Commission on policing began processes of radical (and often sensible and necessary) changes, which nevertheless led to the premature retirement of many senior and experienced officers, in the face of continuing paramilitary violence, an ongoing threat of the full-scale resumption of terrorism, and a rising tide of crime often related to drug abuse.

There is an interesting passage in Michael Heseltine's autobiography *Life in the Jungle* (2000), in which he records a discussion with John Major about developments in Northern Ireland:

> I could understand the community of interest which might, with skill and patience, draw the British Government and that of the Republic together. I could understand that Gerry Adams might be tiring of the endless excuses for wanton violence his position forced him to make and that he might trade it for some share of legitimate power and a much enhanced prospect at the ballot box. All that I could see. What I could not see were the arguments that would persuade the young activists to give up their weapons. They enjoyed power in the community based on cruelty and fear. I could not see them exchanging this to enable others to indulge in the inevitable compromises and fudges of democratic life.

What was all too clear was that the Agreement was characterised by just such compromises and fudges.

It could, I suppose, be argued that those Northern Ireland people – and they are very numerous – who have been disillusioned by the working of the celebrated Agreement, should recall the maxim *caveat emptor*. The Government could not impose the Agreement upon them; they had the opportunity to accept or reject it by referendum. If they bought the proverbial 'pig in a poke', the fault was theirs. They were, after all, adults in a mature democracy.

It is, on the other hand, ludicrous to suppose that the majority of the people will read, let alone fully understand, a document which ran to thirty printed pages in a version posted to each voter. They were going to be heavily influenced by commentary or exegesis as distinct from text; by what media commentators had to say and the arguments for and against an agreement mounted by the principal protagonists. Here there can be no doubt that what came to be called the 'No camp' got off to the better start. This is not surprising. It will always be easier to mount a sharp-edged ideological opposition than to 'sell' an Agreement which is bound to be a 'curate's egg'. Conscious of the need to retain the support of their own electorate in the longer term, parties to such an agreement would inevitably stress their gains and play down their concessions. We had been through all this in 1974 in the aftermath of the Sunningdale Agreement. How could it be, the bewildered citizen might well ask, at one and the same time the first real de facto recognition of Northern Ireland (in the Faulkner version) and a substantial step towards a united Ireland (as imprudently claimed by some members of the SDLP)? Apart from a faintly embarrassing joint appearance by David Trimble and John Hume at a rock concert there was little evidence of pro-Agreement parties forming a common front or presenting a common line. The presentation of the Agreement tended to be defensive in tone.

The personal intervention into the referendum campaign of the Prime Minister, Tony Blair, may very well have been crucial. For different reasons, both the major elements in the nationalist camp – the SDLP and PSF – were firmly pro-Agreement, and although there was worrying evidence of growing republican dissidence (in line with the thinking of Michael Heseltine), there was very little doubt that the great majority of the Catholic and nationalist community would support the Agreement. The problem lay on the unionist side of the fence, where there were growing concerns about prisoner releases and the potential participation in Government of a party backed by an illegal army with huge supplies of weaponry and materiel.

Tony Blair brought to the situation the powerful battery of his presidential talents. We have had few Prime Ministers who could put a better face on any decision, good, bad or indifferent. On a personal visit to Northern

Ireland, the high point – witnessed by a huge television audience – was the physical addition of his signature to five 'personal pledges'. These included the crucial assurances: 'Those who use or threaten violence excluded from the Government of Northern Ireland,' and 'Prisoners kept in unless violence is given up for good.'

Here, apparently, was the Prime Minister of the United Kingdom of Great Britain and Northern Ireland giving us a bankable assurance that politicians linked to terrorism would not become Ministers in a devolved Government, and that the release of prisoners was, indeed, conditional on a genuine and permanent abandonment of violence.

I myself was one of the many upon whom this gesture and these words made a deep impression. I had already taken heart in particular from the new readiness at least on the part of the two Governments to accept and embody in constitutional and statute law the principle of consent. I had seen this as best serving the ends of both communities and traditions. Writing of the consent principle in June 1996 I had argued:

> Under that umbrella parties devoted to a nationalist agenda could begin to break down those barriers of mutual distrust without which any consensual movement towards Irish unity, and certainly any ultimate union of people as distinct from territory, could not occur. Under precisely that same umbrella parties devoted to a unionist agenda could legitimately hope for a growth of solidarity in addressing practical problems in society and the economy, leaving every faction free to argue for its ultimate agenda without acrimony or the threat of force.

I felt, in short, then, that neither the actual Northern Ireland of the present nor a hypothetical united Ireland of the future could offer a decent life and parity of esteem for all its citizens in the absence of clarity about the modalities of self-determination, to be exercised freely and without the threat or use of force.

Impressed as I was by many aspects of the Agreement, I could nevertheless understand – not least as a consequence of my recent dialogue with so many victims of violence – the widespread concern that we could see paramilitary-linked parties in Government and the continuing release of prisoners, including numerous murderers, without any assurance whatever that hostilities had been abandoned for good, validated by concrete evidence of a credible and continuing process to wind down the war machine. This concern related both to republican and loyalist paramilitarism. The loyalist organisations too had their caches of weapons and their 'hard men' anxious for release; but at least it did not seem likely that they would win seats at the Cabinet table even under the projected arrangements for inclusive government.

I could not believe at that time that my Prime Minister would offer a showy commitment to so-called 'pledges' without a sound basis for doing so. Either, one assumed, he was in receipt of confidential assurances from parties linked to paramilitaries that action would be taken within a defensible timescale, or he was prepared, in the absence of acceptable movement, to discontinue the release of prisoners and facilitate formation of a Northern Ireland Executive excluding Sinn Fein.

It is now abundantly clear that either he had received no secret assurances of movement, had misinterpreted 'signals' coming to him (always a danger in such situations) or had been deliberately misled. The possible 'sanctions' mentioned in his pledges were less than robust. There was, first of all, the supposed separateness of PSF from PIRA. It could certainly be argued that the mere act of retention of formidable weaponry constituted an implicit threat of violence. Nor was it to be the case that the Agreement represented a decisive end to violence in Northern Ireland. Admittedly the appalling Omagh atrocity of August 1998 – the worst single incident in the entire course of 'the troubles' – was not attributed to PSF but to the dissidents of the 'Real IRA'. The ceasefire had certainly marked an end to such activities as regular murderous attacks on the security forces. But other violence, much of it attributable to organisations formally 'on ceasefire', continued over the years to come. In particular, whole areas of the Province under the grip of one faction or the other would experience regular 'punishment' action, much of it within communities rather than across lines of confrontation. In any event, the political parties known to have close links with paramilitary groups could be expected to say – and indeed did say – 'If there is violence, it is not coming from our party. It is our conduct, and not that of some group thought be associated with us, that has to be judged.' One was to see this technique of 'distancing' at its classic best in the PSF reaction to the arrest of three Irishmen in Colombia in 2001. In the immediate aftermath, the normally super-articulate spokesmen for PSF were uncharacteristically reticent, and when cornered by the media lacked their customary poise and self-assurance. But of course Gerry Adams, that master of manipulation, had the answer for publication in an Irish-American journal, in the form of an absolute assurance that, whatever the 'Colombia Three' had been doing, they had not been commissioned to do it by Sinn Fein – an organisation, of course, wholly distinct from the IRA. Yet even the skilful Adams let the mask slip occasionally. His notorious jocular reference to the IRA ('They haven't gone away, you know') came very close indeed to a threat of violence if the demands of the republican movement were not met.

There was, though, another reality which eroded the value of one of Blair's key pledges. The innocent unionist voter, anxious to see a restoration of devolved government and quite prepared, however belatedly, to share power with constitutional nationalism, interpreted the Blair words about exclusion from Government as leading to a coalition in which the UUP and the SDLP would be the core members, with the DUP excluded by its own choice and PSF excluded by Government action as a consequence of any continuing threat of violence.

In the real world there was not the slightest chance of this happening. By then both the Irish Government and the SDLP were too deeply committed to the concept of an all-embracing administration, and the SDLP in particular was increasingly nervous about the growing influence of PSF amongst the nationalist electorate. In a very real sense, the pass had been sold by John Hume long ago. He had deliberately allowed similarity of objective (progress towards a united Ireland) to take precedence over difference of method (constitutional politics as against 'the Armalite and ballot box'). Hume's SDLP had appeared to many unionists to have more in common with the nationalism of PSF than with the constitutionalism of the UUP. Hume himself would justify this as the best, and indeed only, way of bringing republicanism in from the cold and committing it over time to the purely political path. He could point to the evolution of the Civil War faction led by de Valera into the democratic party of Fianna Fail.

If, then, Blair had envisaged making good his pledge in terms of excluding PSF, the actual result would not have been devolved government without Sinn Fein, but a continuation of indefinite direct rule.

As for the release of prisoners, there was to be no convincing evidence for a very long time that violence had been given up for good. There was no binding pledge from parties associated with paramilitary organisations, let alone from such organisations themselves, that the 'war' was over and would not be resumed in any circumstances. The retention of weaponry on a large scale, without any evidence – save for a token loyalist gesture – of beginning to put weapons 'beyond use' was itself an implicit and continuing threat of violence. We were to see in days to come increasingly implausible judgements that ceasefires were still 'in place'. Individual prisoners were to be returned to prison for wholly unacceptable behaviour after release; but in general the prisons emptied.

The Prime Minister, knowingly or in naïvety, had given the electorate meaningless assurances. Those of us who had felt such a yearning for peace that we had been prepared to give the new system a fair wind, and had wanted to break away from what we saw, perhaps naïvely, as the cynical negativism of such as Ian Paisley, Jeffrey Donaldson or Robert McCartney, were to be left with the sinking feeling that we had been betrayed and misled by our own Government. Those who had taken assurances on trust were later to pay a heavy political penalty for their leap of faith.

As is well known, the referenda were both carried by a huge majority in the Republic and a substantial overall majority in Northern Ireland, albeit with unionist opinion split right down the middle. The faltering and interrupted progress since then is too well known to require repetition here. The UUP has been humiliated and David Trimble swept away, the Police Service is demoralised, humiliated and reduced in numbers, PIRA disarmament has been so long delayed as to invite scepticism when finally undertaken, Protestant paramilitaries remain active and there is ample evidence of deeply entrenched criminality.

In my memoir *Stormont in Crisis*, published in 1994, I had recorded my reaction to the collapse of the power-sharing Executive twenty years before. I recalled that on that day the carapace of the professional bureaucrat had cracked, and I had wept:

> I wept for the triumph of narrow-mindedness and deeply entrenched prejudice; I wept for the victory of those forces in the Assembly who had so often preferred fisticuffs and ludicrous antics to the logic of debate; I wept for the success of the hard men with the dark glasses, balaclava helmets and pickaxe handles; I wept for the inevitability of a sweeping British judgement that we were all hopeless cases, doomed to endless conflict in an inferno of our own creation; I wept for the eclipse of local democracy.

As my work with the victims of violence had so poignantly demonstrated, many more tears were still to be shed in Northern Ireland after that day, and partly at least as a consequence of it. Reflecting now on the words I wrote at that time, I wonder if I did not exaggerate the degree of local responsibility for our own misfortune. Local people and parties had, of course, made many grievous and avoidable mistakes, as I shall go on to argue. But I have written here so extensively about the decisions of successive British Governments because I return to the fundamental point at which I started this analysis. Those nation-states which are homogeneous in character are deeply fortunate. In language, in popular culture, in religious beliefs they share so much of the social fixative which binds them together. The Irish Free State and the successor Republic remained, over many years, remarkably homogeneous, not least because the Protestant minority was eroded by intermarriage and the implications of the *ne temere* decree insisting on a Catholic upbringing for the children of mixed marriages. Ulster, on the other hand, was heterogeneous because the 'plantation', undertaken as an act of British policy, and reinforcing strong and informal linkages between eastern Ulster and western Scotland, which had already given a degree of distinctiveness to Antrim and Down, implanted amongst the indigenous community a numerous population differentiated by culture and religion. Ever since 1800 the Parliament of the United Kingdom has borne the ultimate responsibility for coping with the consequences of these differences. The failures of that Parliament and of successive Governments answerable to it are a matter of record.

CHAPTER SIX

The Irish dimension

I now turn to examine other significant influences upon events in Northern Ireland, beginning with the role of Irish parties, Governments and interests before moving on to the record of the domestic Northern Ireland institutions and communities. If the reader finds the chapters which follow relatively brief compared with the very comprehensive examination of British policy and behaviour, it is because many of the events already described involved other participants or 'players', and in discussing the interaction of Britain with others involved, much of the relevant ground has already been covered. As far as possible, I am determined to avoid tedious repetition. My objective, however, will be the same as in my analysis of the British role. To paraphrase the wording of the Book of Common Prayer, I shall seek to identify occasions when the Irish have left undone things which they ought to have done, or done things that they ought not to have done.

One must begin by emphasising the very close relationship which developed between the infant Irish state and the Roman Catholic Church. There had not always been such a close affinity between the Church and Irish nationalism, or such reliance by nationalism upon the support of Catholic adherents. It is important to note that powerful Church interests had been favourably disposed to the Union (albeit on the mistaken assumption that Catholic emancipation would rapidly follow). Deep into the nineteenth century eminent clerics remained, in many cases, comfortable members of the establishment and deeply antipathetic to agrarian and other violence. On the other hand, it has to be remembered that the numerous Presbyterian community in the north of Ireland were as affronted as their Catholic neighbours by the privileges extended to the established Anglican Episcopal Church. Wolfe Tone had memorably spoken not just of Protestant and Catholic, but of Protestant, Catholic and dissenter. There had been substantial Protestant involvement in the Rebellion of 1798. One of the founding fathers of my old school, the Royal Belfast Academical Institution, had been William Drennan, an advocate of Irish self-Government and a very early user of the phrase 'the Emerald Isle'. In its earliest years the Academical Institution, founded in 1810, had been college as well as school (before the establishment of the Queen's Colleges at Belfast and elsewhere), and its higher education students had included Roman Catholics who were preparing for ultimate entry to the priesthood as well as to other avocations. However, as the prospect of home rule for Ireland came on the political agenda from the time of Mr Gladstone, and an Irish Nationalist Party (albeit under the leadership of the Protestant Charles Stewart Parnell) attracted growing support in the predominantly Catholic areas of Ireland, an infant unionist coalition with the Orange Order as an influential player began to conjure up the phantom of 'Home Rule is Rome Rule'.

In a perverse way, the determination of unionists in Ulster to remain detached from Home Rule was in itself a reinforcement of the essentially Catholic ethos of the new Irish polity. An Ireland incorporating the six northeastern counties would have been much less homogeneous, incorporating as it would have done a substantial and geographically concentrated Protestant minority. Wisdom, in such circumstances, would have pointed to a more pluralist direction for the infant Irish state; although the attitude of the Northern Ireland Administration to its own substantial minority shows that wisdom does not always prevail in such circumstances. Since the decision of Northern Ireland to opt out of the Irish Free State resulted in an overwhelmingly Catholic Parliament, Government and community, it was hardly a matter of surprise that the Catholic ethos of the new State was all-pervasive. For many years it was to be all too apparent that a rattle of the crozier would bring some recalcitrant Cabinet Minister perilously embarked on the waters of dangerous modernism to his senses. As late as 1951 the effort by the Irish Minister, Dr Noel Browne, to introduce free medical care for mothers and children under sixteen had been stymied by episcopal opposition to such limited state welfare.

It has, of course, to be remembered that the new Free State had itself emerged in circumstances of great controversy and division. In the refusal of a substantial element of the Sinn Fein faction to accept the Treaty with the British, particular sticking points were the retention of exiguous links with the Crown and a remaining 'British presence' in a part of Ireland. It was hardly to be expected, in these circumstances, that the ensuing Civil War would have no impact 'across the Border'.

In May 1921 Sir James Craig, unionist leader, had travelled to Dublin for a secret meeting with Eamon de Valera, then serving as President of the first Dail. While the meeting seems to have been friendly enough in human terms, it led to no meeting of minds. During the 'truce' of July 1921 IRA commanders from the south were infiltrated into the north to stiffen the IRA organisation there.

After approval of the Treaty by the Dail in January 1922 Collins met Craig in his role as Chairman of the Provisional Government of the new State being born. Although there was some useful discussion about the status of Catholics in Northern Ireland, the prospect of boundary readjustment cast a long shadow. In an illustration that there is little new under the sun, the British Government – in the context of what it profoundly hoped to be a final settlement – released IRA prisoners held in the north as well as the south. There followed an appalling period of cross-Border incursions, excessive reactions by security forces in the north, and tit-for-tat sectarian violence.

With the death during the Civil War of Michael Collins, W.T. Cosgrave took on the leadership of the Free State Government. With utter firmness the anti-Treaty faction was put down. On 19 August 1922, with all its energies committed to asserting its authority within its own jurisdiction, the Provisional Government had resolved that 'a peace policy should be adopted in regard to future dealings with North-East Ulster'.

Now it was absolutely clear that Cosgrave, like all his successors in the Irish premiership, wished to complete the process of securing both independence and unity. The ideologues, of course, continued to argue that true independence had yet to be achieved, given a continuing link with the Crown, the presence of a Governor General rather than a President of Ireland in what had been a Viceregal Lodge, and the maintenance of a British presence in the so-called 'Treaty Ports' as well as in Northern Ireland. Though many of these links were largely symbolic in character, they opened up for the Irish Free State the opportunity of a continuing close association not just with the United Kingdom but also with other countries of what came to be called 'the Commonwealth', some of which (such as Australia) had many citizens of Irish lineage. Unhappily that association of states still carried in 1921–22 the description of the 'British Empire', with all its undertones of previous British imperialism. No one could then guess that in years to come it would prove possible to be both a Republic and a member nation of the Commonwealth, or that a State never associated with Britain would be admitted to membership.

However, the process of moving towards independence had involved a deliberate 'distancing' from all things British. Separate music and language, separate sports and games were seen as ways of preserving (or even, to some extent, shaping or moulding) the distinctive Irish national character. Justifiable pride could unfortunately merge with disagreeable intolerance. A member of the Gaelic Athletic Association could be expelled for playing 'foreign' games. Non-Britishness could too readily metamorphose into anti-Britishness. None of this is to underestimate the challenge of avoiding cultural and economic dominance by a much more powerful and populous neighbour. It has never been easy to preserve a sense of distinctive 'Canadianess', when living cheek-by-jowl with the United States of America.

In August 1997 I was asked to present a Northern Ireland perspective at the Merriman Summer School at Ennistymon in County Clare, which had invited a number of speakers to reflect upon how Ireland had used three-quarters of a century of independence. I had said then:

> When an area and a community have long been embodied in another state to which they do not want to belong, it is perhaps inevitable that the first thrust of independence is to emphasise and encourage distinctiveness. This is particularly so when the jurisdiction enjoying a new-found independence is very much smaller in scale than that jurisdiction from which it has separated itself. It is understandable that the mere act of severance needs to be reinforced by emphatic statements of separate identity – from repainting the letter boxes or issuing newly designed postage stamps to matters of greater pith and substance ... Even along as civilised a frontier as that between the United States and Canada, there is inevitably a certain wariness on the Canadian side, flowing from a perception of the overwhelming power and influence of the southern neighbour. The trouble here in Ireland was, I would argue, a schizophrenia of aspiration. The founding fathers of the state wished to see it free, independent and united – that is to say including within its embrace all the people living on the island of Ireland. The new State demonstrated and asserted its new independence by policies and gestures of what I might call 'non-British-ness', a state not always easily distinguished from 'anti-Britishness'. But if you accept that it was a sense of 'Britishness' which, in part at least, characterised the 'separated brethren' of the North, then it was rather as if one cried 'Come over and join us on the other side', while at the same time hacking down a good many of the existing bridges ... I have accepted that in the earliest years of the independent Irish state efforts to establish and underpin its distinctiveness were inevitable. But the consequence was that the Southern jurisdiction came to be seen as more and more 'foreign' by visitors from the North. When you have a customs barrier, when you have a strong official emphasis on the Irish language, when you have a frontier between part of a country at war and a country conspicuously neutral, you create quite a different situation from that envisaged (say) in the Government of Ireland Act 1920.

With the accession of the moderate W.T. Cosgrave to the leadership of the Irish Free State, and the conclusion of the Civil War in the decisive defeat for the republicans, the threat of violent military action against Northern Ireland and its infant Government receded. Immediately ahead, though, lay a further political minefield: the commitment of Article XII of the Treaty to establish a Boundary Commission to determine 'in accordance with the wishes of the inhabitants, so far as may be compatible with the economic and geographic conditions, the boundaries between Northern Ireland and the rest of Ireland'. Not for the first or last time, a document crucial to the future of Northern Ireland would be replete with ambiguity. Collins and his delegation had certainly left Downing Street with more than a hint that the outcome of such a Commission would be to transfer great chunks of territory from 'north' to 'south' (it having to be appreciated that the most northerly part of Ireland in County Donegal was not part of the political entity called Northern Ireland). Craig and his Belfast colleagues were left with matching fears and apprehensions, in spite of being kept more or less in place by 'the Welsh wizard'.

As the Balkan crises of more recent times had demonstrated, political boundaries are not always comfortably aligned with ethnic, religious, linguistic or political communities. While there were, from the outset, areas of Northern Ireland with a clear majority of nationalist or unionist adherents, in many (though not all) of those areas the local minority was nevertheless substantial. Even where there were solid nationalist majorities, they were often isolated from areas of similar allegiance. Most notably, there existed within Belfast, the capital city and heartland of the infant state, a very numerous and well-consolidated Catholic and nationalist community. Any attempt to withdraw such communities from unionist rule would lead to the creation of what became known in South Africa, many years later, as 'Bantustans'. It would, on the face of it, be easier to identify areas adjacent to the Border itself, and with significant nationalist majorities, as potential for transfer. But the issue threw into high relief that 'schizophrenia of aspiration' to which I referred in my Merriman speech so many years later. If one were to abandon any hope of an early movement to Irish unity, it could be regarded as desirable to reduce the number of Catholics and nationalists left under unionist rule to an absolute minimum. In such circumstances, the Northern Ireland State might feel itself less threatened, both by pressure from outside and by disaffection within its borders, and those in Government would feel sufficiently self-confident to participate in close links with the Irish Free State, short of unity, and to make strenuous efforts to protect and encourage a reduced nationalist majority. If, on the other hand, one's foremost aspiration was to promote the conditions for Irish unity, there could be benefits in preserving an entity which was neither homogeneous nor stable.

The question of the boundary came back onto the agenda with the formation of Britain's first Labour Government under Ramsay MacDonald in January 1924. There was an initial impasse when the Northern Ireland Government – increasingly nervous about the possible outcome – refused to appoint a member of the Commission, and it required Westminster legislation to allow the Commission under the chairmanship of a South African judge, Richard Feetham, to proceed with the direct appointment by MacDonald of a 'representative' of Ulster Unionists. By November 1925, with the Conservatives under Stanley Baldwin back in power, it began to become clear as a result of 'leaks' (another frequent phenomenon in the history of Northern Ireland) that any transfer contemplated by the Commission would be comparatively marginal, and could even involve some modest transfer of territory from the Irish Free State to Northern Ireland. This unwelcome news presented a very grave threat to Cosgrave's Government, and at a meeting with Baldwin and Craig it was agreed to revoke the powers of the Commission and suppress its report, to maintain the existing border and to transfer the functions of the Council of Ireland to the Belfast and Dublin Parliaments. As a 'sweetener' to this bitter pill, Cosgrave was able at the same time to secure some financial concessions from the British Government. A tripartite agreement completed in December 1925 then declared the three parties to be 'united in amity ... and resolved to aid one another in a spirit of neighbourly comradeship'.

It is important to emphasise here the great gulf that became evident between the unionist and nationalist views of this course of events. Craig and his successors could emphasise that an Irish delegation had negotiated a Treaty, subsequently ratified by the Dail, which enabled Northern Ireland, if it wished, to opt out of the Irish Free State. Subsequently, as it was entitled by law and Treaty to do, it had exercised that opt-out. It had been obliged, by the ultimate authority of the Westminster Parliament, to face up to the possibility of boundary readjustment and consequent loss of some territory and population. It was, however, the Irish Government who had decided it was not willing to live with the recommendations of the duly appointed Commission. As a consequence it had been brought to acknowledge, in the most formal way, the right of Northern Ireland to exist and had indeed pledged itself to a constructive relationship with its institutions. On the side of nationalist Ireland, reactions were more mixed. The republican ultras, albeit defeated in the Irish Civil War, had 'not gone away, you know', but were regrouping themselves for a fight-back on a political agenda. For them, the Sinn Fein proclamation of Easter 1916, subsequently endorsed by a clear mandate from the people of the whole of Ireland in 1918, had a continuing moral authority which overrode the unacceptable compromises of subsequent 'partitionist' institutions. The moderate and constitutional faction led by W.T. Cosgrave took a less ideologically rigid view. But even those who supported the Treaty had an underlying feeling that it had been an unequal settlement imposed by Lloyd-George under the threat of force. And they had been disappointed with the Boundary Commission debacle, feeling (with some justification) that they had been poorly represented and

outmanoeuvred. There was a sense of disquiet that the substantial nationalist minority in Northern Ireland were to be left without hope of change
or adequate protection for their interests. There was, too, the fact that the
last remaining (albeit largely symbolic) link between the two jurisdictions,
the Council of Ireland, had been abandoned. It is relevant to observe here
that the 1974 attempts to restore a contemporary version of such a Council
proved to be very controversial on the unionist side, in spite of limited initial
functions and an effective power of veto.

Nevertheless, the Agreement of 1925 could have represented real progress
towards a more friendly and comfortable relationship between the two States
and Governments in Ireland, and diminution of the unionist tendency to
regard the nationalist community as a huge Trojan horse in its midst. Certainly
the abstentionist attitude towards the Northern Ireland Parliament began to
break down, as Joseph Devlin and a growing number of other nationalist
representatives entered the Northern Ireland House of Commons, unfortunately to a chilly and distrustful welcome. It could well be argued that, even if
the Free State Government had continued to deal with its northern counterpart 'in a spirit of neighbourly comradeship', it would have been discouraged
and rebuffed by the insecurity and insensitivity of the Craig Government in
Belfast. In any event, that spirit was never to be fully tested, because a most
significant transition was taking place within the Free State itself.

With the end of the Civil War a Sinn Fein slate of candidates led by de
Valera decided to contest the General Election of August 1923, but although
they received substantial electoral support they were not then willing,
because of the requirement to take an oath of allegiance to the King, to take
their seats in the Dail. Subsequently the 'republican movement' was to split
yet again. With a further General Election pending, de Valera was willing
to contemplate taking up seats in the Dail, and in 1927, as leader of a new
Republican Party, Fianna Fail, took the oath with clenched teeth as 'an empty
formality' (as indeed it was). After a period in opposition, Fianna Fail was to
take office as the Government of Ireland in 1932, and to remain from that
time onwards the most formidable political organisation in the Irish State,
and for many years 'the natural party of Government'. This remarkable
transition from civil war through abstention into participation and ultimate
power was a triumph for de Valera personally and indeed for the whole Irish
democracy.

Many learned works have been written about the life and career of Eamon
de Valera, and it is not my intention to add to them here. Suffice it to say
that he was to prove one of the most remarkable Irishmen of the twentieth
century: austere, single-minded, utterly honest and politically subtle; at the
same time uncompromising, inflexible and rooted in visionary concepts of

an ideal Ireland somewhat detached from reality. One shudders to think what he would have made of the 'mohair suits' of the later era of Fianna Fail politics, or the emergence of successors willing to accept personal favours well beyond the bounds of political propriety.

With the accession of de Valera to power, 'the schizophrenia of aspiration' to which I have referred became ever more marked, as the last links of symbolism with Britain were progressively severed. The twilight of Empire had proceeded apace, with the significant enactment of the Statute of Westminster in December 1931 making transparent the equality as well as the partnership between the member states of the evolving Commonwealth. Thus there was to hand a non-threatening instrument for Ireland's free association not only with the United Kingdom but also with other wholly independent states. What was important in Canada or Australia was not the presence of the Governor General representing the Crown, but the reality that he or she could act only upon the advice of local Ministers (as was in practice the case even in Northern Ireland, although its status fell far short of that of an independent dominion). In a process of continuing evolution, Governors General were in course of time to become eminent natives of the Commonwealth country concerned rather than plume-hatted dignitaries parachuted in from London, and member states would be free to declare themselves Republics while remaining within the Commonwealth.

The underlying wish to 'hold Britain at arm's length' can be readily understood in the light of the unhappy past relations between the two islands, and the process of deliberate 'distancing' would not have mattered a great deal if it had not been a declared aspiration and priority to win over the allegiance of a million-strong community which, for a great variety of reasons, valued 'the British connection'. Successively the de Valera Government removed the oath of office and expunged from the Irish Constitution references to the Crown and the Governor General, while preserving only an increasingly tenuous link with the Commonwealth through the Executive Authority (External Relations) Act. All of this was heading towards republican status, and it was perhaps ironic that the final step along this road was not to be taken by de Valera or a Fianna Fail Government. De Valera's political efforts were a strange mixture of boldness and caution.

What was to be of lasting significance was the introduction of a new Irish Constitution in 1937. If it was intended above all to assert absolute independence from Britain and to protect the essentially Catholic ethos of a remarkably homogeneous state, it certainly achieved its purposes. It would be quite wrong to suggest that, since the formation of the Irish Free State, its Protestant citizens had suffered from any persistent or deliberate discrimination. In the business community in particular, Protestants continued to hold positions of influence quite disproportionate to their overall numbers. Nevertheless those numbers had steadily declined, as more and more young Protestants married Catholic partners in circumstances where the Catholic Church insisted that children of a mixed marriage be brought up in the Catholic faith, and many Protestants felt themselves to be essentially tolerated outsiders, somehow held out of the mainstream of Irish political and cultural life.

If, on the other hand, the purpose of constitutional reform had been to advance the ultimate unity of Ireland, then it was expressed in a self-evidently perverse and counter-productive way. Far from seeking to woo or win the good opinions of Northern unionists, or to carry forward the spirit of amity so emptily proclaimed in 1925, the new Irish Constitution was to be characterised by nationalist irredentism and Catholic triumphalism. As has been noted already, the so-called 'territorial claim' embodied in Articles 2 and 3 of the 1937 Constitution was to be defined by the Irish Supreme Court in 1990 as establishing a 'claim of legal right' to jurisdiction over 'the whole national territory' as defined by the Constitution (that is to say, the whole of Ireland) and that consequently the pursuance of the reunification was 'a constitutional imperative'. On the religious as distinct from the political front (although these are in any event closely linked), the Constitution recognised the Catholic Church as enjoying a 'special position'. It could be said that this was a harmless statement of the patently obvious, and the Constitution 'recognised' other religions. However, the 'special position' of the Catholic Church was then further acknowledged by other propositions infused with a Catholic ethos: a constitutional bar to the right of divorce, and a recognition of the rights of the family which was to provide the basis for the Church's subsequent onslaught upon Noel Browne's 'mother and child' scheme. The 1937 Constitution was a deliberate move away from the secular state foreseen by the Free State Constitution of 1922, which had embodied an all-embracing guarantee of religious freedom and equality, to a clerically influenced and Catholic-dominated entity.

Perversely, the great Irish patriot de Valera had raised the most powerful impediment to Irish unity. He had long before – and to his great credit – abandoned any thought of eroding partition by violent means. That left open only two avenues for the realisation of his dream of unity. One day, he hoped, the British might be persuaded to withdraw their support for the Stormont Government, and the unionists would come to terms with their true Irish destiny. Alternatively (and more realistically, since the enduring 'British presence' was in the hearts and minds of people who would go on living in Ireland), the tactic might be to forge ever closer and more friendly relations, to draw unionism out of the laager in which it had so stubbornly entrenched itself. The alternatives, then, could be characterised as the shotgun wedding, a divorce from the existing partner, or a patient courtship.

Now a successful courtship is unlikely to be advanced by hammering loudly on the door demanding to be let in; accompanied by an inference that the personal beliefs of the beloved are, at best, second rate. The 1937 Constitution simply fed the siege mentality of the unionist community, and afforded to unionist politicians the luxury of assured backing for loud cries of 'No surrender' and 'Not an inch'. The Constitution, with its territorial claims and avowedly Catholic character, made it all too easy for a monolithic, complacent and insensitive unionist leadership to remain indefinitely in the trenches.

If headway towards unity was to be made at all, it could only be along the lines of voluntary disengagement. Arguably if Ireland had been content to rely upon all too readily available evidence of unionist discrimination and mismanagement, and to embrace Britain as her friend and ally with ultimate interests well aligned with its own, some progress might have been possible. What actually occurred, however, was a further stage in the business of 'distancing'. Through the Anglo-Irish Agreement of 1938 Britain was persuaded to surrender to full Irish control the so-called 'Treaty Ports' of Berehaven, Cobh and Lough Swilly, retained since 1921. This was to be a further demonstration of the reality of Irish sovereignty and independence; but the inference was that, in some future conflict (as indeed appeared all too likely in the late 1930s) in which Britain would be a belligerent, Ireland would remain neutral.

Now of course the right to remain neutral is a necessary and inherent consequence of any nation's sovereignty. This, however, is to be distinguished from a policy of neutrality. Ireland has not been alone in pursuing such a policy; Switzerland, for example, comes readily to mind. But Switzerland, a landlocked country surrounded by more powerful neighbours, did not stand in the way of such neighbours pursuing their own strategic objectives. In the conquest of Europe, the capture of Switzerland was not necessary, although those who have read extensively about the Nazi fixation with the *Volk* may wonder if, under a triumphant Third Reich, the Germanic element of the Swiss Confederation could have escaped incorporation into the Reich indefinitely. On the other hand, it suited all the belligerents to have some remaining neutral point of encounter, and the Swiss territory was well defended by natural obstacles and a widely armed male population. As long as bigger prizes were there to be won, an assault on Switzerland was simply not worth the effort.

Ireland, on the other hand, was very clearly the back door to Britain, as 'The Year of the French' had illustrated long before. It is not to be supposed that Hitler, if he had decided to tackle British opposition via Eire, would have been deterred for a single moment by the Irish stance on neutrality. Nor could the limited Irish armed forces have offered more than a token resistance to any German invasion, and Britain would inevitably have had to come to their aid, if such a situation had arisen.

What is absolutely clear is that, if the British forces had still been operating from the Treaty Ports, Irish neutrality might well have been quite unsustainable. Although de Valera was widely demonised, both before and after the war, for maintaining diplomatic relations with Nazi Germany and offering formal condolences on the death of Hitler, there can be little doubt that any bending of Irish neutrality was in favour of the Allies, particularly with the entry of the United States into the war. Nevertheless the pro-British United States envoy in Dublin, David Gray, was to comment most unfavourably upon the impact of Irish neutrality on the overall war effort.

At this distance in time it is possible to be more understanding of, if not sympathetic to, the de Valera stance. As he saw it, Ireland was still at the earliest stage of development as a sovereign and independent state, and he did not wish to see all of these hard-won gains put at hazard by a wartime involvement which could be avoided. It cannot be said that the Vatican, whose representatives continued to be influential behind the scenes, did much to assure the most united international actions against the emerging atrocities of the Holocaust. Many of the world's wars have, indeed, been dynastic struggles or bids for power. In the case of the 1939–45 War the principal issue was the suppression of an absolute moral evil, and it is to be regretted that the religious ethos of the 1938 Constitution did not carry across into a convincing assertion of universal moral principles. However, it needs to be remembered that, in spite of their country's neutrality, many individual Irishmen fought with great bravery and distinction against the Axis.

Our primary concern, however, is not with these wider considerations but with the impact of Irish neutrality upon the question of Northern Ireland. Because Labour members of the British wartime coalition had been conscious of the gap in defending the Western Approaches left by the unavailability of the Treaty Ports and shared Churchill's expressed gratitude to Northern Ireland for its continued usefulness in their absence, the post-war Labour administration had no enthusiasm at all for reducing or withholding its commitment to Northern Ireland.

Winston Churchill's own history of the Second World War traces, amongst so many other great events, the course of Anglo-Irish relations during the period of the war. In a 'most secret' minute he sent to the First Sea Lord and others as First Lord of the Admiralty on 24 September 1939, he observed: 'All this talk about partition and the bitterness that would be healed by a union of Northern and Southern Ireland will amount to nothing.

They will not unite at the present time, and we cannot in any circumstances sell the loyalists of Northern Ireland.'

A very clear link between the maintenance of Irish neutrality and British attitudes to Northern Ireland emerges with the greatest clarity in a very long letter addressed by Churchill on 8 December 1940 to President Roosevelt:

> We should ... need the good offices of the United States and the whole influence of its Government, continually exerted, to procure for Great Britain the necessary facilities upon the southern and western shores of Eire for our flotillas, and, still more important, for our aircraft, working to the westward into the Atlantic. If it were proclaimed an American interest that the resistance of Great Britain should be prolonged and the Atlantic route kept open for the important armaments now being prepared for Great Britain in North America, the Irish in the United States might be willing to point out to the Government of Eire the dangers which its present policy is creating for the United States itself. His Majesty's Government would of course take the most effective measures beforehand to protect Ireland if Irish action exposed it to German attack. It is not possible for us to compel the people of Northern Ireland against their will to leave the United Kingdom and join Southern Ireland. But I do not doubt that if the Government of Eire would show its solidarity with the democracies of the English-speaking world at this crisis a Council of Defence of all Ireland could be set up out of which the unity of the island would probably in some form or other emerge after the war.

In a minute addressed to the Dominions Secretary on 31 January 1941, Churchill again not only expressed resentment about the impact of Irish neutrality but also reflected upon the implications for Northern Ireland:

> No attempt should be made to conceal from Mr de Valera the depth and intensity of feeling against the policy of Irish neutrality. We have tolerated and acquiesced in it, but juridically we have never recognised that Southern Ireland is an independent sovereign state, and she herself has repudiated dominion status. Her international status is undefined and anomalous. Should the present situation last to the end of the war, which is unlikely, a gulf will have opened between Northern and Southern Ireland which will be impossible to bridge in this generation.

As we know, however unlikely the British Prime Minister thought it, the 'present situation' (that is to say, the maintenance of Irish neutrality) did last until the end of the war, and the residual bitterness felt by members of the wartime coalition was most evident when Churchill chose to refer at some length to relations with Ireland in his 'victory broadcast' on 13 May 1945:

Owing to the action of the Dublin Government, so much at variance with the temper and instinct of thousands of Southern Irishmen who hastened to the battlefront to prove their ancient valour, the approaches which the Southern Irish ports and airfields could so easily have guarded were closed by the hostile aircraft and U-boats. This was indeed a deadly moment in our life, and if it had not been for the loyalty and friendship of Northern Ireland we should have been forced to come to close quarters or perish forever from the earth.

In reality, the contribution of Northern Ireland itself to the war effort had been less than convincingly impressive, despite the undoubted heroism of its many sons who (in the absence of conscription in Northern Ireland) had served as volunteers in the armed forces. It had taken a long time to gear Northern Ireland industry up to the tempo of war production. Nor had the measures to protect Northern Ireland from air attack been adequate when they had to cope with the prolonged aerial bombardment of Belfast in April 1941, when the Irish Government had responded sympathetically to cries for help as fire brigades raced across the Border. In truth, the main usefulness of Northern Ireland had been to serve, in the first place, as a terrestrial aircraft carrier for the Battle of the Atlantic, and as a marshalling and training ground as American troops entered the war. As Private First Class Milburn Henke from Minnesota stepped ashore at the Port of Belfast, he was to be the first American soldier to enter the European theatre of operations.

De Valera himself was to respond to Churchill's reproaches in a restrained and dignified way, and it is not my purpose here to argue that Irish neutrality did not, in some substantial sense, serve the Irish national interest, but it was in relation to the fulfilment of any aspiration to unity that Irish neutrality had serious long-term consequences. These included an accretion of support to Northern Ireland and disenchantment with the south which persisted for a good many years, and certainly throughout Clement Attlee's post-war Labour Government. They also assisted and encouraged Unionist Governments in Northern Ireland in demonising the south as a jurisdiction unconcerned with the outcome of an historic struggle between democracy and fascism. The gulf which Churchill had prophesied in January 1941 had indeed emerged.

Given the sympathy hitherto shown for Irish aspirations within the Labour Party, nationalist hopes were initially raised by the return of a strong Labour Government. These hopes would be tested and in the end dashed in the context of Ireland's severance of its ambiguous links with the Commonwealth. One might have expected the final push for republican status to come about as a logical conclusion of de Valera's various 'distancing' measures. In the event it was to be John A. Costello of Fine Gael, leader of an inter-party coalition which had sent Fianna Fail briefly into opposition, who declared during a visit to Canada in 1948 that Ireland would proclaim itself a Republic and leave the Commonwealth. Henceforth the country would be known as 'the Republic of Ireland'.

It is interesting to observe here that, for many years, Unionist Governments were to refer instead to 'the Irish Republic', in rebuttal of any assumption that the Dublin Government was entitled to speak for the whole of Ireland. In a sense this was a mirror image of nationalist preference to avoid the use of 'Northern Ireland' or 'Ulster' rather than 'the six counties' or 'the six north-eastern counties' or even – as I vividly remember the term used by a Stormont MP at the time – 'the so-called six county area'. There was some logical justification for this semantic nit-picking, in that the most northerly county of Ireland was not part of 'Northern Ireland'; nor were three of the nine Ulster counties, that is to say, Cavan, Monaghan and Donegal. Further cultural differences were to be illustrated by unionist insistence upon references to 'Londonderry', the city always called 'Derry' by nationalists.

The British reaction to the designation of the Republic and the departure from the Commonwealth was to be complex. On the one hand, there would be formidable difficulties in treating the Irish, so numerous in many parts both of Britain and of the 'white Commonwealth', as out and out foreigners. The Irish were therefore to be accorded a form of 'most favoured nation' status extending well beyond the economic sphere. On the other hand, Sir Basil Brooke's Stormont Government found a sympathetic response from such Ministers as Herbert Morrison to its plea that Northern Ireland's status must be clarified beyond dispute under British law. Thus it was that the self-same Ireland Act 1949, which dealt with other implications of republican status in a pragmatic way incorporated at Section 1 (2) the historic declaration that no part of Northern Ireland would cease to be a part of the United Kingdom without the consent of the Northern Ireland Parliament. I have argued elsewhere that, where no doubt or possibility of future change exists, declaratory provisions of this kind would be totally unnecessary. Moreover, since the United Kingdom (unlike the Irish Republic) did not have a written Constitution, declaratory assurances of this kind were in no sense entrenched. Use of the words 'for ever' in the Act of Union 1800 had not stood in the way of later legislation enabling most of Ireland to leave the Union. Declaratory provisions, like other statutory provisions, were amendable by subsequent Parliaments, and the declaration embodied in the Ireland Act 1949 was indeed to be amended, or indeed replaced, as first of all the 'consent mechanism' shifted from the defunct Northern Ireland Parliament to the people of Northern Ireland, and later the Belfast Agreement led to legislation embodying both options under the consent principle, so that a majority could bring about a movement to unity as well as block it.

Nevertheless, the importance of the so-called 'constitutional guarantee' should not be underestimated, not least because it represented a commitment by one British Government after another. It was to feature, for instance, in William Whitelaw's seminal discussion paper of 1972, *The Future of Northern Ireland*, in these words: 'The United Kingdom Government is bound both by Statute and by clear and repeated pledges to the people of Northern Ireland.'

By 1949 the reality was that, having regard to the consequences of war and the continuing process of 'distancing', there could be no early prospect of bringing about a united Ireland through pressure brought to bear by the British Government. Other than resort to violence, the only available means to pursue the national aspiration (or 'constitutional imperative') for unity was to warm up the relationship with northern unionists and their elected Government, perhaps gaining in the process more sensitive and sympathetic treatment of the northern minority. As we shall see in a later chapter, there had been little in the past conduct or attitude of unionist Governments at Stormont to encourage Irish politicians to believe that this would be an easy process. It would, on the contrary, require great patience and an unremitting effort to win hearts and minds. But rewards might come as an older generation of unionist leaders, still carrying the innate defensiveness of a community under threat from the outset, gave way to younger figures who had less baggage and who had, perhaps, served in the war alongside Catholic and nationalist fellow-citizens.

Unhappily the post-war period was marked instead by an orgy of anti-partitionist propaganda. Stimulated by the Irish Anti-Partition League, a new coalition of nationalist politicians and other interests in Northern Ireland, Sean McBride, a former chief of staff of the IRA, launched in 1946 a new radical republican party, Clann na Poblachta, which began to gain seats from Fianna Fail at by-elections, on the foot of anti-partitionist and anti-British rhetoric. De Valera, faced with the possibility of having his power-base, 'Fianna Fail, the republican party', eroded in a contest for militancy, himself launched a new propaganda drive against partition. Nevertheless, at the General Election of February 1948, sixteen years of Fianna Fail hegemony came to an end, with power passing to a coalition Government headed by John A. Costello. Costello's own party, Fine Gael, had represented the moderate pro-Treaty faction in the Irish Free State but now found itself attached to parties of a very different temper, including McBride's Clan, in order to gain and retain office.

Any student of Israeli politics will have observed how often the policy of Governments in that country has been driven in the direction of obdurate militancy by the disproportionate influence of small extremist factions without which a Government cannot be formed. Now, and not for the last time in the history of the Republic, one was to see the atmosphere of the horse-fair brought into the political arena. These realities were to be reflected in Costello's otherwise improbable role as the midwife of the Republic of Ireland.

The radical 'greening' of Irish politics was to provoke a mirror image at the unsavoury Northern Ireland General Election of February 1949. Funds raised by a national collection in all parishes of the Catholic Church throughout Ireland were ploughed into the electoral contest, which came to be called 'the Chapel Gate Election' and produced the most polarised Stormont Parliament for many years. Moreover, the close link between Irish Governments and the Catholic Church was to be further underlined by the opposition to the 'mother and child' scheme of Dr Noel Browne and his subsequent resignation from the Irish Government.

Far from reaching for a patient growth of mutual understanding, holding out future possibilities of cooperation if not ultimate unity, the Irish politicians had widened the gulf. With the route of peaceful gradualism torn up by those who might march along it, it was hardly surprising that the emphasis shifted towards the 'physical force' tradition in the abortive IRA campaign of the 1950s. However, Fianna Fail returned to power at the 1957 Irish General Election, and de Valera soon showed that he was not prepared to tolerate a breach of his 1938 Constitution's insistence that only the Oireachtas could maintain a legitimate army in the name of the Irish State. In parallel with a similar exercise in Northern Ireland, the Fianna Fail Government invoked powers of internment to remove IRA activists from circulation. Indeed, Sean Lemass, who had succeeded de Valera as Taoiseach in 1959, was to introduce the use of military tribunals as a further deterrent to IRA activity. All of this pressure was to lead to the abandonment of this IRA campaign in February 1962 (but of course without any surrender of either weaponry or aspirations).

The effectiveness of bilateral internment in this specific situation had been demonstrated, but it has to be remembered that in scale and intensity the IRA campaign launched in 1956 was in no way comparable to the later onslaught of PIRA. The final death toll was to be no more than eighteen, and the cost of the damage to property considerably less than a million pounds. The campaign itself had been concentrated in Border areas, and had not provoked large-scale intercommunal disturbances. Nevertheless, the decisive action taken by Fianna Fail, to prove itself 'master in its own house', had indicated a clear abandonment of any idea of eroding partition by force; and it was a wonderful irony that this principled abandonment of violent means had been spearheaded by two of those veterans of the Easter Rising who had subsequently taken up arms against their own fellow countrymen in protest against acceptance of the Treaty.

Although both veterans of the Rising and the Civil War, Lemass and de Valera represented different generations. The visionary formulations of de Valera were now to be replaced by the energy and pragmatism of Lemass, still ideologically committed – as he was bound to be – to the ideal of a united Ireland, but in practice giving the highest priority to economic and social development for the modernisation of Ireland. In this task he was to find an ideal instrument in the fine mind of an outstanding Civil Servant, T.K. (Ken) Whitaker.

At Stormont, though, the changing of the guard was taking longer. Sir Basil Brooke, a man of great charm coupled with utter inflexibility, had lived through the dreadful dangers of Fermanagh in the violent 1920s and saw the Catholic and nationalist community as an ever-present threat. The 'British-ness' of the Brookes could not be doubted. Anti-unionist cynics would sometimes characterise their adversaries as 'more interested in the half-crown than the crown', but the Brookes had an outstanding record of brave military service to Crown and country, culminating in Sir Alan Brooke's crucial role as Churchill's key military adviser (and frequent restraining influence) during the Second World War. Arguably only Churchill himself had made a greater contribution to the British war effort. But Basil Brooke (later Lord Brookeborough) had been Prime Minister of Northern Ireland since 1943, and showed no sign of acknowledging any need for an improved atmosphere either within Northern Ireland or in Ireland as a whole. In his later autobi-ography (1972), Terence O'Neill, Brooke's successor, was to comment with some bitterness: 'He was good company and a good raconteur and those who met him imagined that he was relaxing away from his desk. What they didn't realise was that there was no desk.'

However in 1963, on the resignation of Lord Brookeborough, O'Neill became leader of the Ulster Unionist Party and Prime Minister of Northern Ireland, and it soon became apparent that Sean Lemass was interested in testing the water of a new relationship. In late July 1963, in a speech at Tralee, Lemass took the cautious step of acknowledging that, in Northern Ireland, 'Government and Parliament exist with the support of the majority ...' Not, it may be judged, a very remarkable statement of fact, but nevertheless a change of tone from earlier rhetoric about puppet states and illegitimate regimes. I have commented elsewhere on the fact that by this time the British Government and Parliament were burdened by a great weight of ignorance about modern Ireland. This was to be underlined for me at a later date as I read through the Hansard report of a debate in the House of Commons.

Such reports are conscientiously and meticulously edited; hence my surprise at coming upon a reference to 'the Tralee speech in a tea-shop'. It took a moment to realise that the reporter had misheard and the editor misunderstood a reference to 'the Tralee speech by the Taoiseach'. In later days, of course, terms of art such as Taoiseach, Tanaiste, Oireachtas or Ard Fheis were to trip lightly off the English tongue.

O'Neill gave a cautious welcome to the Tralee speech; while emphasising the desirability of full constitutional recognition of Northern Ireland's status within the United Kingdom, he appealed for concentration on practical issues of concern to both jurisdictions and their populations. It is, however, a truism that exposure to an Irish-American audience often brings out the worst in an Irish politician. When I myself served in New York from 1960 to 1963 I had made some good friends amongst the Irish Government's representatives there. They would sometimes speak with near despair of efforts to inform and interest Irish-Americans in the problems of modern Ireland on the social and economic fronts. But no, this product was not saleable to that particular market. It was 'Brits out' or nothing. It was in just such a setting, in October 1963, that Lemass reverted to the well-worn line of calling for an end to partition. Nevertheless, throughout 1964, there began to develop in the minds of both protagonists the thought that the time was right for a significant personal encounter. Such an encounter would not be absolutely unique, since Craig in his day had met de Valera, Collins and Cosgrave, albeit with few useful long-term consequences. By 1964, however, a fortuitous channel of communication had opened up by the coincidence of O'Neill's embodiment, as Finance Minister, for the first time in 1962, in the United Kingdom delegation to the annual meetings of the World Bank and International Monetary Fund. In that setting both O'Neill himself and his influential Private Secretary, James Malley (a wartime and much-decorated hero of Bomber Command), got to know the Rostrevor-born Ken Whitaker, Secretary of the Irish Department of Finance, the acknowledged leading Civil Servant in the Republic (although no formal headship of the Civil Service existed there) and a close and trusted confidant of Sean Lemass. It was impossible not to like and trust Whitaker, a most dedicated and selfless public servant, and it was along the Malley–Whitaker axis that the idea of a visit to Belfast by Lemass was canvassed.

Even though the formal invitation was issued from the Northern participant, the willingness not merely to meet the Northern Ireland Prime Minister but to meet him in Belfast represented a courageous risk on the part of Lemass. The Irish Republic was far from ready to abandon its formal constitutional claim; nevertheless, the act of entering the grounds of Stormont, the epicentre of anti-partitionist daemonology, would represent a very striking gesture of de facto acceptance, and a positive manifestation of the spirit of Tralee.

With the Lemass visit of January 1965, a new and apparently promising phase in north–south relations began, and was to be carried forward in further meetings both in Dublin and Belfast by Lemass and his successor as Taoiseach, from 1966, Jack Lynch. Initially the meetings were more relevant on the symbolic than on the practical front. Indeed, the joint communiqué on 14 January 1965 acknowledged that the currently insoluble issues had been sidestepped with the bland words:

> We have today discussed matters in which there may prove to be a degree of common interest, and have agreed to explore further what specific measures may be possible or desirable by way of practical consultation and co-operation. Our talks – which did not touch upon constitutional or political questions – have been conducted in a most amicable way, and we look forward to a further discussion in Dublin.

As one of the principal draughtsmen of this terse communiqué, I still find it humorous to note the pretext that this most political of encounters did not touch upon political questions! The series of north/south ministerial talks subsequently concentrated on purely practical issues. There was, for example, discussion of the possibility of showing some of the Lane Bequest pictures from time to time in Belfast, and the possible linkage of the Erne and Shannon waterway systems made its first appearance on a cooperative agenda. It has to be appreciated that, even in less propitious times politically, the two Governments had been able to achieve cooperative agreements relating (for example) to the Foyle Fisheries, the operation of the Great Northern Railway linking Dublin to Belfast, and the generation of hydro-electric power.

This developing, and potentially benign, dialogue was soon to be overtaken by the growing disorder in Northern Ireland and the reaction to it. After the resignation of O'Neill, his successor James Chichester-Clark had attempted unsuccessfully to stabilise the situation. With the events in Londonderry on 12 August and widespread sectarian clashes elsewhere in Northern Ireland, the Taoiseach Jack Lynch, in a broadcast on the evening of 13 August, expressed the view that the Stormont Government was no longer in control of the situation. He called for the intervention of the United Nations peacekeeping force and spoke of field hospitals being made ready to cope with casualties across the Border. While it is easy to understand the emotions stirred amongst people in the Republic by the ugly scenes of violence in Northern Ireland, and the consequent conviction of Lynch that he must react in some positive way, the inevitable result was an abandonment of cross-Border dialogue and the resumption of 'megaphone diplomacy'. Chichester-Clark's response was to characterise Lynch's broadcast as 'inflammatory and ill-considered', and in a formal statement the following day he returned to the language of the Irish cold war: 'We must, and we will treat the Government which seeks to wound us in our darkest hour as an unfriendly and implacable Government, determined to overthrow by any means the state which enjoys the support of a majority of our electorate.'

In acknowledging the bitterness of these exchanges, it needs to be borne in mind that the leading personality on each side was, in most circumstances, notably level-headed and unflappable, and not easily attracted by hyperbole.

No rapprochement was likely as the situation in Northern Ireland continued to deteriorate. Violence moved up a further notch with the widespread rioting in Belfast on the night of 14 August, including a mini-pogrom in which Protestants burned down houses in Catholic streets, and ill-advised and indiscriminate use of firearms by the police. Dr Hillery, the Irish Minister for External Affairs, pressed for the intervention of a United Nations or Anglo-Irish force but was rebuffed by the British Government. That evening, at the British Embassy in Dublin, windows were broken and the Union flag torn down and burned by a hostile crowd. On 20 August, the Security Council of the United Nations adjourned consideration of the Republic's request for United Nations involvement.

It may have been inevitable that the Irish Government reacted as it did in the emotional atmosphere generated by the events of August 1969. Nevertheless, the rupture of developing decent relationships across the Border between the two Irish Governments represented a grave setback to the growth of mutual confidence and the calming of the fearful and defensive mindset of the unionist community. It was, indeed, about this time that the distinguished journalist, Harold Jackson of *The Guardian* first drew attention to the phenomenon of the dual minority: on the one hand, the Catholics of the north, the actual minority there fearful of oppression by the Protestant and unionist majority in Northern Ireland; on the other hand, the Protestants of the north, the potential minority in any future united Ireland, equally fearful of oppression by the nationalist majority of the whole island, and with evidences of relatively recent clerical domination readily to hand.

It is also important to stress that when James Chichester-Clark had met Harold Wilson at 10 Downing Street on 19 August 1969 the subsequent 'Downing Street Declaration' had not only reaffirmed 'the clear pledges made by successive United Kingdom Governments that Northern Ireland should not cease to be a part of the United Kingdom without the consent of the people of Northern Ireland' but also 'that responsibility for affairs in Northern Ireland is entirely a matter of domestic jurisdiction'. In other words, and in spite of historic sympathy for the Irish cause within the Labour Party, the Irish Government was being bluntly advised to keep out. Jack Lynch then backed off from the implications of his broadcast of 13 August by a calming statement made (coincidentally) once again in Tralee, of reassurance that his Government was not seeking a reunification of the Republic and Northern Ireland by violence. Although Chichester-Clark, on 23 September, welcomed that reassurance, he went on to make it clear that he saw no basis for unity by agreement: 'I will say with emphasis that we need to maintain inviolate our link with Britain. This is our fundamental policy on which our electorate has many times declared itself.'

The suspicion remained that, while the use of violence was renounced, the Government of Northern Ireland could be subjected to other means of duress, whether through the British Government, the United Nations or Irish America. In reality, the essentially moderate Lynch was uncomfortably caught between two stools. While unionists could be expected to characterise any comments on developments in Northern Ireland as an unwarrantable intrusion, he could be criticised from other quarters as weak and irresolute in defence of national interests and security. Certainly the latter was the line adopted by the People's Democracy firebrand Michael Farrell at a speaking engagement in Lynch's home city of Cork. More serious and menacing was the intervention of the republican-minded Neil Blaney, Dail Member for County Donegal and Lynch's Minister of Agriculture. On his 'home patch' of Letterkenny, and in plain breach of Lynch's recent reassurances, he declared that Fianna Fail as a party had never decided to 'rule out the use of force as circumstances demanded it in Northern Ireland'. In his early and more militant days in 1928, Sean Lemass had described Fianna Fail as 'a slightly constitutional party', and its long tenure of office had not removed the traces of the violent ethos from which it had sprung. The later Lemass had shown more concern that people should live and prosper in Ireland; yet the legend of 'blood sacrifice' lived on, stimulated by much nostalgic rhetoric in annual ceremonies at Bodenstown remembering and honouring republican heroes. The potential fission within Fianna Fail was to be further illustrated when on 12 December the Tanaiste Erskine Childers (a future President of Ireland and the son of a famous father) called for the formulation of a policy which would persuade Northern unionists that they could benefit from Irish unity. What was at issue here was a question of the most fundamental importance. Did 'Irish unity' mean a final victory of Catholic and republican Ireland over unionism and 'the Brits', with the shoe of dominance shifting firmly to the other foot, or did it mean a growing together by patient and peaceful means on terms widely acceptable throughout the island? Once again, a hard choice between the shotgun marriage of north and south, the pressure for Great Britain to divorce Northern Ireland, or the sensitive courtship resting neither on force or other pressure but a build-up of mutual understanding and mutual interest. Lynch's uncomfortable position in a party embodying both moderates and ultras was to be well illustrated in exchanges in the Dail on 18 December. After the Taoiseach had declared that partition would be solved by peaceful means, he went on (in what was probably no more than a careless use of words) to say that his Government would rely on attaining unification by peaceful means 'so far as it could', but under further questioning replied unambiguously that 'force is ruled out'.

There was now a serious division at the heart of the Irish Cabinet. Neil Blaney and Kevin Boland were well known to be militantly anti-partitionist in sentiment, but were to be greatly reinforced by the adherence of a rising force in Irish politics, Charles Haughey. He had been one of the contenders for party leadership on the departure of Sean Lemass, to whose daughter he was married, but had previously shown an interest mainly in practical issues of Government as a forceful and energetic Minister, first at Justice, then at Agriculture and, as the Northern Ireland troubles accelerated, at Finance. Haughey had, however, family links across the border in Northern Ireland, and events in the Derry Bogside and in north and west Belfast convinced him that those he acknowledged as fellow countrymen and fellow nationalists across the Border were under great threat. Articulate and obviously deeply concerned nationalists from the north were visiting Dublin to stress the need, as they saw it, for something more than sympathetic noises from the south. They wanted more than sympathy or humanitarian aid; they wanted weapons with which to defend themselves.

Of equally great relevance was the split in Sinn Fein / IRA. Under the influence of leaders such as Thomas MacGiolla the official orientation of Sinn Fein had moved steadily leftwards towards a kind of domestic Marxism. The rise of a strongly supported socialist party was viewed with deep suspicion and apprehension by the mainline Irish parties, and particularly by Fianna Fail, which behind the 'radical chic' attributed externally to anti-partitionism concealed a deeply conservative approach to the development of society. Although the immediate cause of the split in the 'republican movement' was an Army Council decision to give at least token recognition to the three Parliaments in Dublin, London and Belfast, the formation of PSF in January 1970 shifted the emphasis away from the achievement of social justice throughout Ireland to the 'good old cause' of getting 'the Brits' out. A new leadership, strongly based in the north, was anxious to restore credibility with those nationalist supporters who, finding themselves undefended in the summer of 1969, had surmised that henceforth 'IRA' could stand for 'I ran away'. In the evolving situation, armed support for communities in the north might have the added advantage of shifting the focus of IRA activity firmly away from the south.

There was to be great subsequent controversy and confusion about who exactly had been involved in the supply of weaponry to elements in Northern Ireland, and under what authority they had done so. What is incontestable is that the whole issue broke out into the open on Wednesday 6 May 1970 after Lynch accepted the resignations of two of his Ministers (O'Morain and Boland) and dismissed two others (Blaney and Haughey) following allegations about the illegal importation of arms into the State. Subsequently Haughey and Blaney were arrested and charged with conspiracy to import arms and ammunition. The charges against Blaney were dropped and in October 1970 a Dublin jury acquitted Charles Haughey.

All of this did not represent a very favourable setting for the development of confidence between the several interests of Dublin, London and Belfast. An unexpected, unannounced and (so far as the British Government was concerned) unauthorised visit by Dr Hillery in July 1970 to the nationalist Falls Road in Belfast led to criticism, not only from the Northern Ireland Government but also from the British Foreign Secretary, Sir Alec Douglas-Home, who characterised the visit as an error of judgement and a serious diplomatic discourtesy. On 11 July, on the eve of the annual Orange parades throughout Northern Ireland, Lynch nevertheless declared a continuing interest and role for the Republic. 'It is', he said 'for political leaders to govern wisely and justly. I accept the guarantees of the British Government that it will do so. My Government is the second guarantor.'

One of the reasons for Lynch's widespread popularity throughout the Republic had not only been his charm and affability (he was competitive with Harold Wilson as a meditative pipe-smoker), but also his previous fame as a renowned exponent of hurling, a tough and vigorous Gaelic sport, and not one in which the faint-hearted were likely to flourish. He had been a constructive participant in cross-Border talks with the Northern Ireland Government, and before the eruption of serious and prolonged violence seemed the ideal man to pursue the 'patient courtship' approach. Unhappily the crises of 1969–70 were to reveal him as a weak leader, not necessarily in terms of his own personality or character but in terms of his underlying political position. He had been a compromise choice in the contest to succeed Sean Lemass as Taoiseach, and he was to lead a deeply riven party and Cabinet, in spite of winning successive votes of confidence within his Parliamentary party. He had tried, ultimately unsuccessfully, to keep everyone on board. Belligerent language used in August 1969 – 'the Irish Government can no longer stand by and see innocent people injured and perhaps worse' – was shadow rather than substance. Its use was to lead to comment by the Tribunal presided over by the magisterial Mr Justice (Leslie) Scarman, which reported in April 1972 on the factors underlying the outbreak of the troubles: 'There is no doubt that this broadcast stemmed from the will of the Bogsiders to obstruct any attempt by the police to enter their area, and to harass them by missile and petrol bomb attacks, whenever they appeared on the perimeter.'

This comment was not necessarily a criticism. Some would certainly argue that preceding events had given 'the Bogsiders' good cause to resist the entry of the police into their area. But it did demonstrate that words as well as bullets had consequences. Above all, Lynch did not exercise sufficient discipline over members of his Cabinet willing to initiate freelance activity in support of the Catholic population, even if this led to a strengthening of PIRA.

For the remainder of Lynch's first term as Taoiseach, which ended with the defeat of Fianna Fail in 1973, he continued uncomfortably to straddle both sides of the fence. When his emphasis on a policy of cooperation with the north at the Fianna Fail Ard Fheis (or conference) of February 1971 drew from Chichester-Clark a welcome coupled with a rejoinder that the whole situation could be transformed if the Irish Government were to discard its claim to jurisdiction, Lynch felt bound to react on the BBC's *Panorama* programme on 1 March to the effect that the claim to jurisdiction was fundamental and could not be abandoned. Yet on a visit to the United States later that month he was resolute enough to tell an Irish-American audience that 'every act of violence is retarding the ultimate reunification of Ireland. We don't like to have British troops in Ireland, but it seems they are necessary.'

A further escalation of violence was to occur in Northern Ireland following the introduction of internment (in Northern Ireland alone) on 9 August. Lynch's immediate reaction was to observe: 'In the present situation in the North it is imperative that further parades are banned there and that the law be administered impartially, and that a conference of all the interested parties take place in order to obtain a new form of an administration for Northern Ireland.' This statement, issued at a highly emotive moment, was noteworthy for its emphasis on desirable reform within Northern Ireland rather than on arguments for Irish unity. Further developing this thesis Lynch called in a statement on 12 August for the establishment of administration in which power and decision-making would be 'equally shared' between unionist and non-unionist.

At this stage, though, any right of intervention by the Republic in the internal affairs of Northern Ireland was still being firmly resisted, both in London and Belfast. On the same day as Lynch's advocacy of 'power-sharing' Edward Heath rejected suggestions of a tripartite meeting, bringing in Lynch as well as Faulkner, to discuss the situation in Northern Ireland. The following day Brian Faulkner utterly rejected the right of Mr Lynch to dictate a political settlement in Northern Ireland. Indeed, relations – on the face of it at least – continued to deteriorate. On 17 August, in a message to Heath, Lynch called for an end to internment and indicated his Government's support for 'passive resistance' in the north. This approach was immediately rebuffed by the British Prime Minister as an unjustified and unacceptable interference in the domestic affairs of the United Kingdom. Lynch in turn rejected this charge, and renewed his proposal for multilateral talks. In this unpleasant atmosphere, the question of 'incursions' inevitably raised its head, with Lynch claiming thirty such incursions by the British Army into the territory of the Republic over the previous two years.

There were elements of shadow-boxing in these exchanges. While Lynch was obliged to maintain his stance on the desirability and inevitability of ultimate unification, he was much more concerned with the medium-term aim of facilitating more stable Government within Northern Ireland. While Heath was obliged to oppose the right of another country to interfere in the internal affairs of a part of the United Kingdom, he had to recognise that the support of Lynch could be crucial in winding down the alarmingly escalating violence. It is not to be assumed that when Heath met Lynch at Chequers over more than eight hours on 6 September, the discussions were confined to Anglo-Irish trade or attitudes towards development of the EEC. The offer of a tripartite meeting, along the lines earlier suggested by Lynch, showed a distinct and significant shift in the British stance. When imminent tripartite talks were announced on 11 September, Faulkner was at pains to emphasise that his agreement to participate was on the clear understanding that 'neither the constitution nor the Border would be an issue nor subjects of discussion'. This was not how Mr Lynch interpreted the situation; on 3 September he emphasised that the forthcoming meeting was to be 'without preconditions'.

As Deputy Secretary to his Cabinet, I was to be one of those from Northern Ireland who accompanied Faulkner to the deeply significant discussions at Chequers on 27 and 28 September 1971 (and indeed I still have in my possession – albeit slightly battered in the bombing of my home seventeen years later – a copy of the official history of Chequers signed by the three protagonists, Lynch, Heath and Faulkner). The focus of the communiqué issued at the conclusion of the talks would be on the agreed need to wind down both violence and the internment and other emergency measures set in hand to cope with it. The emphasis was on reciprocal de-escalation. The communiqué contained no embarrassing references to the Border or constitutional issues, and indeed it was inconceivable that at that time any common ground could be found on that front. Nevertheless, the unprecedented tripartite meeting could be regarded as the first tacit recognition of the so-called 'Irish dimension' acknowledged in the discussion paper of 1972.

A further crisis in Anglo-Irish relations was inevitably provoked by the events of 'Bloody Sunday' in Derry on 30 January 1972, when thirteen civilians were shot dead by soldiers of the Parachute Regiment. Although Lynch himself had called on the introduction of internment for the banning of all further parades, the shootings had occurred on the occasion of an illegal march organised by the Derry Civil Rights Association. In the Republic, an immediate expression of public and political outrage was inevitable. Lynch himself, who had conceded the previous year in the United States that 'we don't like to have British troops in Ireland but it seems they are necessary', now characterised the events of 30 January as 'an unwarranted attack on unarmed civilians'. The Taoiseach called for an inquiry into the events in Derry, announced a day of national mourning, and recalled the Irish Ambassador from London. On the day of mourning itself, 2 February 1972, a huge crowd gathered around the British Embassy in Dublin and burned it to the ground.

Although Edward Heath had announced in Parliament on 1 February the establishment of a judicial tribunal of inquiry under the sole direction of the then Lord Chief Justice Widgery, his ultimate report, made in April 1972, was to be presented in the radically different situation following the suspension of the Stormont Parliament and the introduction of direct rule. Widgery's findings have ever since proved to be so controversial, and in particular so unacceptable to most of the population of Derry in particular, that today an international inquiry is teasing through a mountain of evidence. The painstaking care being taken in this process is in vivid contrast to the rapid conduct of the Widgery tribunal over a period of a few weeks. Lynch himself was deeply critical of the Widgery conclusions and expressed a desire for an international examination of the conduct of the Army on that fateful day; an examination which now, after a lapse of many years, has come to pass.

The whole context was to be utterly changed by the introduction of direct rule. That search for 'a new form of administration for Northern Ireland', for which Lynch had called on the introduction of internment, was now to take place. In addition, the incoming first Secretary of State for Northern Ireland, William Whitelaw, was determined to explore the possibility of bringing the PIRA campaign to an end, and willing to take real political risks in that cause. Not for the last time, the 'political process' and a 'peace process' were to run in parallel. On this latter front, that of the search for peace, it is noteworthy that the Irish Government of the day did not seek to involve itself in the process as Albert Reynolds in particular was to do at a later date. Fianna Fáil had shown its profound disapproval of the IRA by its willingness to introduce internment during the earlier terrorist campaign. Having painfully climbed the ladder to constitutionalism and political power, the party was not willing to concede to any other interest the right to speak for the Irish State or to deploy armed forces on its behalf. As for Fine Gael, which was able to form a new coalition Government after the Irish General Election of 28 February, the new Taoiseach Liam Cosgrave had attacked Lynch's Government at the previous year's Fine Gael Ard Fheis for failing to stamp out the IRA in the Republic. Both the outgoing and incoming Dublin Governments were anxious to keep the IRA at arm's length.

The new national coalition in Dublin, embodying Fine Gael and Labour, had some striking figures in its Cabinet, including the philosophical but energetic Garret FitzGerald (himself a future Taoiseach) and a maverick polemicist, Conor Cruise O'Brien, advancing along the journey from composing old-fashioned anti-partition propaganda as a professional Irish diplomat to his ultimate apotheosis as a supporter of the unionist right. It was to be a peculiarly similar journey to that made in England by other able and angry young men, such as Paul Johnson from the liberal left to the authoritarian right. FitzGerald, a questioning intellectual and experienced journalist, had a close personal knowledge of people and events in Northern Ireland. I myself, in early 1960, had been interviewed by him for the *Irish Times* about my posting to New York to pursue inward investment opportunities there. Liam Cosgrave personally, with his reticence and horsey interests, was to develop a good relationship with Brian Faulkner.

As Whitelaw's attempts to achieve a lasting ceasefire faded, the political agenda became a leading priority. Since August 1970, nationalism in Northern Ireland had been represented effectively for the first time by a strong and coherent new party, the SDLP, under the leadership of Gerry Fitt. Its contribution to the initial debate on the future governance of Northern Ireland was to propose a form of condominium or joint sovereignty, coupled with a declaration by Britain in favour of Irish unity. Although leading members of the SDLP, such as John Hume, maintained regular contact with the Irish Government, it does not follow that the latter would have been happy to adopt the role proposed for it by that party. The idea of sending a joint international expedition to the upper slopes of a still active volcano was not particularly appealing.

However, a new framework for Irish intervention in the political process was created by the British Government's discussion paper issued in 1972, in the crucial section headed 'The Irish Dimension'. The key passage read:

> Whatever arrangements are made for the future administration of Northern Ireland must take account of the Province's relationship with the Republic of Ireland: and to the extent that this is done, there is an obligation upon the Republic to reciprocate. Both the economy and the security of the two areas are to some considerable extent interdependent, and the

same is true of both in their relationship with Great Britain. It is therefore clearly desirable that any new arrangements for Northern Ireland should, whilst meeting the wishes of Northern Ireland and Great Britain, be so far as possible acceptable to and accepted by the Republic of Ireland ...

These propositions were to be taken a significant step further in the White Paper *Northern Ireland Constitutional Proposals* (March 1973). The British Government now declared that it favoured, and was prepared to facilitate, the formation of some kind of Council of Ireland, but warned that

if a council is to be set up not merely as a statutory concept, but as a useful working mechanism in north–south relations, it must operate with the consent of both majority and minority opinion in Northern Ireland, who have a right to prior consultation and involvement in the process of determining its form, functions and procedures.

Given the expressed need for consent, the British Government announced that it intended to invite to a conference representatives of the Republic of Ireland and the leaders of the elected representatives of Northern Ireland opinion, to discuss how three objectives of the discussion paper might best be pursued, that is:

(a) the acceptance of the present status of Northern Ireland, and of the possibility – which would have to be compatible with the principle of consent – of subsequent change in that status;

(b) effective consultation and cooperation in Ireland for the benefit of north and south alike;

(c) the provision of a firm basis for concerted governmental and community action against terrorist organisations.

Following the publication of this White Paper, the political process was to be carried forward in two distinct stages. First, following elections to a new Northern Ireland Assembly, leaders of parties elected to that body would be brought together under the chairmanship of the Secretary of State to seek a broadly agreeable basis for the future discharge of legislative and executive functions in Northern Ireland. The context would be the British Government's declared policy that the formation of an Executive could no longer be solely based upon any single party, if that party were to draw its support and its elected representation virtually entirely from only one section of a divided community. There would, in simple language, have to be 'power-sharing'. But agreement reached about this internal dimension could only be conditional. The White Paper pointed to a need to address also the 'Irish dimension', and the SDLP (backed by the Irish Government) could be expected to insist upon acceptable progress on this front as the final coping stone of any wide-ranging settlement. To use the terminology bandied about in much later exchanges, 'nothing is agreed until everything is agreed'.

History records all too vividly how this entire process ended in failure and deep disillusionment; in the collapse after a few months of a fragile and divided Northern Ireland Executive, a reversion to direct rule with its truncated legislative procedures and colonialist flavour, further decades of violence and a growing alienation between Northern Ireland communities at grass-roots level.

It has to be said that all parties concerned were facing an immensely difficult task and were burdened by a great weight of history. No attempt to solve through a single agreement such complex and long-lasting problems could be assured of success. The negotiating processes were to be inherently weakened by the deliberate absence of the DUP and anti-Faulkner Unionists, and by the fact that many prime movers of terrorism were just over the wall of the conference chamber. All parties to the process showed real courage; some also made serious mistakes.

In particular, far too little attention was paid, even by its authors, to the warning that a Council of Ireland would have to be in such a form as to 'operate with the consent of both majority and minority opinion'. Faulkner's precarious electoral mandate enabled him to enter the talks process, but did not ensure that its outcome would be tolerable even to his own supporters, let alone to dissidents. Both the Northern Ireland and British Governments had long stood out against intervention by any Irish Government in the domestic affairs of Northern Ireland as part of the United Kingdom. Proposals for a Council of Ireland were 'external', in the sense that the Irish Government would have to be a party to them; but they were also 'internal' in that they would impact upon functions previously discharged by the Northern Ireland Government. Nor was 'power-sharing' an easy concept to sell to unionist supporters. As recently as October 1971, a Northern Ireland Government discussion paper, *The Future Development of the Parliament and Government of Northern Ireland*, had expressed the following conviction: '... suggestions for reform of "PR Government", where parties in Parliament would be represented within the Executive in proportion to their strength, are fundamentally unrealistic ... any such formula would simply not be workable in Northern Ireland conditions given the deep divisions of opinion which exist on quite fundamental issues.'

It was because of their fear that Faulkner would be exposed to damaging criticism for far exceeding his electoral mandate that a number of politicians sympathetic to him were to argue that the outcome of talks should be endorsed by referendum.

As I shall argue later, Faulkner was to make a fundamental (if wholly honourable and understandable) mistake in agreeing in broad principle in the first ('domestic') stage of the talks that a future Council of Ireland should have some executive functions, in relation to matters yet to be defined. It is to be assumed that the SDLP made it brutally clear that, without assurances there would be a meaningful Council, it would not think it worthwhile to pursue the process to a conclusion. But the SDLP, under the chairmanship of a Secretary of State desperate for a constructive outcome, pressed the Faulkner unionists very hard. In the Assembly elected in June 1973 unionists 'pledged' to the support of Faulkner gained only twenty-four seats (some of them occupied by the faint-hearted and unreliable) as against twenty-seven gained by the two coalition partners, the SDLP and Alliance. While the SDLP was prepared to concede the post of Chief Executive to Faulkner, it could only be persuaded to allow the Faulkner unionists a slender majority within the Executive (or Cabinet) if they in turn accepted a non-unionist majority in the Administration (or Government) as a whole. On a fundamental issue, then, Faulkner could be sure of commanding a Cabinet majority; but in reality (as events were to demonstrate all too clearly in the months to come) the division on such an issue would precipitate the destruction of the Executive itself. In a sense, the right of Faulkner to commit political suicide was reserved to him.

However, no blame can fairly be allocated to Cosgrave's Irish Government for Faulkner's fundamentally weak position as he entered the crucial Sunningdale Conference in December 1973. They must, however, bear the responsibility, alongside the British Prime Minister Edward Heath, for driving Faulkner and his unionists to the wall, and utterly failing to deliver the objectives of the 'Irish dimension' set out in the British Green and White Papers.

First of all, the Sunningdale communiqué committed the participants to a Council of Ireland 'with executive and harmonising functions' as well as a consultative role. The rule of unanimity in reaching decisions in the proposed Council of Ministers was clearly intended to reassure unionists that nothing could be imposed over their heads. Yet from the outset there was a probability rather than a possibility that the Council proposals would fail to meet the test of acceptability in the unionist community. While not disputing that he had agreed in principle to some degree of executive powers for a Council during the Whitelaw-chaired talks at Stormont Castle, Faulkner was to express at the beginning of the Sunningdale Conference the gravest doubts about his ability to sell such a package back home.

A future and relatively early crisis was made inevitable by the failure to make convincing progress on the issues of constitutional status and security. The last words of the final Northern Ireland Government had been embodied in its departing document *Political Settlement* (1972), reproducing statements issued on 24 March 1972. The statement made that day on behalf of the outgoing Northern Ireland Government had reviewed proposals made to the British Government in the weeks before the introduction of direct rule:

> We suggested a far-reaching effort to securing a constitutional 'new deal' in Ireland as a whole, under which Northern Ireland's right to self determination would be recognised by Treaty, there would be a common policy and action for the suppression of illegal organisations, including the concept of a 'common law enforcement area in Ireland', making the return of a fugitive offender automatic, and a joint Irish Inter-governmental Council would be set up with equal membership from the Belfast and Dublin Governments, to discuss matters of mutual interest, particularly in the economic and social spheres.

It was entirely understandable, and almost certainly prudent of the Irish representatives at Sunningdale to rule out, at that stage, any question of a referendum to amend Articles 2 and 3 of their Constitution embodying the 'territorial claim'. It has always been clear that, if this issue were to be addressed with any prospect of success, it would have to be with the endorsement of a Fianna Fail Government. All oppositions have a disposition to oppose; Fianna Fail regarded it as almost unnatural to be out of power; and the precarious inter-party coalition could not afford be vilified as 'the faint hearts who sold out the national aspiration'. But the result of this prudence and recognition of political reality was a grotesque fudge in the Sunningdale communiqué. While the British declaration firmly asserted that 'the present status of Northern Ireland is that it is part of the United Kingdom', the parallel Irish declaration solemnly declared that there could be no change in the status of Northern Ireland without majority consent, but did not clarify what that status was or confirm any acceptance of it. At best it embodied a political view taken by the Irish Government then in power; but the constitutional case brought by Kevin Boland was soon to flush out the reality that the provisions of the Irish Constitution, rather than the wording of any political communiqué, embodied the definitive declarations about the status of Northern Ireland. On the issue of terrorism and fugitive offenders, some limited progress was made, and the Irish Government undertook to introduce arrangements to try within its own jurisdiction people accused of murder in Northern Ireland; but wider issues – including the ideas floated by Faulkner and his colleagues before direct rule – were characterised as presenting 'problems of considerable legal complexity' and remitted to a joint British–Irish Commission of jurists.

In my view the Irish, pushed and (to a considerable degree) misled by the SDLP, had committed a terrible error of judgement. Throughout this long unhappy story of Northern Ireland, parties have been remarkably insensitive in considering the realities on the other side of the political fence. Thus we have seen again and again sorties by political generals who, when looking behind them, find that their troops have remained in the trenches. What was Faulkner now being asked to sell to a sceptical unionist electorate? Indefinite loss of all those 'law and order' functions whose withdrawal had precipitated the resignation of the whole Stormont Government led by him; the constitution of a new-style Cabinet incorporating Ministers who had recently been backing acts of civil disobedience, such as a 'rent strike'; the creation of an executive all-Ireland body which, however circumscribed by unanimity rules or otherwise, could be presented as an all-Ireland Government in embryo; a meaningless fudge on the emotive issue of status; and extremely limited progress in confronting the ongoing problem of terrorist violence. Even for a politician as self-confident and articulate as Brian Faulkner, it was a hopeless manifesto to present to the people who wished to preserve the Union. This became all too evident in a very short time after the conclusion of the Sunningdale Agreement. The man who presided over the new power-sharing Executive, which assumed office on 1 January 1974, was to be repudiated by the Ulster Unionist Council (the ruling body of his party) on 4 January, leading to his resignation as UUP leader on 7 January. Long before the catastrophic United Kingdom General Election of February 1974, it was perfectly clear that, in particular, the proposals for a Council of Ireland were not saleable to the unionist community. With the support of over 50 per cent of the total electorate at the polls, the three parties constituting the UUUC gained eleven of the twelve Northern Ireland seats at Westminster.

A more patient policy on the part of the Irish Government and the SDLP would have sought to create, rather than to assume, mutual confidence between previously conflicting interests. One cannot know the extent to which concentration upon the perceived evils and dangers of a Council of Ireland masked a less readily acknowledged dislike of the idea of Catholics and nationalists in Government. It cannot be taken for granted that the power-sharing Executive would have prospered even in propitious circumstances. As it was we were heading for a double catastrophe: not only the collapse of well-meaning efforts to reach a comprehensive settlement, but a flaccid acceptance of its destruction by unacceptable and illegitimate methods.

Too late in the day, the Irish Government began to understand the vulnerability of Faulkner. Accompanying the Chief Executive to a meeting at Baldonnell with Liam Cosgrave, I found the latter sympathetic to Faulkner's predicament, and willing to recognise the damage inflicted on Faulkner's credibility by the line of pleading necessary to rebut Kevin Boland's contention that the Sunningdale declarations had been unconstitutional. This was to be clearly recognised by Garret FitzGerald in his autobiography published in 1991:

Legally, we had an impeccable defence – and it succeeded. Politically, in its impact on Unionist opinion, it was totally disastrous. The subtle legal arguments used to defend the agreement were not merely lost on unionists: they totally destroyed the value of the declaration, undermining Faulkner's already shaky position and leaving a legacy of distrust that contributed to, without being in any way the prime cause of, Unionist rejection of the Anglo-Irish Agreement 12 years later. If when we had prepared for Sunningdale we had realised fully what our careful drafting of the 'status' document implied from the point of view of the defence against constitutional challenge we might perhaps have given more serious consideration to a constitutional referendum.

Quite so. Faulkner had also emphasised to Cosgrave his growing pessimism about acceptance in the unionist community of a Council of Ireland.

On the 'status' front, Cosgrave promised to do what he could without prejudicing the Irish Government's response to the pleadings of Boland. In the event it was not to be until 13 March that the Taoiseach felt able to declare in the Dail: 'The factual position on Northern Ireland is that it is within the United Kingdom and my Government accepts this as a fact.'

While the legal and constitutional impediments (not to speak of the domestic political realities) prevented him from going further, this statement inevitably fell far short of unconditional recognition. It was rather as if a father, maintaining that his son was wholly innocent on a charge of murder, were to say, 'The factual position of my son is that he is in the death cell, and I accept this as a fact.' Meanwhile the business of putting flesh on the bare bones of the Sunningdale Agreement relating to a Council of Ireland was rolling ahead, under the broad direction of an Intergovernmental Steering Group of officials who were overseeing bilateral exchanges between individual Northern Ireland Government Departments and their counterparts in the Republic. These exchanges revealed a significant contrast, and at times a tension, between functional departments of the Irish Government and the 'centre', represented in particular by the Department of External Affairs. By and large those responsible on either side of the Border were not markedly enthusiastic about surrendering to a new and untried all-Ireland body control or influence over some important domestic service in their own jurisdiction. They sought to be guided by the objectives of 'harmonisation' formulated at Sunningdale, that is to say

(1) to achieve the best utilisation of scarce skills, and expertise and resources;

(2) to avoid, in the interests of economy and efficiency, unnecessary duplication of effort; and

(3) to ensure complementary rather than competitive effort where this is to the advantage of agriculture, commerce and industry.

These objectives, with their emphasis on demonstrable benefit, were sensible and realistic. The notion that all competition for (to take an example) foreign inward investment could be eliminated was naïve. But while the departmental officials seemed prepared to reflect the spirit of the stated objectives, those closest to the political centre in Dublin showed a much more ideological cast of mind, and a determination to shift as much responsibility as possible on to an all-Ireland basis. This inflation of executive responsibility was bound to give further strength to the arguments of the anti-Sunningdale unionists, that a Council of Ireland would be a Government for all-Ireland in embryo.

It has to be said, though, that the list of potential functions considered at a joint meeting of Irish and Executive Ministers was unsensational, particularly given the unanimity rule, and that when Faulkner told his Executive partners in the SDLP that he could not proceed without a stay on the introduction of Executive functions, the Irish were prepared to accept any outcome acceptable to the Executive as a whole. Unfortunately no such outcome could be reached until the UWC strike was already under way. The rapid descent into disintegration has already been described elsewhere.

It seemed to me, in the aftermath of this very sad collapse, that a great opportunity had been missed. Nationalist Ireland, as represented by the Irish Government, would have done well to recognise that it would be better to feed and nurture a tiny plant than to establish an outsize bush on barren soil. The unionists allowed themselves to be frightened by scare stories about a cooperative monster in their midst, from reaping the benefits of an historic rapprochement through an alliance with parties committed to wholly peaceful means. The British had presided over these developments – relating, after all, to part of their own country – with Tory insensitivity after the replacement of Whitelaw and real mismanagement at critical moments by Wilson and Rees.

The next politically significant involvement by an Irish Government occurred in December 1980 at a meeting in Dublin between Margaret Thatcher as Prime Minister and Charles Haughey as Taoiseach. It can be taken for granted that, in the course of briefing for this meeting, Mrs Thatcher had been very fully informed about the distinct whiff of sulphur hanging over Haughey's reputation since the arms trial. She was, too, almost jingoistically patriotic and intellectually and emotionally supportive of the Union. But this many-sided character was to display from time to time a certain weakness for rather raffish men. While I have referred elsewhere to 'the lizard-like gaze' of Mr Haughey, he could when he wished withdraw from his armoury of talents a powerful battery of charm and flattery. She led to Dublin a very powerful delegation, including the Chancellor Geoffrey

Howe and the Foreign Secretary Lord Carrington. Carrington, in particular, as we have already seen had previous experience of dealing with Northern Ireland and had not come away with a high opinion of the unionists.

The setting for this important meeting was the deteriorating public order situation in Northern Ireland. The prolonged hunger strikes by republican prisoners were having deeply worrying consequences, and in August of the previous year there had been a mass slaughter of soldiers at Warrenpoint and the murder of Lord Mountbatten. It can well be imagined that, for various reasons, both the Foreign Office and the Ministry of Defence in London had a powerful interest in trying to break the political impasse, and a sense that better progress would be made with the Republic as a partner rather than an adversary.

In her memoirs *The Downing Street Years* (1993), Margaret Thatcher is disarmingly frank about the apparent significant shift in policy recorded after the Dublin meeting with Haughey:

> This meeting did more harm than good because, unusually, I did not involve myself closely enough in the drafting of the communiqué and, as a result, allowed through the statement that Mr Haughey and I would devote our next meetings in London 'to special consideration of the totality of relationships within these islands'. Mr Haughey then gave a press briefing which then led journalists to write of a breakthrough on the constitutional question. There had of course been no such thing. But the damage had been done and it was a red rag to the unionist bull.

This is, when you think of it, a fairly astounding admission. Everyone knows that it is not Ministers but officials who, following a meeting between their masters, get into a huddle and haggle about the wording of a draft. The Irish, in my personal experience, are highly skilled in this black art, and often capable of slipping beneath the radar of the ineffable self-confidence of certain British officials. Nor should it be assumed that all British officials present on such an occasion would have shared Mrs Thatcher's instinctive unionism. But the crucial completion of such a process is not the drafting but the authorising of the statement. A strong-minded and strong-willed leader needs to think carefully at that stage not only about the gloss or 'spin' they can place on any communiqué but also about the emphasis likely to be given by their interlocutor. The plain fact of the matter is that, in authorising the release of this communiqué, Margaret Thatcher had presented Charles Haughey and the Irish with a benchmark for the future. The seeds of what became the John Hume-branded 'three-strands strategy' had been sown.

At the end of 1982, however, Haughey and Fianna Fail lost office, and Garret FitzGerald became Taoiseach. In his autobiography (1991), FitzGerald gives a revealing account of his state of mind as he returned to power:

I had come to the conclusion that I must now give priority to heading off the growth of support for the IRA in Northern Ireland by seeking a new understanding with the British Government, even at the expense of my cherished, but for the time being at least clearly unachievable, objective of seeking a solution through negotiation with unionists.

In reaching this conclusion, FitzGerald had been heavily influenced by the growing prospect of PSF overtaking the SDLP as the majority party of the nationalist community. Here, though, we come very close to the heart of the matter. As long as the unionist/loyalist and republican/nationalist communities remained unreconciled, one faced the danger of a shift towards greater militancy on either side of the great political divide. The politics of domestic reconciliation would be good for the UUP and the SDLP; politics of continuing animosity would be good for the DUP and PSF. The continuing failure of discussions within Northern Ireland to make any useful progress triggered a growing impatience in Dublin and London. Yet, as we shall see, a purported 'settlement' on terms unacceptable to a large part of the population would have an inherent weakness and instability.

The first move in the new game was to be for nationalist Ireland to 'get its act together', and the medium for this was to be the New Ireland Forum. It had been John Hume's idea to propose a nationalist Council for a New Ireland, and although FitzGerald was anxious to broaden this concept to include all parties in the Dail and anyone else willing to join in talks with them, it was certainly clear from the outset that no unionist political party could or would discuss the future of Northern Ireland in a Dublin Forum where they would be greatly outnumbered by nationalist politicians, north and south. Moreover, in spite of the Irish emphasis upon the famous 'totality of relations', the underlying assumption was that progress could be made in an Irish context without any reference to the British links and loyalties of unionism. It was to be the first manifestation of the imbalance that characterised the negotiations for the Anglo-Irish Agreement and their outcome in 1985.

The New Ireland Forum, meeting for the first time in May 1983, was to produce its Report on 3 May 1984. In the absence of the unionist parties, there had been little challenge to comfortable nationalist assumptions, apart from the honourable effort by the McGimpsey brothers as individuals to explain the unionist point of view, and some devastating presentations from the distinguished economists, Sir Charles Carter and Dr Louden Ryan, demonstrating that any united Ireland would be unable to afford the standard of services made possible in Northern Ireland by British Exchequer support.

The Report was, in a number of respects, disastrously insensitive. Garret FitzGerald himself was later to admit 'the nationalist bias of the historical section and the ritual obeisance to the concept of a unitary State'. Faced with the choice between withdrawal of Fianna Fail support for the Report or conceding to Haughey's demand that a unitary state should be the 'preferred option', FitzGerald had opted for the latter. So it was that the Forum Report embodied a clear preference for a unitary thirty-two county state, but also tabled the other options of a federal arrangement or joint authority. The Report also stated that 'the parties in the Forum also remain open to discuss other views which may contribute to political development'. The Forum professed itself keen to safeguard, under any foreseeable alternative arrangements, the ethos of the Protestant/unionist community in Northern Ireland, but in its analysis signally failed to acknowledge that this ethos was about 'Britishness' as well as Protestantism. In short, everything about unionists was to be respected, with the exception of their unionism.

I have discussed elsewhere the initial reaction of Mrs Thatcher to the Forum options ('out, out, out') and the reaction of the unionist parties and communities can be imagined. In the interests of preserving a façade of nationalist unity, Garret FitzGerald had allowed his authority to be attached to a biased analysis and an unrealistic preference. Haughey had proved to be the better poker player.

In the section of this book dealing with the role of the British Government, I have dealt very fully with the events leading to the signing of the Anglo-Irish Agreement in 1985. On the face of it, it was a great triumph for Irish diplomacy to shift Mrs Thatcher from her outraged denunciation of the Forum options to the concession of such a substantial and continuing involvement in the affairs of Northern Ireland. The outcome reflected, as well as the determination of certain British officials to circumvent the essential unionism of Mrs Thatcher, the consummate skills of experienced Irish officials such as Dermot Nally and Noel Dorr, for both of whom I had and have the utmost respect.

I fear, though, that even the Irish – much better informed in many ways than their English counterparts – greatly underestimated the strength and duration of the unionist reaction to the Agreement. While the British and Irish were brought together regularly across the table at meetings of the Intergovernmental Conference, the unionist community drifted away into growing alienation both from its nationalist neighbours and a British Government incapable or unwilling (as they saw it) to represent their interests. The joint Anglo-Irish Secretariat at Maryfield, located behind barricades (indeed initially picketed or even attacked) and invisible from the road, assumed in the unionist mind the sinister and mysterious connotations of a Lubianka. Since the exchanges there were secret, disaffected unionists could conjure up thoughts of sinister conspiracies, rather than the mundane business often conducted there. It says something, though, for the degree of insensitivity shown to unionist opinion, that at one early moment there was pressure to locate this Secretariat in the grounds at Stormont. In spite of denials, there was an impression of the substance if not the form of joint authority. While Dublin Ministers were free to appoint, and sometimes did appoint, their political or even financial supporters to important public positions in the Republic, no post of any significance in Northern Ireland could be filled without considering recommendations from the Irish, often bearing the fingerprints of the SDLP. The Irish Government had a direct and the SDLP an indirect input into developing policy totally withheld from unionists elected by large majorities to the House of Commons. Its architects would still characterise the Anglo-Irish Agreement as a success; if not 'the final solution' to the Northern Ireland problem, certainly a significant step on the way towards it. Let us, then, acknowledge its failures and deficiencies. It left the 'constitutional imperative' hanging in the air; it did not promote or encourage movement towards devolution in Northern Ireland; it did not promote greater sympathy or understanding between separated communities; it did not check, over the longer term, the rise and rise of Sinn Fein.

Developments from 1985 to the present have been very fully discussed and analysed in my section about British involvement. In this section I would wish to emphasise one further point about these later events. From start to finish it has been quite apparent that John Hume has deployed a remarkable influence upon the policies of successive British and Irish Governments. I will discuss much more fully in the next section his performance within Northern Ireland and as leader of the SDLP. Over years he clearly became as invulnerable to criticism in Ireland as Nelson Mandela in post-apartheid South Africa. Lionised by Irish America, the White House and congressional leaders, using to the full a platform in New York or at Westminster as well as back home, receiving columns of laudatory journalism and described in hagiographic books, loaded with honorary doctorates, citations and distinctions, Hume would at many moments have been sure of unopposed election to the presidency of Ireland. Very often John Hume's personal policy was (as we shall see) synonymous with SDLP policy; and no Irish Government wanted to incur the displeasure of the northern guru. Occasionally, but only occasionally and with the utmost tact, he would be reined in. Albert Reynolds, in particular, was to prove too shrewd and sensible to consume the meal precooked by Adams and Hume, and characterised by an abundance of green vegetables. In joining with Major to make the Downing Street Declaration, Reynolds formulated the soundest and most promising policy in relation to Northern Ireland of any Irish Taoiseach.

CHAPTER SEVEN

The politics of Northern Ireland

In this final section of analysis, I turn to the role played in events in Northern Ireland by its domestic political parties. The reservation to this stage of comment upon their actions or inactions does not imply that these were less important or significant than those of the other major players. It reflects, rather, the reality that these domestic political or other interests played their part within a framework established by the Crown in Parliament, and reflecting, on some occasions at least, agreement between the sovereign Governments in London and Dublin.

While there was, of course, political activity – centred upon elections to the Parliament of the United Kingdom – in the years between the Act of Union and the Government of Ireland Act 1920, I wish to concentrate here upon the period from the establishment of the Northern Ireland Parliament up to the introduction of direct rule in 1972, throughout which the UUP was the dominant force in local politics and in continuous control of the Stormont Government; and also the period following direct rule, during which powers to govern in Northern Ireland were either shared or withdrawn.

With the establishment of the first Dail early in 1919, attended by Sinn Fein members unwilling to participate any longer in a British Parliament, it became clear that a peaceful transition to a Home Rule Parliament within the United Kingdom was no longer achievable.

I have already discussed elsewhere the background to and nature of the Government of Ireland Act 1920. It is sufficient to repeat here that only in Northern Ireland (defined as six counties of the old province of Ulster) was it possible to work the Act. Since the area as defined was clearly the most extensive within which unionism could be assured of a governing majority, it was hardly a surprise that the UUP, now led by James Craig, won a significant majority (forty out of the fifty-two seats) in the new Northern Ireland House of Commons at the first Northern Ireland General Election of 24 May 1921. The remaining twelve seats were shared equally between the nationalists and Sinn Fein. Given the high poll (of 89 per cent) and the use at that stage of proportional representation at such elections, this can be taken as an undistorted reflection of party and communal loyalties immediately after partition. Unionists were clearly the dominant force; nevertheless, election returns from the outset underlined the reality that a significant proportion of Northern Ireland voters were unreconciled to the partition settlement, whereas in Southern Ireland Sinn Fein had won 124 seats out of 128.

So it was that the task facing the new Government of Northern Ireland was not only to provide public services for the benefit of all, but also – if possible – to draw a divided community closer together. From the outset it was vain to suppose that Catholics and nationalists would resile from the dream of a truly united and independent Ireland; but could they be persuaded, at least, that they would be equal citizens in a new mini-state, free from discrimination and unfairness?

The judgement of history has to be that, for too much of its long tenure of office, unionism failed to honour that second responsibility. But the blame for such a failure must lie partly upon the Catholic and nationalist minority and its representatives. If nationalists felt entitled to look to a unionist Government to deal fairly with them and their interests, so the unionists felt entitled to look not for the abandonment of aspirations to unity, but for a willingness to play a constructive and responsible part in the organs of the new jurisdiction.

The new Government had come into being at a time of violent activity by the IRA both north and south of the Border. Protestant communities in areas close to the Border came under particular pressure, leading to a reincarnation of the UVF and the activity of Protestant vigilantes in such areas as County Fermanagh, where a member of a distinguished aristocratic and military family, Sir Basil Brooke, was soon to play a leading role. It was to be the British Government, prior to the election of the first Northern Ireland Government, which thought it best to canalise this spontaneous commitment to self-defence into a new Ulster Special Constabulary, whose most numerous element, the B Specials, would be a part-time uniformed and armed force. Inevitably this new Constabulary was to be overwhelmingly Protestant in composition, setting the scene for a growing Catholic conviction that the forces of law and order in Northern Ireland were not concerned with their interests or protection.

At the state opening of the new Northern Ireland Parliament in June 1921, King George V made a heartfelt appeal 'to all Irishmen to pause, to stretch out the hand of forbearance and conciliation, to forgive and forget, and to join in making for the land which they love a new era of peace, contentment and good will'.

A new phase opened with the signing of the Anglo-Irish Treaty in

December 1921. This was followed by a period of intense and prolonged violence in Ireland, north and south. In Northern Ireland there was extensive sectarian conflict, cross-Border incursions, notorious murders, house-burning and other activities all too familiar in more recent times. Craig met Michael Collins in London in March 1922 and the two leaders associated with a declaration of peace a number of specific understandings, including efforts to draw Catholics into the Special Constabulary, but when this agreement proved ineffective Collins began to supply weaponry to northern units of the IRA.

It was, then, hardly surprising that, in an atmosphere of crisis and with the very survival of its new institutions at stake, the Government of Northern Ireland deemed it necessary to introduce draconian special powers legislation, including powers of internment. This legislation, prepared for and justified by a demonstrable state of emergency, was to linger on the statute book through more peaceful times to come, exposing successive Northern Ireland Governments to criticism for an alleged disregard for civil liberties. In spite of such new powers, the situation went from bad to worse; great and sometimes historic houses were burned down, businesses attacked, and people shot dead in the street. But this wave of violence began to subside as the full energies of republicans, pro- or anti-Treaty, were committed to a civil war largely fought out in the south.

With the conclusion of the Irish Civil War in May 1923, the willingness of the Unionist Government to deal fairly with all its citizens could be put to the test in more normal and peaceful conditions. Craig's middle-aged and middle- or upper-class Cabinet Ministers included some, such as Lord Londonderry, who were conscious of the need to demonstrate genuine even-handedness, but other colleagues continued to view Northern Ireland as an entity under permanent siege and threatened within its own walls by an element disloyal to it. From the outset the new Northern Ireland Civil Service was predominantly Protestant in composition. Perhaps unsurprisingly in the prevailing circumstances, relatively few of those who chose to transfer to Belfast from the Irish Administration at Dublin Castle were Catholics, although one of these was the splendidly named A. Napoleon Bonaparte Wyse, the Permanent Secretary to the Northern Ireland Ministry of Education, who nevertheless kept his home in Dublin and travelled back to it every weekend. Catholic interest in the Civil Service could hardly be encouraged by the prominence within its ranks of Wilfred Spender, first as Secretary of the Cabinet and thereafter as Head of the Northern Ireland Civil Service. Spender, in the past, had been prominently active in the unionist cause, both politically and militarily. On the other hand, it has to be said that a necessary condition of adequate Catholic representation in the ranks of the Northern Ireland Civil

Service was a matching willingness and desire to serve within it; and for a long time those who chose to serve the State, whether as civil servants or policemen, ran the risk of being stigmatised as 'West Britons' or lackeys of the Crown and its local agents.

Unfortunately Craig's Government, even when the storm of the 1920s had passed over it, showed in its policies and legislative programme little concern for Catholic or nationalist opinion. The abolition of the use of proportional representation at local government elections; the redrawing of electoral boundaries with indefensible examples (as in Londonderry) of gerrymandering; and the concession to the Protestant churches of excessive influence in the State (and de facto Protestant) schools; all of these developments enhanced the conviction in the Catholic community that the organs of the State were working against their interests. By 1930 there were, in effect, two separate and distinct systems operating side by side in Northern Ireland. In their fixed determination to retain complete control over Catholic schools albeit on a basis of less than full funding, the Catholic hierarchy had missed the opportunity to argue before the Judicial Committee of the Privy Council that the education legislation infringed the terms of the 1920 Act. The stance of the Catholic Church in this matter was, of course, in line with its universal teaching that, wherever possible, Catholic children should be educated in a Catholic religious environment. But the separateness of the education systems sowed the dragon's teeth of the future. Generations of children would grow to adulthood in ignorance and fear of 'the other'. Of course, any attempts to persuade the unionist majority to take a more generous and far-sighted view were undermined by the original stance of nationalists elected to the Northern Ireland Parliament not to take their seats. And even as this abstentionism broke down in the later 1920s, political nationalism was on the whole poorly focused and poorly led, and refused to take on the role of an official opposition. The atmosphere was certainly not improved by the introduction in February 1929 of the Bill to abolish proportional representation in elections to the Northern Ireland Parliament. With this step, accompanied by a redrawing of electoral boundaries, unionism reinforced its dominance in the House of Commons, making the outcome of voting so predictable that there was a steep rise in the number of uncontested seats. By the death of the leading nationalist Joseph Devlin in January 1934, Northern Ireland had become an almost completely polarised society: in its politics, in its education, in its written media, and in sporting and cultural life. The unionists were the more greatly to blame in that they disposed of the ultimate political power. Yet in truth, each side was the mirror image of the other. An Orange, Protestant, anti-Irish unity faction confronted a Hibernian, Catholic and anti-partition faction. Debates in the local Parliament were dry and dusty affairs. Nationalist representatives were often, by intent, absent, and even when present more concerned to reiterate grievances than to play a constructive role in addressing economic or social issues. Unionist representatives were lazy, complacent and confident of carrying in Parliament whatever they chose. In large measure they left it to a professional Civil Service to develop new policy; 'Glengall Street', or Unionist Party Headquarters, was less a think-tank than a cis-Atlantic Tammany Hall.

To the extent that there was any inclination to hold out the hand of friendship towards nationalism, this was further subdued by Eamon de Valera's appointment as Prime Minister of the Irish Free State in March 1932. The accession to office and power of the bogeyman of extreme nationalist republicanism, he who had opposed the Treaty and fought against it in a bitter civil war, inevitably reinforced the siege mentality of Ulster unionism. Moreover, the great International Eucharistic Congress held in Dublin in June 1932 demonstrated to Ulster Protestants the strongly Catholic character and spirit of the Irish Free State. In the heightened atmosphere of these events, the leaders of Ulster unionism were drawn to employ profoundly divisive rhetoric, Craig declaring 'ours is a protestant government' and Basil Brooke (the future Prime Minister) arguing that 'Roman Catholics were endeavouring to get in everywhere and were out with all their force and might to destroy the power and constitution of Ulster.' How useful it is, one reflects, in all too many past and present jurisdictions to be able to sweep real practical problems under the carpet by sounding an alarm against the barbarians alleged to be at the gates; how easy to be elected by the simple device of wrapping oneself in a flag.

Sectarian rioting in Belfast in 1935 could not be quelled by the action of police alone; military support had to be sought, and was provided, in aid of the civil power. Alienation was taken a step further when, on 1 July 1937, the electorate of the Irish Free State approved by referendum de Valera's new Constitution embodying the irredentist claim to Northern Ireland and recognising the special position of the Catholic Church. From the outset, a number of the wiser politicians and officials in the Free State saw that these claims, far from advancing the cause of Irish unity, could only reinforce resistance to it. In February 1938, massive support for Craig's unionists at the Northern Ireland General Election, which he had fought on the single issue of partition, showed that de Valera had if anything copper-fastened unionist hegemony.

From 1939 to 1945 the principal focus, in all parts of the United Kingdom, was upon the impact of 'total war'. Unwisely Craigavon (as James Craig had now become) pressed the British Government to extend conscription to Northern Ireland but Neville Chamberlain wisely refused, understanding

the risks likely to be involved in attempting to conscript unwilling nationalists. In the event, the volunteers joining the armed forces from Northern
Ireland included, in the Catholic James Magennis, the Province's only VC
of the Second World War. On his death in November 1940 Craigavon was
succeeded as Prime Minister of Northern Ireland by a senior colleague J.M.
Andrews; but by and large the Cabinet of ageing figures remained unchanged,
and their ineffectiveness was underlined by the slow pace of gearing up the
war effort in Northern Ireland.

The general unpreparedness of Northern Ireland was illustrated by its
terrible vulnerability to the German air-raid of 15/16 April 1941 on Belfast,
with at least 900 dead (the largest loss of life from a single air-raid on one
night outside London). It deserves to be remembered that, on de Valera's
authority, fire brigades from across the Border raced to the relief of Belfast
and its citizens on that dreadful night. There was a growing conviction that
Northern Ireland must seek a Government more demonstrably capable
of responding to the needs and challenges of war. Even the most dyed-in-
the-wool unionist could see that the ageing coterie who had launched the
Northern Ireland State alongside Craig were no longer capable of coping
with events; and so, after a 'palace revolution' within the ruling party, Sir
Basil Brooke was invited on 1 May 1943 to form a new Government. While
he brought into the Cabinet some new and energetic figures – such as John
MacDermott, later Lord Chief Justice of Northern Ireland and a Law Lord –
he went no closer to forming a 'Government of all the talents' than bringing
into office Harry Midgley, from a background in Northern Ireland Labour.
It must be doubtful if any nationalist would have agreed to serve; certainly
none was invited.

Brooke's rise to power reflected accumulated concern about Northern
Ireland's contribution to the war effort and response to its challenges. At
that level at least, some progress was secured, not least by the placing of
younger and more energetic men in positions of responsibility. At the political level, however, Brooke's inheritance was a sterile and unpromising one.
In the years since 1921, unionist Governments had signally failed to build, or
even to design in outline, any bridge between too deeply sundered communities. This failure had many causes: these included real fear of subversion
of the State, rooted in the violent origins of Northern Ireland and the early
abstentionist approach of nationalist politicians, but also in a real failure
of energy and imagination, and in a total insensitivity to the outlook of
those not represented in Government. Everywhere in the world, regimes
entrenched in power for a long time veer towards arrogance and dogmatism.
By 1943 unionism had already been in office without interruption since 1921.
The outcome of elections, throughout this period, could be forecast pretty

accurately in advance on the basis of a sectarian head count. Under a system of winner-takes-all executive Government, nationalism was not merely excluded from office, but could see no realistic prospect of ever achieving it in the foreseeable future. Where power alternates between parties, a party temporarily in opposition moderates its conduct in the knowledge that it too may in time return to power and to the responsibilities of power. At Westminster the monarch's 'loyal opposition' feels itself to be a significant part of the machinery of the State. At Stormont nationalism had found itself excluded from power, office and influence like some orphan child gazing into a brightly lit and richly furnished shop-window. Unionist Governments had done little to question the desirability of having civil and police services so unrepresentative of the wider community in their composition. Rather had they taken every opportunity to entrench themselves in power: by abandoning proportional representation, by gerrymandering of electoral boundaries, by easy acceptance of segregated education, and by the enactment and employment of draconian special powers.

So it was that Basil Brooke inherited a field sown with dragon's teeth. He was, significantly, deeply rooted in the border land of County Fermanagh, where his exposure in the early 1920s to IRA attack had led him to take a leading role in the development of the B Special Constabulary. He was an aristocrat of deeply conservative instincts, but he brought to his new position an effortless charm and ease of manner which assured his intense popularity amongst the unionist community. They respected, too, the conspicuous contribution made by the Brooke family to the profession of arms; indeed a close relative, Sir Alan Brooke, was to be acknowledged in time as second in importance only to Winston Churchill in Britain's contribution to the Second World War.

By the end of that war, Brooke was flying high in terms of popularity and prestige, at least in his own community. He could draw upon the credit he had established with Labour Ministers who had taken part in the wartime coalition and had contrasted Northern Ireland's participation with the Free State's neutrality. This sympathy was demonstrated by the embodiment in the Ireland Act 1949 of the so-called 'constitutional guarantee'. With the support of Whitehall and Westminster the Stormont Government – often starved of resources in the pre-war period – was able to put into place the extensive (and expensive) social and other services introduced by the Attlee Government. When faced with the choice between their essentially conservative instincts and the potential practical benefits of 'parity', Northern Ireland Ministers prudently opted for the latter.

During the Brooke era, which was to last from 1943 to 1963, there was to be no violent challenge to established order comparable to earlier onslaughts upon the infant Northern Ireland State; while the IRA was to mount a Border campaign in the 1950s, its relatively modest scale compared with the later 'troubles' may be judged by a total death toll of eighteen, of whom twelve were republicans and six members of the RUC.

How, then, did Brooke use his mandate, his exceptionally long hold on the premiership, and the relatively favourable economic, security and political conditions within which he operated?

On the vitally important front of education, a relatively liberal Minister of Education, Samuel Hall-Thompson, was able after a bitter struggle to secure some improvement in State support for Catholic schools, and a greater degree of religious freedom in State schools, but throughout Brookeborough, as he had now become, tolerated or even encouraged Orange and Protestant resistance to Hall-Thompson's modest reformism, leading ultimately to the latter's resignation and replacement by the populist Harry Midgley, who had by then travelled very far from his Labour origins.

If many Protestants were resistant to an increase in State support for Catholic schools, it has to be said that for their part Catholic bishops were deeply suspicious of undue reliance upon State funding. They were to regard a retention of control as more important than a maximisation of Government support. Similar fears of a submergence of a Catholic ethos were to impede for many years the entry into the State NHS system of the important Mater Hospital in Belfast, which had to fall back on support through a system of football pools.

It has to be recognised that, in spite of his very real popularity, Brookeborough had to reckon with the continuing conviction of all too many adherents that the equitable treatment of Catholic fellow-citizens would be a concession to a potential treason. Disputes about Orange parades in such locations as the Longstone Road in County Down and Dungiven in County Londonderry exposed Ministers who sought to ban such events as offensive to the local inhabitants to severe criticism and political embarrassment within their own party. In matters such as this, there was little evidence of any broad policy or controlling influence from the centre of the Government. Ministers of more liberal tendencies were not prevented from taking decisions in accordance with their conscience and convictions; but nor could they depend upon backing and encouragement if and when they subsequently came under fire from the ultras.

Generally evident, though, was a tendency which was to persist over many years. This was to speak for 'Ulster' – 'Ulster' wants this, 'Ulster' wants that – in a way which equated that term with the Protestant and unionist population only. In later years I was also to notice in the remarks of a senior unionist politician rather regular use of the phrase 'the folk'. 'Folk' wanted this or wanted that; I could not help recalling how often in Nazi Germany leaders had spoken of the *Volk*. When in 1959 first Sir Clarence Graham, then Chairman of the Standing Committee of the Ulster Unionist Council, and thereafter Brian Maginess the Attorney General, advocated the acceptance by the Unionist Party of Catholic party members and candidates, Brookeborough lined up with Sir George Clark, Grand Master of the Orange Lodge of Ireland, in rejecting these heterodox doctrines.

At this point I should make it clear that, from the first day of 1956 until 15 April 1991, I occupied a series of positions relatively close to the centre of Government in Northern Ireland. I do not intend in what follows to reveal any information not already in the public domain. I am conscious, too, that when I attribute failings to successive Governments in Northern Ireland I was myself a servant of those Governments in a position of some influence and to that extent implicated in what they did or failed to do. Certainly my relatively brief but close relationship with Brian Maginess as his Private Secretary at the Ministry of Finance in 1956 demonstrated to me that there were leading unionists conscious of the dangers inherent in the continuing divisions and tensions within our community.

All this time the Government in London maintained a placid and complacent role, holding itself aloof from Northern Ireland's problems and explosive possibilities. Only once in the Brookeborough era was a stop light flashed in the way of the Stormont Government. This was when they conceived the crazy plan to break parity in the social services in the area of family allowances, in order to be less generous to large (and this was widely interpreted as Catholic) families. For once Whitehall took a clear stand and Stormont beat an ignominious retreat. But the Brookeborough Government's fear of fundamentalist Protestantism was to be strikingly illustrated when Whitehall extended an offer to locate in Northern Ireland the headquarters operation for the Premium Bonds, with the prospect of creating a large number of new jobs in an area of high unemployment. Fearful of clerical criticism for encouraging gambling, Stormont rejected this generous offer.

Brookeborough's tenure of office had almost certainly been prolonged by a cruel stroke of fate. His Finance Minister and potential heir, Maynard Sinclair, had been one of the victims of the *Princess Victoria* ferry disaster of January 1957, and the subsequent early death from cancer of the able and impressive Morris May removed another politician of prime ministerial potential. In the event it was to be the economic and employment issues which precipitated the belated resignation of Brookeborough, amidst widespread disappointment at the failure of the so-called Hall Report on the Northern Ireland economy to offer any convincing alternative to excessively high rates of unemployment.

Over this period of some twenty years, Brookeborough had done little more than maintain the status quo. Elections continued to be fought on the Border and the Flag; and even modest advances by the Northern Ireland Labour Party failed to widen the political horizons of the Brookeborough Government. He had been faced, it has to be said, by divided and ineffective representation of nationalism, fully as committed to their old slogans as he had been to his. But a period of relative peace and stability had been wasted. The clock was already ticking towards disaster. The Education Act of 1947 had provided for the first time a platform for able Catholic children to advance steadily through the education system, to analyse and question their subordinate and often humiliating status, and to bring in time to the political arena the passion and the skills of a more self-confident generation of young Catholics. In 1963, as the Brookeborough era came to an end, Bernadette Devlin was sixteen years of age.

On a vacancy in the office of Prime Minister, the Unionist Party of those days had no electoral system to identify a new leader. As in the Conservative Party of the day, informal consultations and the 'usual channels' were the basis of choice. The death of Morris May had removed from the field a formidable contender for the succession, but there were in the party many admirers of the undoubted talents and energy of Brian Faulkner, who was felt to be the most likely to maintain the 'traditional unionism' of Brookeborough while giving it a more acceptable public face. Faulkner, it has to be remembered, had led a controversial Orange parade along the Longstone Road in 1955 and had then seemed entirely comfortable with the politics of 'no surrender' and 'not an inch'. Whether, if he had secured the premiership in 1963, that highly acute and intelligent man would have held to this traditional course must be a matter of speculation. One recalls how later unionists, drawn to the support of David Trimble by his postures on the Garvaghy Road in Portadown, found they had secured more than they had bargained for. Tenure of the highest office can sometimes bring with it a heightened sense of responsibility with an exposure to new realities.

Be this as it may, the choice fell not upon Brian Faulkner but upon Terence O'Neill. It is very doubtful if this would have been the outcome of a poll of unionist MPs or party members at the time. But O'Neill had important friends and allies at this vital moment. As Finance Minister a vigorous speech on the economy, in reaction to the Hall Report on the prospects for the Northern Ireland economy (the so-called 'Pottinger Speech'), had caught the attention and won the admiration of the influential editor of the *Belfast Telegraph*, Jack Sayers. Within the party he was at that stage, and ironically, in the light of later events, favoured by the influential Chief Whip, Bill Craig, as well as the Party Secretary Jim Bailie at Unionist headquarters in Glengall Street. At the time of the Brookeborough resignation, O'Neill had given no real indication of the liberal tendencies which could have caused heart-searching on the unionist back-benches. In spite of a brief spell at Home Affairs, the core of his ministerial experience had been at Finance, and it was his good fortune to be a contender at a moment when the main focus of political interest was on unemployment and economic affairs, where his credentials were good. And so it came about that the name of O'Neill was submitted to the Governor and his appointment as Prime Minister was followed by his election to be leader of the UUP.

The O'Neills were a deeply political family. Terence's father – a traditional unionist, supporter of the gun-running and the UVF – had been the first MP killed in the First World War (and indeed Terence's two brothers were in turn to die in the Second). His uncle, Hugh O'Neill (Lord Rathcavan) had served as the first Speaker of the first Northern Ireland Commons and as a junior Minister in a British Government, while his cousin Phelim had also been an MP. Another cousin Sir Con O'Neill, one of the foremost diplomats of his generation, was to play a leading part in Britain's adherence to the EEC. Terence O'Neill himself was a descendant through his mother of the first and last Marquess of Crewe, a leading figure in Asquith's great Liberal Government of all the talents and earlier, as the young Lord Houghton, a Lord Lieutenant of Ireland.

Unfortunately, O'Neill's own roots in Northern Ireland were comparatively shallow. On the death of his father, O'Neill's mother had eventually remarried with a member of the British Consular Service, taking the young boy to the exotic Legation at Addis Abbaba. Later experiences at Eton, as a young-man-about-town in pre-war London and as a Captain in the Irish Guards had left him with little in common with, or sympathy for, the typical member of the Ulster Unionist Council. Unlike his predecessor, he lacked the common touch. He was an implant, an exotic, with his carefully modulated Etonian English and his shy diffidence, too easily (if unfairly) attributed to arrogance. As part of his entrance strategy into unionist politics, O'Neill, on return to Northern Ireland, had joined the Orange Order, which in those days was an implicit qualification for selection as a candidate. Originally he had aspirations to a seat in Parliament (where indeed he might have been more at home), but the family associations ultimately secured his selection for and election to the Stormont constituency of Bannside in deeply loyalist territory later to be represented both in Parliament and at Stormont by the Reverend Ian Paisley.

There is no reason to believe that O'Neill came into office with any grand strategy to improve community relations. His early priority was to gear up physical, social, economic and environmental development. This involved commissioning Professor Tom Wilson of Glasgow University to develop a comprehensive economic plan. There were ambitious initiatives to develop new 'growth centres' at Lurgan/Portadown (later Craigavon) and at Antrim/Ballymena. The opportunity to give a much higher priority to the city of Londonderry, with its unionist-controlled Council amongst a majority Catholic and nationalist population, was missed. Insensitivity to nationalist views and perceptions, rather than overt and conscious discrimination, led to the unthinking acceptance of a recommendation by the independent Lockwood Committee that Northern Ireland's second university should be located in Coleraine, leaving the fate of the long-established Magee University College in Londonderry in limbo. If the extensive development of higher education in Londonderry, undertaken in more recent times by the University of Ulster, had been conceded or foreseen in the 1960s, the growing sense of alienation 'west of the Bann', might have been held back. No one then in Government had the breadth and generosity of vision to appreciate that, whatever the detached judgement of the Lockwood Committee might be, there was an opportunity through the university project to reach out to the minority community and its Derry heartland. Some, of course, would argue that a New University of Ulster established in the conflict zone of the late 1960s and early 1970s would have struggled to survive. A counter argument is that generosity in this and other fields could have prevented the later conflagration. What is beyond doubt is that the campaign for a second university at Derry brought to prominence many of those who would later spearhead the wider movement for civil rights.

On the community relations front, the O'Neill regime was initially distinguished by reformist rhetoric. O'Neill began to speak of 'building bridges in the community', of the need for the efforts of 'a united people' and of his hope for a response 'without too much concern for party lines'. Specifically he accepted that it was essential 'to convince more and more people that the Government is working for the good of all and not only those who vote unionist'. Unhappily some ill-chosen words after his retirement from the premiership were to reveal a rather naïve hope that, if nationalists were enabled to share in economic and social progress, they would in time become neo-unionists.

Unlike his predecessors, however, O'Neill went out of his way to express an interest in, and respect for, Catholic interests and institutions. He sent a message of sympathy to the Catholic hierarchy on the death of Pope John XXIII and visited Catholic schools in Ballymoney and Ballynahinch. At least one local newspaper went out of its way to obtain and publish a picture of the Prime Minister with a crucifix over his head, in the process feeding the growing opposition to O'Neill on the wilder fringes of unionism as 'a Protestant traitor' or 'Lundy'. It is a demonstration of the extreme state of polarisation in Northern Ireland tolerated by his predecessors that this simple gesture of courtesy caused such a stir at the time.

The hard truth of the matter was that the rhetoric (for much of which, as O'Neill's regular speech writer, I was responsible) and the sympathetic gestures far outran O'Neill's ability or capacity to deliver real improvements in the circumstances of the Catholic and nationalist minority. A significant early opportunity was missed to make progress in the first days of the O'Neill premiership. Two leading lay Catholics, Brian McGuigan and J.J. Campbell, came forward with a devastating analysis of Catholic under-representation over a wide range of significant public bodies. As a close adviser to O'Neill at the time, I accept a full share of the blame for not responding constructively to the démarche. We fell back upon frankly specious arguments – justifying, for example, under-representation of Catholics on economic bodies by the fact that relatively few Catholics then held senior positions in commerce and industry. We did not ask ourselves, or press the Prime Minister to ask, why the Catholic community occupied so few key positions in either the public or the private sector. The Campbell/McGuigan démarche was written off as just another propagandist effort to embarrass a unionist Government, rather than as a genuine effort to persuade Stormont to change its ways.

If progress in securing equal rights for Catholic citizens was slow, striking developments – albeit once more largely symbolic in character – were to take place on another front. Nationalists had, by definition, never abandoned their sense of being citizens of an all-encompassing Ireland, and yet cooperation between the two jurisdictions had been at a low-key level and of a workaday character. In discussing the role of Irish Governments, reference has already been made to the change of tone which became apparent as Sean Lemass succeeded Eamon de Valera. The O'Neill/Lemass exchanges of January 1965 represented the first high-profile effort since the abortive Agreement of 1925 to establish a neighbourly relationship and practical cooperation at the highest political level. At the time the Lemass visit to Belfast had great impact, and was widely hailed as the dawning of a brighter day for the whole of Ireland.

But this bold démarche sowed the seeds of future trouble for the O'Neill administration. The plans for the encounter were made known in advance only to O'Neill's circle of intimate advisers, and not shared with or endorsed by his Cabinet colleagues. He had made a judgement that any such proposal would divide the Cabinet, lead to endless procrastination, and postpone if not prevent a healing initiative. It was also the case that the secrecy of his approach was typical of a somewhat aloof and insecure personality. Although no colleague at the time took a sense of resentment as far as resignation, and although O'Neill was subsequently to fight a very successful General Election, the issue of cross-Border cooperation began to build up suspicion and potential outright opposition both in the Cabinet and in the parliamentary party. The truth was that unilaterally, and on his sole authority, O'Neill had breached a principle consistently maintained by his predecessors over many years; that neighbourly relations would only be possible if the Republic of Ireland withdrew its irredentist constitutional claim to Northern Ireland.

The O'Neill/Lemass meetings, and the further intergovernmental exchanges which followed it, represented the first of three great leaps of faith made by unionist leaders: O'Neill's exchanges with the Government of the Republic; Faulkner's acceptance in principle of executive functions for a Council of Ireland; and Trimble's acceptance of the Belfast (or Good Friday) Agreement.

One early reward for O'Neill's risky venture was the acceptance by the Nationalist Party, following a visit to Dublin by its veteran leader Eddie McAteer, of the role of Official Opposition at Stormont. This was potentially a significant step. It did not alter the nationalist stance on what the state of things ought to be – that is to say, a united Ireland – but conveyed a heightened acceptance or at least grudging toleration of things as they were. It has to be said that the core Nationalist Party at Stormont sitting alongside other nationalists from minority parties, contained a considerable number of reasonable and moderate men who could and would, if given the opportunity, have made constructive contributions to the political life of Northern Ireland. In this respect they were rather different from McAteer himself, a gruff and grizzled veteran, steeped in negativism and the politics of protest. At an earlier point in his career he had published a notorious blueprint for civil disobedience, and his brother Hugh had at one time been Chief of Staff of the IRA. Yet there were others such as the Nationalist Senator Paddy McGill, who was sufficiently intrigued by that institution to make it the subject of a PhD thesis. At any rate it was clear that O'Neill had opened a door to future progress; but would there be significant movement through it?

Growing restlessness within the Parliamentary Unionist Party was led by the brilliant and vituperative barrister Desmond Boal. Of even greater significance within the majority Protestant and unionist community was the inexorable rise of the Reverend Ian Paisley, certainly one of the most striking figures in the history of Northern Ireland. The fissionary qualities of Ulster Protestantism are well illustrated by the proliferation of sects. As early as the first half of the nineteenth century the Presbyterian Church had been riven by accusations of 'heresy'. While the Catholic Church spoke of central authority and the Anglican Church of Ireland established a clearly hierarchical system, other Protestant churches empowered individual congregations and recognised the force and authority of individual conscience. The individualism of the Protestant, as contrasted with the collectivism of the

Catholic, carried forward into both political and ecclesiastical organisation. The old undivided Unionist Party was not an easy organisation to lead. While in Great Britain the Conservative organisation in Parliament had created a mass movement to serve it, both the national Labour Party and the UUP were the deliberate artefacts of pre-existing organisations and movements; hence, for many years, the great continuing influence of the trade unions in the one and of the Orange Order in the other. Unionist leaders were not appointed to tell their followers what to do, but rather to deliver what their followers told them to deliver. Thus a constituency organisation, advised by unionist headquarters at Glengall Street to nominate a candidate supportive of the leader and the party line, was only too likely to do the precise opposite.

Ian Paisley was certainly not the first vehement Protestant fundamentalist to enter Northern Ireland politics. In the 1950s Norman Porter, Secretary of the Evangelical and National Union of Protestants, had been elected to Stormont as an Independent Unionist, displacing the sitting member Hall-Thompson, who had not been forgiven his modest generosity to the Catholic schools when Minister of Education. Porter's arrival and his contributions to debate underlined the reality of a powerful strain in Protestant thinking, but he himself – personally affable if impossibly narrow in his views and opinions – never attracted a really large following.

Ian Paisley was a horse of a different colour. From a base in his own Free Presbyterian Church, established in 1951, he began to establish a political presence early in the O'Neill era, when he organised a march to protest against the lowering of the Union flag over Belfast City Hall to mark the death of Pope John XXIII. He moved closer to centre stage through events during the British General Election of 1964. In the cockpit constituency of West Belfast supporters of the republican candidate Liam McMillen decided to display a small Irish tricolour in the window of their headquarters in Divis Street. The initial view within the Stormont Government was that, however much it opposed the symbol of the flag, there should be maximum freedom of political expression consonant with the preservation of law and order, and in this case the emblem in question was unlikely to give offence in a strongly nationalist and republican area of the city. At that time, under a controversial Flags and Emblems Act, the police had discretionary powers to remove such a flag where its display could create a threat to public order. Paisley now created precisely such a threat by declaring that if the authorities took no action, he himself would lead a march up Divis Street. In the face of this threat the proposed march itself was banned, but the police moved to remove the contentious flag, provoking in the process the most serious sectarian rioting in Belfast since 1935. This was a foretaste of things to come, and an appalling precedent from which many drew the lesson that the otherwise legitimate activities of other interests could be impeded by threats to make those activities the occasion of disorder.

With the O'Neill/Lemass meetings, the political activity of Paisley intensified. O'Neill's initiative was characterised as 'treachery' and 'O'Neill must go' rallies and meetings were harangued by Paisley's emphatic and belligerent rhetoric. It was, once again, the first scene in a very long performance, since virtually every successor to O'Neill in the governance of Northern Ireland, whether Prime Minister, First or Chief Minister or Secretary of State, was in time to receive similar advice about departure times.

In 1966 Northern Ireland entered a fulcrum year. On the social and economic front things were looking up; a new city at Craigavon (albeit not the most tactful choice of names in a divided community), a new university at Coleraine, a new building dock at Queen's Island. A new era of better relations with the Republic seemed to have made a sound beginning. A more cooperative Opposition at Stormont awaited the conversion of reformist rhetoric into real action against discrimination and disadvantage.

But Ireland, north and south, is plagued by a plethora of historical recollection, and 1966 was to be the year of two emotive fiftieth anniversary commemorations: in nationalist Ireland, north and south, the Easter Rising; in unionist Northern Ireland, of the huge sacrifices made by the 36th Ulster Division (basically the pre-war UVF) at the Battle of the Somme. These commemorations were to be like trumpet calls summoning communities back to old allegiances. A polity in Northern Ireland which O'Neill (perhaps vainly) hoped to draw together by comprehensive social and economic development now ran the risk of falling apart into separate and conflicting factions. From the start, O'Neill himself was deeply apprehensive about the outcome, and Paisley took every opportunity to exploit apprehension in the Protestant community. The sectarian face of what was coming to be termed 'Paisleyism' was demonstrated at a noisy protest during the meeting of the Presbyterian General Assembly against its alleged 'Romeward trend'. In the course of this demonstration the then Governor of Northern Ireland, Lord Erskine, with his wife and church dignitaries, were roundly abused. Of course anyone with the slightest knowledge of the Presbyterian Church in Ireland, whether at that time or later, would know that its alleged drift towards Rome was a ridiculous piece of mischief. What was at issue here was nothing more and nothing less than common courtesies between fellow Christians. Paisley, however, was determined to pursue allegations of 'treason' amongst the political establishment and of 'ecumenism' (an even more pejorative label in his eyes) amongst the mainline Protestant churches. Promoting and feeding on the fears and suspicions of puzzled people in a changing world, he was able to recruit more and more adherents to his Free Presbyterian Church and to the politics of Protestant 'no surrender'. As an outcome of the events outside the General Assembly, Paisley was bound over to keep the peace, declined to enter into a bail bond and as a consequence served a brief term in prison. His original and principal church had been called the Martyrs' Memorial; now Paisley had the further credential of martyrdom to add to his growing reputation amongst disaffected Protestants.

Since Paisley, in every sense a large, complex and able personality, can when he wishes dress himself in the apparel of the conscientious public representative serving all his constituents without regard to class or creed (and able to produce evidence that he does so), it is important to place on record the authentic flavour of the invective flowing at that time from this faction of Ulster Protestantism. One of the principal channels for this was a strident newspaper entitled the *Protestant Telegraph*.

The flavour of this publication can best be conveyed by a very typical report of a speech given by Paisley at the Ulster Hall on 19 June 1966 on the theme of 'why our protest against Rome must continue'. The article included the following words.

> He exposed the Roman harlot and questions his hearers as to what fellow-ship light could have with darkness. As Protestants it is our duty to separate ourselves from every form of compromise or union with the antichrist and to dedicate our lives to the furtherance of true religion in the Province ... As Protestants, however, we were not prepared to be silenced or bullied by the Stormont regime, but depending on the God of our fathers for help, we would continue our protest against Rome and Romanism in Protestant circles.

In an article in the *Protestant Telegraph* on the theme of 'O'Neill the Dictator' the following terms were used: 'Since the Church of Rome determined to make Ireland a serfdom of the Vatican – ecclesiastically and politically – Ulster Protestants have been the great hindrance to supreme papal domination.' O'Neill, on the other hand, had used a speaking engagement at Corrymeela to warn of the dangers which he now saw emerging: 'No democratic society can afford to allow itself to be intimidated by violence or pushed around by noisy minorities ... Let us shed the burden of traditional grievances and ancient arguments.'

Unhappily the 'traditional grievances' were not about to disappear, but rather to be reinforced. In the very week during which O'Neill was to attend commemorative ceremonies on the battlefield of the Somme, a young Catholic barman was shot at a public house in Malvern Street in the Shankill area of Belfast by an organisation styling itself the UVF. O'Neill flew back to Belfast, secured the agreement of his Cabinet colleagues to proscribe the 'new UVF' as an unlawful organisation, and in the Stormont House of

Commons on 28 June used for the first time the analogy of a crossroads: 'We stand at the crossroads. One way is the road to progress which has been opening up before us with all its promise of a richer and fuller life for our people. The other way is a return to the pointless violence and civil strife of earlier years.'

The Malvern Street murder, for which one Gusty Spence was ultimately to be convicted, proved in truth to be the first shot in a very long politico-sectarian war. Attempts were made at the time to link Paisley personally with the emerging violence, but no such credible link was ever established. No one, on the other hand, can discount the potential effect of ceaseless and belligerent rhetoric directed at a confused community.

Amidst the tensions and difficulties of 1966, the atmosphere was not propitious for decisive reformist action by O'Neill. There were growing signs of dissidence in the Unionist Parliamentary Party fomented by Desmond Boal, and unsuccessful attempts were made to mount a palace revolution around the formidable person of Brian Faulkner. It was a very great misfortune that O'Neill and Faulkner had never developed a relationship of mutual confidence. Faulkner undoubtedly felt (and I would judge rightly in my own close working experience of both men) that in 1963 he had been passed over for a man of less executive capability and with a weaker hold on the loyalties of the mass party. For his part, O'Neill, conscious of Faulkner's previous reputation as an assertive law-and-order figure, saw him throughout as an impediment to reform and a dangerous rival to himself. He was, in the event, greatly to overestimate Faulkner's willingness to mount or support a coup against him. Faulkner was, in fact, deeply unsympathetic to the sectarian crudities of Ian Paisley, and had many contacts and friendships in the Republic (where he had indeed gone to school) through the Freemasonry of horsemanship.

In truth, by the second half of 1966 O'Neill was uncomfortably confined between a rock and a hard place; under growing pressure from the Wilson Government in London, exposed to criticism from Paul Rose and others in Parliament, exhorted to press ahead with the reform programme by London broadsheets, yet all the time conscious of growing mutterings in Cabinet and Party, with Boal increasingly supplying intellectual muscle to the growing Paisleyite onslaught. Stung by implicit criticism in a report by *The Times* news team O'Neill wrote on 28 April 1967 a long article for that newspaper reflecting on the event of 1966 as having 'made many people realise that harmony in a previously divided community cannot be achieved overnight, but demands a long and patient process of social and political education'. He stressed decisions to abolish university representation and plural voting in elections to the Stormont Parliament, to set up a permanent impartial Boundaries Commission and to reform local government on completion of an exhaustive re-examination of its functions, areas and financing. Crucially, though, he made no reference or commitment to move from a 'ratepayer franchise' at local government elections to the universal suffrage enjoyed in Great Britain.

By now the rhetoric of O'Neillism – the mellifluous speeches and articles – was in real danger of heightening expectations without delivering adequate results. Those of us who at the time pressed O'Neill to move faster and more boldly had to accept the hard fact that it was he and not we who would face the prospect of spelling out unpalatable realities to traditional unionists gathered in geographically and intellectually isolated Orange Halls, seduced by Paisleyite arguments that O'Neill was heading full pelt for a submission to Rome and the authority of a Dublin Parliament. It should be said that no such ideas had ever entered his head. He was a sincere and practising Anglican, and was moved by the conviction that many Catholics could be brought to recognise and accept the benefits of the Union. The greatest potential threat to that Union, as he often expressed it to me, lay in any conflict between loyalism and the authority, of Parliament and the forces of the British state.

However, the crucial trigger for the next phase of events was the development in the Catholic community of a movement for civil rights. Many different factors had a bearing upon its emergence in 1968. The Catholic sons and daughters of the Education Act of 1947 were coming to maturity, bringing to the pursuit of Catholic grievances a new self-confidence and intellectual authority far surpassing the dreary and negative performance of old-fashioned representation at Stormont. Big events were loose in the wider world; the movement for black rights in the United States, the events in Paris and the emergence of student firebrands, such as Tariq Ali and Danny Cohn Bendit. Working in the wings for the rapidly approaching moment were their Northern Ireland equivalents in such people as Eamon McCann, Bernadette Devlin, Michael Farrell or the Protestant supporter of civil rights, Ivan Cooper. In Derry Paddy Doherty and John Hume (who had been spurred on by the 'University for Derry' campaign) were rising forces.

The initial flashpoint of 1968 centred around the issue of housing. In Derry and elsewhere, outrageous gerrymandering of electoral boundaries had assured a unionist dominance in spite of nationalist preponderance in the population. Housing allocations – other than those made by the upright and high-principled Housing Trust – were made by many local authorities with an eye to preserving the sectarian balance in key wards or electoral districts. Personal patronage was used by nationalist as well as unionist counsellors. Thus allocations too often reflected political expediency rather than individual need. The pressure for civil rights arose originally out of an outrageous allocation of a council house at Caledon in County Tyrone, in reaction to which the young nationalist MP for the area Austin Currie (eventually to hold ministerial office both in Northern Ireland and later as a member of the Dail, in the Republic) squatted in the house. The escalation of events from that point onwards is too well known to require extensive repetition here. Northern Ireland entered a dangerous era of demonstration and counter-demonstration, the imposition of banning orders and the pursuit of demonstrations in defiance of such orders, all moving to a spectacular crescendo in Londonderry on 5 October 1968 when the RUC batoned demonstrators, including the MP Gerry Fitt, in the presence of parliamentary observers from London and to the astonishment of a world-wide television audience. With an honesty which deserves great respect, Austin Currie admitted in his autobiography published in 2004 that he would never have initiated the era of protest if he had known to where it would ultimately lead in terms of so many avoidable deaths.

These alarming developments represented both a challenge and an opportunity for Terence O'Neill. He now inevitably faced growing pressure from the United Kingdom Government, which had hitherto fended off criticism from its own back-benchers with advice to 'trust O'Neill'. It was now to make it clear that early action to satisfy civil rights demands was an imperative. Speaking in the House of Commons on 21 October 1968, Harold Wilson recalled that he had previously paid tribute to O'Neill and his attempts to pursue liberalisation in the face of very great difficulties. He added: 'But I do not think anyone in the House is satisfied with what has been done and in particular the feeling that he is being blackmailed by thugs who are putting pressure on him is something that this House cannot accept.'

As a consequence O'Neill, when urging upon an unenthusiastic Unionist Party a move forward from the rhetoric to the reality of reform, was able to deploy the powerful argument that his Cabinet could either look for the credit of willing change, or accumulate the odium of change forced upon it. It was, however, an illustration of the harsh political realities facing O'Neill that he could not reckon upon a united Cabinet. Because he saw the importance of exposing senior colleagues to the real risk of United Kingdom Government action over their heads, he decided to be accompanied by Brian Faulkner and Bill Craig to a meeting at 10 Downing Street. Craig in particular chose to regard Wilson's warnings, whether delivered in public or in the privacy of the Cabinet Room, as a bluff. He was persuaded in the last resort that the long-established convention of non-intervention would hold, and that concessions made under the pressure of violence would simply feed the appetites of unionism's obdurate opponents.

Since the attitude and activities of Craig would have a significant influence on the development of events of this time and later, some further reference should be made to his record as a member of the O'Neill administration. As Chief Whip he had played an important role in O'Neill's accession to the premiership, and for a time as Minister of Development had demonstrated the energy and visionary qualities which had singled him out as a rising man. He was personally quiet-spoken and agreeable, and included not a few Catholics amongst his circle of friends. Unfortunately his move to Home Affairs in 1966, following upon the Prime Minister's judgement that Brian McConnell had been weak and ineffective in that post, brought out a stubborn and intractable side of his character. His reaction to the events in Londonderry on 5 October, in the context of a ban imposed by him as Minister of Home Affairs, was to retreat into unreasoning obduracy. In some interesting respects, his attitude echoed that of politicians in the southern states of America on the eve of the Civil War, in asserting 'states' rights' as against the powers of the central Government.

While Craig represented the main rallying point of hard-core resistance to change, he was certainly not an isolated voice in the O'Neill Cabinet. Some there already saw in the civil rights movement the hand of militant republicanism, or believed that its well-meaning frontmen would be manipulated by people with an anti-partition agenda. Thus, while the publicly proclaimed demand was essentially for equal citizenship within the United Kingdom, they feared that any concessions would be consumed as a mere hors d'oeuvre, before calling for the main course of subverting or undermining Northern Ireland's position within the United Kingdom.

Brian Faulkner was, of course, another key player at this time. As an energetic and successful Minister of Commerce, he had by then established himself as clearly the second man in the Government and its ablest political operator. He was not – as his later role both in the Chichester-Clark and his own administration was to show – at all antipathetic to reform per se, particularly where pragmatism pointed to its necessity. Temperamentally, though, he was not a man who took well to the thought of acting under duress.

In truth, O'Neill had a limited number of secure and reliable allies within his own Cabinet, and this was vividly illustrated by the fact that almost seven weeks were to lapse after the events of 5 October before O'Neill was in a position, on 22 November, and after a series of tense Cabinet meetings, to announce a five-point reform programme: a fair point system for the allocation of public authority housing; the appointment of an Ombudsman; the abolition of the company vote at local government elections; a review of the controversial and contentious Special Powers Act; and the setting up of a Londonderry Development Commission. These proposals, which owed a great deal to the support of James Chichester-Clark and his able MP brother Robin, certainly addressed some of the main areas of legitimate criticism, and in particular the manipulation of housing allocations for electoral purposes, and the control of Londonderry by a self-centred and unrepresentative unionist oligarchy.

After more than five years of the O'Neill premiership, characterised by much talk about reform and too little real action to secure it, the first fruits of change were at last available. Would all of this have happened without belated pressure from London, or could it have been delivered earlier, and ideally hard on the heels of the cross-Border exchanges and the acceptance by the Nationalist Party of a formal Opposition role at Stormont? My own view is that, while his heart was in the right place throughout, in many other respects Terence O'Neill was singularly ill-suited to the task of shifting the centre of gravity of a very conservative, defensive and suspicious Unionist Party. His party roots were shallow and his manner and upbringing distanced him from the mass of his party's supporters. Earlier reform might, just might, have been sold to the party by a firm alliance and a common policy between O'Neill and Brian Faulkner. They had, in truth, gifts and assets which were potentially complementary. Just as Tony Blair and Gordon Brown were to constitute a formidable if sometimes uneasy 'dual monarchy' at the top of the Labour Government, so an O'Neill/Faulkner campaign for reform would have had a better chance, albeit not an assurance, of success.

Building upon the decisions announced on 22 November, O'Neill moved ahead to secure the support of his party (achieved only on the basis of 'no further changes without prior consultation') and of a wider community. The medium for the latter was the *Ulster at the Crossroads* television broadcast of 9 December, the immediate response to which was a massive manifestation of popular support, with letters or telegrams arriving at Stormont Castle from around one in ten of the whole population. The Prime Minister's credibility with the reform lobby was further enhanced when, on 11 December, O'Neill called for Craig's resignation from the Government. This had become inevitable after his flagrant breaches of collective responsibility, criticising the idea of an Ombudsman on 2 December, repeating similar remarks on 5 December and finally on 10 December openly challenging the Prime Minister's broadcast reminder that Northern Ireland could experience United Kingdom Government intervention in its affairs.

At the year's end, things looked promising for O'Neill, for reform and for Northern Ireland. He had displaced an obdurate opponent, received evidence of massive support within Northern Ireland, been backed (albeit grudgingly) by the Unionist Party, and improbably chosen by readers of the *Irish Independent* as their man of the year. There was still a mountain of change to be climbed, but at long last there had been movement forward from base camp. Those of us who were, at the time, O'Neill's closest aides, were encouraged and optimistic. O'Neill himself remained gloomy and communicated a sense of foreboding. We were wrong, and he was right.

How, then, did the slide begin, and who was primarily responsible for it? There were, at that time, various factions involved in the demand for change. At Stormont, the clapped-out Nationalist Party deployed a declining influence. At the political level, of much greater importance was the ability of Gerry Fitt as a Westminster MP to engage the interest and sympathy of a growing number of Labour MPs, including members of the Government. The umbrella organisation termed the Northern Ireland Civil Rights Association brought together a strange mixture of apolitical Catholics, communists and other left-wing interests and certainly, from the outset, some people associated with militant republicanism. Thus Craig was not alone in suspecting that, for some at least, the overt agenda of 'equal citizenship' was cover for a covert agenda of anti-partitionist disruption. Indeed by March 1969 the Association had come increasingly under the control of militants.

I have already argued that, in some respects at least, events in Northern Ireland at this time took their cue from radical movements in other countries, often drawing upon the daring, idealism and iconoclastic tendencies of students in higher education. To this point Queen's University in Belfast had remained relatively detached from the political turmoil. This was to change when a radical group calling itself 'the Peoples' Democracy' (PD) was formed at the University on 9 October 1968. That day a large number of students marched to Belfast City Hall, sat down in the street for three and a half hours, and later presented to representatives of Government demands for 'one man, one vote' at local government elections; repeal of the Special Powers, Public Order and Flags and Emblems Acts; appointment of an Ombudsman; Human Rights legislation; allocation of housing by use of a point system; redrawing of electoral boundaries; fairness in employment opportunities; and an impartial inquiry into police actions in Londonderry on 5 October. It can be noted that some of these demands were in fact met by the Government statement of 22 November, while others were to feature in initiatives taken by successive Governments in time to come. Most prominent in the PD's committee of ten were three remarkably articulate and able people in Bernadette Devlin (later to be elected to Parliament), Kevin Boyle (today an eminent and respected Professor of Law) and Michael Farrell.

In the course of his broadcast on 9 December, O'Neill, after reiterating the reforms to be introduced by his Government, had made a direct appeal to those who had been demonstrating for civil rights in these terms: 'Perhaps you are not entirely satisfied; but this is a democracy, and I ask you with all sincerity to call your people off the streets and allow an atmosphere favourable to change to develop.'

This plea was well received by many of those to whom it had been directed. But the young activists of PD scorned the O'Neill reforms as inadequate, and as Bernadette Devlin was to admit subsequently, they sought quite deliberately to 'break the truce'. Thus they conceived the idea of a seventy-five-mile civil rights march from Belfast City Hall to Londonderry, after the pattern of Martin Luther King in the United States.

It has to be said that, over a great many years, a certain breed of unionist or 'loyalist' has had only to see an elephant trap to leap headlong into it. Inevitably such a march would pass through or close to staunchly unionist communities, but the march consisted of a relatively small ragtag and bobtail army which ignored and unmolested would have passed any given point in a very short time. This was no massive insurgency; indeed responsible nationalist leaders, including in particular John Hume, had advised strongly against it, as all too likely to provoke sectarian violence.

In the event, serial harassment of the relatively small group of marchers culminated in an outrageous assault at Burntollet Bridge near Londonderry, with some two hundred 'loyalists' attacking the marchers, thirteen of whom sustained injuries requiring hospital treatment in spite of rather derisory police efforts to protect those under attack. The ultimate arrival of the marchers in Londonderry on 4 January 1969 was the occasion of sectarian rioting and serious allegations of police brutality in the Catholic Bogside.

Bernadette Devlin and others had set out to end the truce, and had most certainly achieved it. Yet the effects might have been relatively short-lived had not Terence O'Neill been led at this stage into a serious error which did much to withdraw from him a growing support and sense of confidence amongst some elements of the nationalist community. Not only O'Neill himself, but also I and his other close advisers and intimates, were furious that an irresponsible initiative by the PD had put at risk all the potential gains from the new commitment to reform. So it was in a spirit of resentment that we fashioned for issue by the Government a statement which emphasised condemnation of the marchers rather than contempt for the large number of loyalist thugs who had assaulted this smaller number of young people, who, however irresponsible their conduct or questionable their motivation, were entitled to pass along a public road in safety.

Thereafter we entered a period of continuing communal conflict and political instability. A Cabinet decision to appoint a 'high level and independent Commission to enquire into and report on violence and civil disturbance in Northern Ireland since October 5th 1958' (later to be chaired by the Scots judge, Lord Cameron) precipitated the resignation of Brian Faulkner from the Cabinet, together with William Morgan. This event was marked by a distinctly acrimonious exchange of correspondence. Faulkner argued that, in remitting crucial issues to a Commission, Government was abdicating its own central responsibility. The party should either, in his view, resist the pressure for further change or (which would be his own preference) accept the desirability of introducing adult suffrage in the local government franchise. In response O'Neill accused Faulkner at some length of persistent failure to lend him as Prime Minister the support to which he felt entitled. At that time I was inevitably in the O'Neill camp and helped to draft his rather bitter contribution to the debate; in retrospect, and having worked closely with Faulkner as well, I have to conclude that the latter emerges with greater dignity from these exchanges. Indeed, looking back upon the one-sided reaction to Burntollet and the response to Faulkner's resignation, I would have to accept that those of us who were at the centre of events were, under very great pressure, losing any sureness of touch. O'Neill now faced an increasingly alienated nationalist minority and a divided Unionist Party.

At the beginning of February 1969 the opposition to O'Neill began to take on a more coherent and coordinated shape. No fewer than twelve Unionist back-benchers had gathered at a hotel in Portadown to prepare a challenge to O'Neill's leadership at a party meeting. These included the machiavellian Desmond Boal, William Craig, John Taylor and Lord Brookeborough's son John Brooke. In response to this direct challenge, O'Neill took the extraordinary risk of calling for a dissolution of the Northern Ireland Parliament, setting in train what could only be described as a 'coupon election'. For the first (but certainly not the last) time the Unionist Party was about to enter a General Election deeply divided. The choice of candidates lay with constituency Unionist Associations, and in many of those constituencies enemies of 'O'Neillism' – members of what had come to be called 'the Portadown Parliament' – were deeply entrenched. Inevitably, then, voters might find in a particular constituency an official Unionist Party candidate supportive of O'Neill, an official Unionist Party candidate opposed to O'Neill, or an unofficial Unionist Party supporter of O'Neill seeking to displace an officially nominated candidate opposed to him. The concept of the Unionist Party as a 'broad church' crumbled under the pressure of the crisis, and it soon became transparently clear that O'Neill would be happy to see official party members opposed to him replaced by unofficial candidates pledged to support him.

In the event the outcome of that election recalls Wellington's description of the Battle of Waterloo as 'a damnably close run thing'. The return of thirty-nine unionists represented a gain of two since the previous General Election; official unionists in support of O'Neill and unofficial unionists sympathetic to them won 44 per cent of votes cast; independents, such as Tom Caldwell and Robert McConnell, won striking victories in the O'Neill interest; and in solidly unionist Larne, the surgeon Hugh Wilson, a total political novice, came to within 654 votes of displacing Bill Craig. On the other hand, most of the leading anti-O'Neill unionists had been returned, there had been little clear evidence of support for O'Neill across sectarian lines and, most significantly, O'Neill had won his own long-held constituency of Bannside by a majority of only 1,414 over Ian Paisley and (given substantial support also for Michael Farrell of the PD) on a minority of the total votes cast in Bannside. This was no electoral disaster, but nor was it the significant breakthrough for which O'Neill had hoped and taken such enormous political risks.

From this point things were to run ever more rapidly downhill. At a by-election in mid-Ulster on 17 April 1969, the 21-year-old Bernadette Devlin was returned to Parliament, the youngest woman ever to be elected to Westminster. An early physical assault on the complacent Reggie Maudling on the floor of the House of Commons did not dissuade some facile commentators from greeting her as a latter-day Joan of Arc. Her youth, enthusiasm, zeal and extraordinary articulacy concealed, for a time at least, the anarchic barrenness of her ideas.

With a growing conviction that his time was limited and his usefulness diminishing, O'Neill at last persuaded his Cabinet to agree to the introduction of universal adult suffrage at local government elections. But this belated victory had been won at a great cost; on 23 April James Chichester-Clark, hitherto regarded as a wholly reliable member of the O'Neill camp, resigned from the Cabinet. It is difficult to believe that he took this step without consultation with his brother Robin, who, as an MP, was within the inner circle of the Conservative Party and a friend as well as an ally of Terence O'Neill. (It is, incidentally, curious that so many commentators continued to describe O'Neill and the Chichester-Clarks as 'cousins'; their cousinage was, in fact, a great many times removed, although it was the case that the defunct baronial title of 'O'Neill' had been revived for a member of the Chichester family.) James Chichester-Clark's public explanation of the rationale for his resignation was the strangely unconvincing one that, while he was not opposed in principle to 'one man, one vote', he did not agree with its timing. Perhaps the real motivation was a growing conviction that O'Neill had simply exhausted his political usefulness. It is to be noted that, in the aftermath, O'Neill was to vote for Chichester-Clark as his successor and the latter was to press ahead with the promised voting reform. At any rate, in the aftermath of Chichester-Clark's resignation, O'Neill was able to carry the Parliamentary Unionist Party (from the Commons and Senate) by only twenty-eight votes to twenty-two.

So precarious was O'Neill's position by this time that any substantial shock was likely to displace him. This was provided by a series of explosive attacks upon key points beginning on 30 March with the destruction of an electricity sub-station at Castlereagh near Belfast and continuing on 24 and 25 April with further attacks on water pipelines and electricity pylons. So monocular at the time was the vision of the RUC that these assaults were initially assumed to be the work of the IRA. In fact they were subsequently proved to be the work of loyalist extremists. While it is perfectly true that republican violence has been for many years the most grave threat to life and limb, the 'physical force' tradition in Ireland is certainly not confined to nationalist or republican sympathisers. The old UVF gun-running set the ball rolling in 1912, the murder committed by the new UVF at Malvern Street represented the first fatality of the present cycle of violence, and it was loyalists who were first to use explosive devices to sabotage vital services in the interests of achieving a political result.

Finally, on 28 April, Terence O'Neill had had enough and resigned. The following evening, in a farewell broadcast, he said:

> I have no regrets for six years in which I have tried to break the chains of ancient hatred. I have been unable to realise during my period of office all that I had sought to achieve. Whether, now, it can be achieved in my lifetime I do not know. But one day these things will be and must be achieved.

That lifetime was to end in June 1990, in exile from Northern Ireland where he had long ceased to feel welcome. A rather thin congregation attended his memorial service in St Anne's Cathedral, Belfast. That peace which had been his goal remained unachieved.

Historians and commentators will continue to argue about the verdict to be reached on the premiership of O'Neill. There are those on the loyalist wing of Protestantism who would see him as the man who lowered the defences of unionism, abandoned the principle of no dialogue with Dublin in the absence of formal constitutional recognition, and began an endless and demoralising cycle of concessions to violence and intimidation. There are those from a nationalist background who would accuse him of pursuing, rather than a reconciliation between unionism and nationalism, a wholly unrealistic objective of converting nationalists into unionists. Somewhere in the middle ground were those who characterise him as ultimately ineffective, creating expectations he could never fulfil, and converting rhetoric into genuine reform only at the eleventh hour in the face of irresistible pressure from London.

One who, like myself, was closely associated with him throughout his premiership cannot pretend to complete objectivity. Certainly the O'Neill regime made some serious mistakes. There was a failure to build that alliance with Faulkner, which might have given more muscle to a thrust for change (if, indeed, Faulkner had at that time been willing to acknowledge it). There was a weakness in party management on the part of a shy and aloof figure, who shrank fastidiously from the masculine bonding of tea room or Orange Hall. There was an excessive confidence that carefully crafted articles and speeches, which won high praise from Jack Sayers of the *Belfast Telegraph* and other liberals of an intellectual stamp, and which raised the profile of O'Neill outside the Province, would significantly shift opinion in the wider unionist community. There was the rash alienation, in ill-judged remarks after Burntollet, of a good deal of potential sympathy and support amongst the Catholic population. There was the failure to secure through the unprecedented and risky medium of a 'coupon election' that overwhelming mandate without which he could not move further. Those of us at Stormont Castle who had been bedazzled by the avalanche of support expressed after the 'crossroads' broadcast had been naïve to suppose that there could be any more favourable outcome than a deeply divided party, even if O'Neill remained leader of its larger faction. On the other hand, it has to be appreciated that O'Neill was attempting the Herculean task of bringing out of its entrenched positions a largely divided Cabinet and unenthusiastic party. And from 1966 onwards not only he, but all his successors in unionist leadership, had to struggle to be heard above the bull-bellowing din of Ian Paisley, spraying everywhere – like some outbreak of chemical warfare – his allegations of treasonable submission to the wiles of Rome. At a time when the eighteen-year-old Paisley was concentrating upon a life of thundering from the pulpit, O'Neill had been wounded at Nijmegen as the Irish Guards tried to break through to the enclave at Arnhem. In truth, O'Neill did his best to bring fundamentally decent instincts to bear upon the deeply entrenched problems of a divided community. He was cautious in his efforts to make progress; later experience tends to show that there were good grounds for such caution. Not for the last time, unionism had lost an opportunity to achieve a reconciliation on relatively favourable terms, for at that stage it can be argued that most Catholics would have accepted an assurance of equality of rights and opportunities, without insisting upon seats in Government. We shall see, as we move forward, the ratchet effect of repeated unionist failure to grasp reconciliatory opportunities: movement of the focus of minority demands from equality under a Stormont Government to participation within a Stormont Government, participation plus an 'Irish dimension', and in due time the inclusion within Government even of parties clearly linked to private armies.

With O'Neill's resignation, the Unionist Party faced a fateful decision about its future leadership. Some initial soundings were made to establish whether the affable and well-liked Jack Andrews, son of a former Prime

Minister, might be willing to stand for election as a caretaker premier. However he was then nearly sixty-six years of age, conscious of the unhappy experience of his father when displaced by Basil Brooke, and personally modest and unambitious. In a party which remained very deeply divided by recent events, there was a most conscious and deliberate effort and determination to 'keep Faulkner out'. The O'Neill loyalists saw him as the man who, by his resignation, had precipitated the downfall of the outgoing leader. Thus it was that they settled on the rather unlikely champion of James Chichester-Clark. Tall, grave, soldierly and honourable, Chichester-Clark had very limited departmental experience, having been appointed Minister of Agriculture as recently as 1967. He was judicious but slow-moving, and an unimpressive communicator. Inevitably his rival for the highest office was to be Brian Faulkner himself. By some, the contest was seen as a choice between continuing reform and a return to reaction. The reality was a great deal more complex. It was an interesting straw in the wind that the former Cabinet Minister William Morgan, who had resigned from O'Neill's Government alongside Faulkner now endorsed the latter as a leader from whom reforms would come more quickly. Chichester-Clark, on the other hand, had chosen as the occasion for his resignation the key decision to change the local government franchise. For the first time, the choice would be made by the vote of the Parliamentary party. The outcome could not conceivably have been closer. Chichester-Clark won possession of the poisoned apple by seventeen votes to sixteen. Ironically, O'Neill's vote was to be cast, as he later put it, for the man who had brought him down recently rather than the man who had been trying to bring him down for years. The politics of unionism had become indecently personal.

As I shall seek to demonstrate, Chichester-Clark responded honourably, and with some skill and courage, to the heavy burdens which fell upon him. I would nevertheless conclude today – as someone very close to O'Neill and at the time firmly in the anti-Faulkner camp – that it would have been much better for Northern Ireland if Faulkner had won the premiership at that time rather than two years later. He was to prove, both in office under Chichester-Clark and during his own brief premiership, energetic and imaginative in pursuit of necessary reform. Unhappily long-serving politicians tend to acquire at an early stage stereotypical images which they later find difficult to shed. The image of Faulkner as a crude 'law and order' man, was to persist in spite of his deployment of other gifts, and to be reinforced in many minds by his ultimate resort to internment. In 1969 the ship of State had taken some heavy hits on its superstructure but it was not yet taking in water or failing to respond to steering. Two years later, Faulkner had to hoist his broad pennant on the mast of a sinking vessel.

On his appointment, Chichester-Clark moved rapidly to alleviate tension in the community. One of his first acts was to declare an amnesty for those convicted of, or charged with, political offences since 1968: and amongst those benefiting from this gesture was Ian Paisley. The new Prime Minister offered an olive branch to the opposition, appealing to them in vain to join him in a declaration that Northern Ireland was at peace and would remain so. The Chichester-Clark premiership was to be dominated by three events: the disorders of 1969 and their political consequences in terms of relationships with London and Dublin; the deployment of the Army as the dominant security force in Northern Ireland; and the transformation of the political map of Northern Ireland amongst both the unionist and the nationalist communities.

While the Northern Ireland Civil Rights Association had announced on 8 May 1969 its postponement of a planned campaign of civil disobedience, ten days later it was to threaten street demonstrations unless it had received within six weeks a Government timetable for meeting its agenda of demands: 'one man, one vote' at local government elections; votes at eighteen; an independent Boundary Commission; a points system for housing; machinery to remedy local government grievances; laws to prevent discrimination, particularly in employment; a review of the Special Powers Acts; and disbandment of the B Special Constabulary. For his part, Chichester-Clark had already promised an extension of Ombudsman powers to cover complaints against local authorities, and after talks at Downing Street with Wilson and Callaghan he stated that a model points scheme for housing allocation had been drawn up. There began to be evidence of a growing divide on the nationalist side between moderate nationalists who advised a reserved judgement on the delivery of commitments to reform, and radicals, such as Bernadette Devlin and Eamon McCann, who wanted to maintain continuing pressure through street demonstrations and protests. As Civil Rights rallies resumed, Ian Paisley, who had initially expressed confidence that Chichester-Clark would redirect the Unionist Party onto traditional paths, now began to demand that the new Prime Minister get rid of 'O'Neillites' within his Government.

Disorder became more frequent; in Armagh, in Lurgan, in Dungiven, in Belfast. In an environment of mounting disorder and sectarian antipathy, Chichester-Clark and his liberally minded Minister of Home Affairs, Robert Porter, had alarmingly limited resources with which to keep the peace. The regular establishment of the RUC was of no more than 3,000 officers, only a proportion of whom could be on duty at any one time; there was not, as in Great Britain, the option of easy reinforcement from neighbouring forces; the only locally controlled auxiliary force, the B Specials, were regarded as politically partial and quite unsuitable for deployment in conditions of civil disorder; tactical means of holding mobs at bay, such as CS gas or 'tear smoke' were available for use only under stringent conditions imposed by the Home Office; and the ultimate resort of appealing for military assistance 'in aid of the civil power' could, it was already being whispered to London lobby correspondents, have 'consequences' not explicitly defined but clearly implying a reduction or even withdrawal of the powers of the Government of Northern Ireland.

The events in Belfast and Londonderry in August 1969 led not only to the involvement of the Army in the maintenance of law and order, but to a period of intense and direct Government pressure on the Stormont authorities, and in time to further radical measures. These were to include the disbandment of the B Specials and the formation of the Ulster Defence Regiment, the external examination of police organisation through the Hunt Report and the virtual imposition of Sir Arthur Young to command the RUC, the withdrawal of housing powers from local authorities and their concentration in a central housing authority committed to fair and impartial location and allocation of public housing, and the abandonment of earlier work on the reorganisation of local government while a review team led by Sir Patrick Macrory worked out a radical new pattern for the delivery of services.

At this stage, the Stormont Government had become a glove puppet rather than a self-regulating centre of political authority. Without Army support there could be no hope of containing a rising tide of disorder, and the national Government could and did attach to such support whatever wider political requirements it wished. Long before, Henry Ford allegedly quipped that you could have a Model T in any colour you wanted as long as it was black. Now the Stormont Government could pursue any policies it wanted, as long as they were acceptable to Callaghan and Wilson. Such transparent subordination made a mockery of the very idea of devolved government, and led to Stormont having responsibility without power, to turn the Baldwinian wisecrack on its head. Chichester-Clark knew very well, for example, that acceptance of the disbandment of the B Specials would do him enormous political damage, but had not understood that this was to be the consequence of his fatal meeting at Downing Street.

It has to be said that throughout this most trying period, Chichester-Clark for the most part behaved in a responsible and measured way, but two consequences should be noted. Perhaps inevitably, the reaction of Jack Lynch and his Government in Dublin brought to an abrupt halt those cross-Border exchanges initiated by O'Neill in 1965. The reality, of course, was that harsh words from Lynch were to be preferred to rash actions by some of his more hard-line colleagues. Secondly, at a press conference in Belfast on Sunday 17

August Chichester-Clark gave an account of events in the city, placing the main odium on extreme republicanism and failing to appreciate the scale of Protestant attacks on Catholic areas, which attracted the scorn and ridicule of journalists who had been present on the spot.

Chichester-Clark agreed to designate the GOC, Sir Ian Freeland, as the person with ultimate responsibility for security in Northern Ireland, including control of the Special Constabulary as essentially a paramilitary force. While the RUC remained under the command of its own Inspector General, and would continue on its own initiative to cope with that which was later described by the acronym ODC (ordinary decent crime) the Army would be in the lead in directing security and anti-terrorist operations. This decision stood upon its head the accepted principle underlining military aid to the civil power in a part of the United Kingdom. Much of the remaining period of Chichester-Clark's unhappy premiership was to be taken up with pressures to eliminate 'no-go areas', protect communities from terrorist outrages and 'root out' those responsible, for which he had in reality ceded responsibility to the Army and the United Kingdom Government. He was to beat a drearily repeated path to No. 10, the Home Office and the Ministry of Defence to press for more vigorous action, sometimes acknowledged by a modest addition to available forces but without any transforming impact on the situation.

Perhaps the most significant development, though, during Chichester-Clark's term of office, was the extent of change on the political scene, where for decades a unified and dominant UUP had faced a jaded and ineffective Nationalist Party with a few flankers and outriders. In this transformation scene, the key personalities were Gerry Fitt, John Hume and Ian Paisley.

Now that John Hume has been recognised as a kind of lay saint throughout nationalist Ireland and the overseas Irish diaspora, it is sometimes forgotten to what extent the late Gerry Fitt was a mould-breaker. From his arrival at Westminster in 1966 he used his friendly and engaging personality to make many political and personal friends amongst the ranks of the Labour Party. It was largely out of respect and sympathy for him that Labour Party observers were present in Londonderry on 5 October 1968 to see their friend battered and bloodied. Coming from a working-class Catholic background as he did, he was inevitably anti-partitionist in sentiment, and indeed would never have been elected to Stormont or Westminster on any other basis. Yet at his roots he was a populist, egalitarian socialist. One of the reasons why he fitted so comfortably into Parliament was that he found it possible to be proudly Irish without being anti-British. He was, indeed, to develop a great respect and even love of British institutions and serve in turn in both Houses of the Westminster Parliament. As a merchant seaman he had played his part in the war effort in hazardous Arctic convoys, and when his moderation and aversion to violence exposed him to personal danger and physical attacks upon his home and family, he was to seek and find congenial refuge in England.

John Hume must be ranked alongside Ian Paisley and Gerry Adams as one of the dominant political influences of the late twentieth century in Northern Ireland. Active at first in the civil rights movement through the Derry Citizen's Action Committee, his election to Stormont at the General Election of February 1969, unseating in the process the long-standing leader of old-fashioned nationalism Eddie McAteer, was the harbinger of a new direction in Catholic and nationalist politics. He was ultimately (from 1983) to be a member of the United Kingdom Parliament and also (from 1979) a member of the European Parliament.

Both Hume and Fitt were to be prime movers in the effort to consolidate a number of distinct groups of nationalism into a single modern and purposeful party. Seven Stormont politicians initially came together from three different political parties to form the Social Democratic and Labour Party: Gerry Fitt and Senator Paddy Wilson (later to be the victim of an atrocious murder by one of our current 'politicians') from Republican Labour, the young and energetic Austin Currie (squatter at Caledon in the earliest days of the civil rights movement) from the Nationalist Party and Paddy Devlin from the Northern Ireland Labour Party, together with the three independent MPs closely associated with the civil rights campaign, John Hume, Paddy O'Hanlon and the Protestant Ivan Cooper. The stated objects of this new party were to secure equal rights for all, to foster north/south cooperation in Ireland and to build support for the eventual unity of Ireland through the consent of the majority of people, north and south. The first leader of the party was to be Gerry Fitt and its deputy leader John Hume. It is significant that the foundation of the SDLP, on 21 August 1970, occurred in the same year as the split in Sinn Fein/IRA, leading to the establishment of a political party, Provisional Sinn Fein, which in time to come – abandoning previous policies of total abstention – would contest with the SDLP not just for nationalist votes but for nationalist seats. Thus in 1970 there emerged not merely the prospect of a much more forceful and skilful pursuit of nationalist interests, but of a future argument as to whether or not these should be pursued solely by non-violent means.

This potential split in the nationalist monolith was paralleled by an actual split in the unionist monolith. In April 1970 Ian Paisley and his adherents had made a significant move into active politics. Paisley, as already described, had pressed Terence O'Neill very hard in the contest for Bannside in February 1969. Now, in the following year, a so-called Protestant Unionist Party was to win two seats at Stormont by-elections – Paisley himself, at the second attempt, being elected for Bannside and his colleague the Reverend William Beattie, another minister in Paisley's Free Presbyterian Church, for South Antrim. From these roots there grew in time the Democratic Unionist Party founded in September 1971 by Ian Paisley and Desmond Boal, who became its first chairman. This most able and effectively vituperative barrister had long been a thorn in the side of the UUP leadership, voicing vehement criticism of Brookeborough, O'Neill, Chichester-Clark and Faulkner in turn. He had been prominent in the promotion of dissidence on the UUP backbenches after the O'Neill/Lemass exchanges, and had been removed from his position as counsel to the Attorney General after he defended the rights of Free Presbyterians to protest outside the General Assembly. In Boal's vision the new party would be 'right wing in the sense of being strong on the Constitution, but to the left on social policies'. In truth, the DUP brought together in a potentially strong alliance people who supported Ian Paisley for a variety of motives: Free Presbyterians and other evangelical and traditional Protestants who saw the moderator of the Free Presbyterian Church as a God-given bulwark against popery and erroneous backsliding; a Protestant underclass who had resented the capture of the centres of power within the UUP by a commercial and professional middle class with different mores and aspirations; and a growing number of energetic and ambitious younger men with solid educational attainments who were attracted by the forcefulness and charisma of the Paisley leadership. Since this chapter discusses a litany of errors, it has to be acknowledged that the old unionist establishment for too long grossly underestimated the skills and abilities of a formidable populist politician. While the televised crudities of a debate in the Oxford Union, with Paisley mocking the wafer consecrated for the mass, may have offended the fastidious, such demonstrations of open antipathy to Catholicism and all its works won him growing support amongst the ranks of 'no surrender' and 'no pope here' Protestantism. Paisley's erosion of O'Neill's majority at Bannside, followed by his own election for that Stormont constituency, were belated wake-up calls.

As the DUP grew into a mass party of the unionist community, comparable in strength with its rival the UUP, it inevitably acquired support from those more interested in its political than its sectarian agenda. Yet this party was to be comparable only with a later Hume-led SDLP in terms of its dominance by a single overwhelming figure at its head. Whatever the view of some of its later supporters, Paisley himself was driven by a sincere and passionate belief in separation from and resolute resistance to error; and while he saw many Protestant churches as having strayed too far from the paths of revealed truth, he continued to see the Catholic Church and the papacy as the source and fountain of sinful error. His unionism was of that variety which proclaimed its loyalty to 'the Crown being Protestant', but this was never synonymous with deference to Her Majesty's Ministers, whether in the Northern Ireland or the United Kingdom Government, or unquestioning submission to the laws made by the Crown in Parliament, where these too deviated in his view from the path of righteousness.

There were to be those who saw in the growing breakdown of the old unionist/nationalist paradigm an opportunity to promote the politics of reconciliatory centrism and looked to the reintroduction of proportional representation as a hopeful means of strengthening 'the middle ground'. In truth, changes in the electoral system, which were to occur after the introduction of direct rule from London, persuaded relatively few people to leap across, or seek to straddle, the great sectarian divide. Their long-term impact was to make the UUP in particular impossible to lead, since proportional representation enabled the persistence within the party of deeply divided factions. The search for a healing centralism had its origins in the New Ulster Movement, which developed in early 1969 a demand for non-sectarian politics and practical reform. Out of this movement was to grow in time the Alliance Party, launched in April 1970. In its heady early days it was to attract significant support from active politicians disillusioned with their previous party affiliations – such as Phelim O'Neill, a former Unionist Cabinet Minister or Tom Gormley, previously a nationalist MP. Up to and including the Sunningdale Conference of late 1973, Alliance was able to play a useful moderating role, but its longer-term fate was to be squeezed by the rallying to traditional flags in the face of sustained and continuing violence.

All of these developments were visible to the whole community. What was less apparent at the time was the increasing sense of desperation in official circles at Stormont about the growing divisiveness and dangerous alienation of the minority community. Much careful thought was given as to how, short of their participation in executive government, the elected representatives of nationalism might be afforded an opportunity to play a more constructive and fulfilling role. A blueprint was therefore prepared to introduce at Stormont an advanced system of parliamentary scrutiny by committee, within which chairmen drawn from the Opposition benches would play a prominent part. These proposals, when unveiled to Parliament and the public by Brian Faulkner as Chichester-Clark's successor, were to make a profound initial impact, too soon to be overwhelmed by adverse developments elsewhere and nationalism's reaction to them. It is arguable that such proposals, which were available to the Chichester-Clark Government, could have been introduced by that Government into a more favourable atmosphere and with better prospects of success. But the Cabinet of the day failed to grasp the nettle of parliamentary reform at that time. In other respects, though, the Chichester-Clark Government drove forward its programme of reform with some energy. On 29 August, during a memorable visit to the Province by James Callaghan, the Northern Ireland Cabinet joined with the Home Secretary in a joint communiqué embodying commitments to equality of opportunity in employment and other vital areas; to protection against incitement to hatred on grounds of religious belief; to guaranteed fairness in the allocation of public housing with need as the sole criterion; to effective means for the investigation and redress of grievances; and to proper representation of minorities both in elected and appointed bodies. British as well as Northern Ireland officials were to be involved in the consequential programme of work. It was pretty apparent to all that, while Chichester-Clark himself was fundamentally sympathetic to reform, in many respects the Home Secretary had presented the Stormont Cabinet with a table d'hôte menu.

It has to be said that, in driving this programme forward, no colleague was more supportive and effective than Brian Faulkner, who – whatever his disappointment at the outcome of the 1969 leadership election – was to prove throughout a most loyal and effective lieutenant to Chichester-Clark.

While many unionists were apathetic about, or even opposed to, the wider reform programme, the main threat to Chichester-Clark arose on the 'law and order' front. At the Downing Street talks, Chichester-Clark thought he had agreed only to the standing down of the B Special Constabulary in the current explosive atmosphere, and as late as 22 August 1969, when the GOC Sir Ian Freeland, using his new powers as overall security supremo, recalled Ulster Special Constabulary arms into central armouries, he avowed in response to a question that the Special Constabulary was not being disarmed and disbanded. As against this, Harold Wilson himself on the very day of the Downing Street meeting had spoken of their being 'stood down'. When in due course a committee on policing led by Lord Hunt recommended an unarmed RUC supported by a locally raised (and largely part-time) regiment of the Army, it became pretty clear even to the most naïve that the replacement of the Special Constabulary had been part of the scenario all along. In October, on publication of the Hunt Report, the Unionist Cabinet had little alternative but to accept the demise of the Constabulary and replacement of Mr Anthony Peacocke as Inspector General of the RUC by a Chief Constable, Sir Arthur Young, appointed from the City of London. The immediate impact was a direct confrontation in Belfast between loyalist mobs and the forces of the police and Army. O'Neill's gloomy foreboding was indeed coming to pass.

Chichester-Clark was now in a most unenviable situation, caught between the Scylla of loyalist riots and barricades in Belfast and the Charybdis of the growing emergence from the shadows of militant republicanism. Reference has already been made to the implication in these events of some members of the Lynch Government in Dublin. The year 1970 saw a steady ratcheting up of violence, with no fewer than 153 explosions compared with nine in 1969. The pace picked up still more alarmingly in 1971 with 374 explosions between January and July of that year. A new level of frightfulness was reached on 10 March when three young Scots soldiers, off duty and in civilian clothes, were lured to their deaths by shooting. Chichester-Clark pressed, without much confidence of success, for some striking new security initiative to contain the rising violence, but with the very modest result of a reinforcement of the garrison by a further 1,300 troops. Chichester-Clark was sure this reinforcement would make little difference, and indeed himself unsure (as a former soldier) what kind or dimension of initiative would be capable of doing so. He was by now in the intolerable position of being the person to whom the electorate looked for greater security, without any effective control of the situation. Even the honeyed diplomatic tones of Lord Carrington, sent to Belfast in a last-minute effort to persuade him to stay, could not overcome his growing mood of powerless despair. It was significant that, in his brief resignation statement on 20 March, Chichester-Clark made no specific criticism of the British Government's stance, but said he could 'see no other way of bringing home to all concerned the realities of the present constitutional, political and security situation'. What were these 'realities'? They were that the British Government had stripped the Northern Ireland Government of all credibility and effective autonomy within the powers devolved by the Act of 1920. The illusion was being promoted, through the Hunt Report, that the law and order situation in Northern Ireland was, or could rapidly become, comparable with that in the Home Counties, and responsive to the persuasions of the friendly local 'bobby'. It was rather as if the chiefs of the Mafia were to be kept in order by Dixon of Dock Green. A 'civilianised and normally unarmed force' was indeed an appealing ideal; but how much normality could Northern Ireland expect?

Now, at last, the formidable energy and executive ability of Brian Faulkner was to be harnessed to the governance of Northern Ireland, after his overwhelming endorsement by the UUP, in preference to Bill Craig, by twenty-six to four. He moved at once to see if he could heal wounds in the UUP suffered in recent divisions. Sensing how important it was to hold together unionist support 'beyond the Bann', he recalled to the colours as Minister of Agriculture a significant figure in Harry West. West had been dismissed from O'Neill's Government as long ago as 1966 after an acrimonious disagreement as to whether a disposal of land to a public authority breached a 'conflict of interest' code for Ministers promulgated by O'Neill. In the aftermath West, a personally warm and likeable personality with particularly strong links with the farming community, had drifted into a progressively more oppositionist stance. He had been a prime mover in the so-called West Ulster Unionist Council, which criticised reform – and in particular local government reform and the move to a central housing authority – as inimical to the best interests of unionism. Faulkner's ability to put all this behind him was all the more remarkable in that he himself, as Minister of Development, had been the main driver of these specific reforms. His Cabinet-making had other interesting features. Taking advantage of a previously ignored provision of the 1920 Act, which permitted a person to serve as a Minister for not more than six months albeit not holding a seat in either House of Commons or Senate, Faulkner gave the Community Relations portfolio to David Bleakley, who had served as a Northern Ireland Labour MP from 1958 to 1965. His removal in that year at the first General Election fought by Terence O'Neill has often been criticised as removing from Stormont one of the few truly effective Opposition voices. I would judge such criticism to be naïve. Fighting an election in the same year as the controversial meetings with Lemass, O'Neill faced a political imperative to achieve the most impressive mandate he could; and Northern Ireland being what it was, he could not look to staunchly nationalist constituencies for any gains. Now the inclusion of Bleakley in a Faulkner Cabinet was a signal of his willingness to broaden the basis of Government as much as he could. Unfortunately the Ministry of Community Relations was never one of the big beasts of the governmental jungle. With its modest budget and a permanent head at a lower hierarchical level than his departmental colleagues, the acid test would be not what the Ministry of Community Relations itself could do, but what it could persuade other departments and Ministers to do or to avoid. Had such a department existed, for example, at the time of the Campbell/McGuigan approach on public appointments, the issue might well have been given the attention it deserved. A further appointee to the new Cabinet was the 34-year-old Liberal Unionist, Robin Bailie.

Both at the time and subsequently, Faulkner's Cabinet dispositions were to be viewed in some quarters as a cynical and machiavellian balancing act. He himself would have seen it somewhat differently as a recognition of the need to pull his own party together, before working to pull the wider community together. However, Anne Dickson, a Liberal Unionist MP, resigned the Party Whip as a protest against West's inclusion, while at the same time West was criticised by Bill Craig for his readiness to resume office. Faulkner's thrust for inclusiveness had not reached as far as Craig. In the event Faulkner's capabilities as Prime Minister were to be tested for the very brief span of a single year in office as the last head of a conventional unionist administration.

It was to be a truly dreadful year of ever escalating violence. Since Faulkner had, in days gone by, taken a strong 'law and order' stance, there were some who from the outset expected him to give the primacy to questions of security, and saw the eventual resort to internment as conclusive evidence that this had always been his planned master-card. In reality he was to come to that fateful step only after much agonising, imaginative attempts to improve the overall political climate, and in the absence of significant movement sought by other means. Indeed, at his first meeting with the Ulster Unionist Council as its new leader on 29 March 1971, Faulkner promised he would never make a 'blanket condemnation' of any section of the community, or support a proposition to 'get tough with Catholics'. 'My Administration', he said, 'will be scrupulously fair to everyone under the law.'

The precarious condition of the ice upon which Faulkner was skating was brought starkly home on 6 April, when in a House of Commons speech Harold Wilson revealed that the Labour Government had drafted a Bill for imposing direct rule as a last resort and that this Bill was now in the hands of the Conservative Government which had succeeded his own.

As the result of an amnesty for the surrender of unlicensed arms announced on 30 March, a very substantial arsenal (446 revolvers, 47 automatic pistols, 585 rifles, 240 shotguns, 300 air guns, almost 100,000 rounds of ammunition, 64 grenades, 4,427 detonators, 16 bayonets and knives, 13 magazines, 24 starting pistols, 5 incendiary devices, 12 ignitor charges, 663 ammunition clips and 89 thunder flashes and flares) had been handed over to the police. Of all the guns, some 85 per cent had been illegally held. Under the monitoring machinery of the Joint Security Committee, chaired by Faulkner himself as Minister of Home Affairs (as well as Prime Minister), a close eye was kept on potential confrontation at forthcoming parades. In carrying the very heavy burden of his dual role, Faulkner was supported, as Minister of State at the Ministry of Home Affairs, by John Taylor. Generally regarded as hardline in his views and attitudes, Taylor's role was not well received by the SDLP or the wider nationalist community. Whatever his political views, he was a man of personal courage, as his refusal to be silenced by a later assassination attempt, in which he was most gravely wounded, was to show. In spite of the abundant harvest from the arms amnesty there was sustained rioting and civil disorder in both loyalist and republican areas, and daily evidence of the growing strength of both factions of the IRA, shown in mounting explosive attacks.

The great irony was that, in the midst of all this escalating mayhem, the entity of Northern Ireland was about to celebrate its fiftieth birthday. On 14 May, an 'Ulster 71' exhibition opened in Belfast's Botanic Gardens, to the notes of a merry jingle not to be found in any anthology of any Irish poetry:

Ulster 71
Come and join in the fun

Incongruously, on the opening day, photo-journalists ever eager for a new angle were able to depict Brian Faulkner at the wheel of a dodgem car. He must already have been all too well used to being buffeted both from before and from behind. It was manifestly a time to be extraordinarily careful in the use of words. On 25 May Faulkner used the following words: 'At this moment any soldier seeing any person with a weapon or acting suspiciously may fire to warn or with effect, depending on the circumstances, without waiting for orders from anyone.' When, inevitably, this rather loose use of words triggered suspicions and allegations of a 'shoot to kill policy', it was necessary for Lord Balneil as Minister of State for Defence at Westminster to reiterate the well-established doctrine of minimum force. The Army, in any case, were throughout under the control of the Ministry of Defence and the GOC, both of whom understood that the use of force by any soldier might have to be justified in a court of law. The shrewd and diplomatic GOC of the time, Sir Harry Tuzo, was to make it clear that no permanent solution could ever be achieved by military means; the task of the Army was to win a 'gradual ascendancy' over the IRA and create the conditions in which local politicians could work out an acceptable settlement.

On 22 June 1971 Faulkner gave eloquent expression to his desire for a broadly acceptable political solution. With careful planning, the new Prime Minister's reply to the Queen's Speech at the opening of a new session of Parliament had been timed to take place exactly fifty years after the official opening of the first Northern Ireland Parliament on 22 June 1921. Faulkner had given the greatest care and attention to the construction of a speech designed to heal and reconcile. However belatedly, Governments now brought forward those proposals for effective parliamentary participation which had been an effort to reshape the mould of politics, if not to break it. In addition to this, Faulkner tabled a further proposal for round-table discussions about resolving the current crisis between Government and opposition. The first meeting of these inter-party talks, involving the UUP, the SDLP, the Nationalist Party and the Northern Ireland Labour Party, took place at Stormont on 7 July and the statement issued afterwards commented: 'Nothing of this sort involving private and completely frank exchanges has been attempted before,' and continued: 'We all think it worth to continue with this experiment in patient discussion and intend to meet again for further talks.'

But this first meeting was also to be the last. During rioting in Londonderry on 8 July two men were shot dead by the security forces. The immediate reaction of John Hume was to demand a full-scale inquiry into the circumstances of the deaths of the two men, Seamus Cusack and Desmond Beattie, as he believed from his own investigations that neither had been armed. On 12 July Hume toughened up his stance; unless the inquiry he had sought was conceded, the SDLP would withdraw from the Northern Ireland Parliament and set up an alternative Assembly of its own.

The leading role played by John Hume, rather than his party leader Gerry Fitt, was significant and a portent of things to come. It has often been said that for elected politicians all politics are local, and certainly Hume has at all times kept very close to his Derry base. To adopt such a hard line, so soon after evidence of genuine attempts by Faulkner to seek a broader consensus, was a signal that Hume's long-term strategic objectives were beyond the capacity of the Stormont Government to deliver. Hume, too, was over the long term interested in a broader consensus, yet not one to be found on the centre ground but rather through the willing or unwilling movement of unionism in the direction he favoured.

Hume's attitude was, of course, a very bitter blow to Faulkner. He had embodied his proposals of 22 June in a wide-ranging speech of a markedly conciliatory character. Now, he said on 15 July, Opposition Members had to make a choice between real and effective participation in affairs or what he characterised as 'the instant politics of exploiting every issue as it arises without consideration of the long-term effects'.

An inquiry was not conceded; the SDLP and other nationalist members began a boycott of Parliament; and a crucial watershed was reached with the introduction of internment. The judgement of history is bound to be that the introduction of internment and the way it was carried into effect were horrendous mistakes. Hindsight is a wonderful thing, and it is difficult to argue that a measure which failed was anything other than a bad idea. Yet the background to the decision has to be appreciated. Violence was steadily building up to unprecedented and intolerable levels. The strongest possible measures – and not just from the Protestant community – were being brought to bear upon Faulkner to get rid of the incubus of terrorism once and for all. The British Government, without whose support and participation internment could never have been introduced, had no credible alternative strategy to offer. Previous Governments, not just in Northern Ireland but in the Republic as well, had found internment a useful and effective measure. Where the Northern Ireland Administration erred was in failing to appreciate that internment only on one side of the Border could have at very best a limited effect, and the political atmosphere in the Republic at this time was not favourable to a cooperative move against the IRA. Faulkner's security advisers were unaware that much RUC intelligence about republicanism was woefully inaccurate and out of date. Nor was there a convincing effort to show that the enemy was terrorism, whatever its origin, rather than simply the IRA. A substantial swoop on loyalist extremists could have underlined a more obviously even-handed approach.

In spite of Faulkner's later indignation about the introduction of direct rule, it was highly likely from the start that, if internment failed, radical measures for the future governance of Northern Ireland would come onto the agenda. With violence bursting out with renewed vigour after internment, and with the Stormont Parliament devalued and embarrassed by the withdrawal of the nationalist opposition, Faulkner threw himself with desperate vigour into efforts to find a political way forward.

So, in October 1971, the Stormont Government launched a consultative document or 'Green Paper' on *The Future Development of the Parliament and Government of Northern Ireland*. It fleshed out the committee proposals of the previous June; discussed possible methods of election to Parliament that were alternatives to the first-past-the-post system; pointed to strong arguments for an increase in the size of the House of Commons; and canvassed possibilities for changing the size, compositions and role of the second chamber or Senate.

More significantly, perhaps, the consultative document discussed the crucial issue of responsibility for the executive government of Northern Ireland. It recognised the reality of fifty years of government by a single party, and said:

> It may be argued by some that a permanent majority/minority situation creates problems for the smooth operation of the democratic process. In many ways the British democratic system, with its virtual assurance that those who control the executive will also control the legislature, represents a much greater concentration of power than (say) the American system, based as it is on a deliberate diffusion and separation of powers. Between General Elections the power of a British Government is, in some respects, as absolute as democratic power can be, but this exercise of power is accepted by a Parliamentary minority who know that sooner or later their turn to exercise it will come. Where that expectation does not exist, there is clearly a risk of disenchantment with the democratic Parliamentary process. Because of this, it has been argued in some quarters that means must be found to give 'the minority' in Northern Ireland a share in the effective exercise of power. The Government believes that this important issue should be openly and dispassionately considered by Parliament and people.

However, the consultative paper explicitly rejected what it called 'PR Government', where the parties in Parliament would be represented in the Executive in proportion to their strength, and went on to argue that the powers of government could not be shared with those who failed to accept certain 'over-riding principles', and in particular 'the maintenance of Northern Ireland as an integral part of the United Kingdom in accordance with the statutory guarantee of the Ireland Act 1949'. On the other hand, it stated as a 'general principle' that 'it would be very desirable to promote a situation in which members of both religious communities who accept unreservedly the [overriding] principles ... could take part in the executive government of the country'.

What was the real significance of this complex and rather guarded wording? The day following the publication of his consultative paper, Brian Faulkner for the first and only time invited a Roman Catholic, G.B. Newe, to join a Northern Ireland Cabinet. Newe had hitherto been socially rather than politically active. He made it clear that he was not and never had been a member of the UUP, and while he recognised the social and economic benefits of the link with Great Britain, he asserted the absolute right of people to work peacefully for a united Ireland.

Some, at least, chose to regard the overriding principle earlier quoted as implying that a Catholic could only be a member of a Northern Ireland Government if he was, without being a party member, in some sense a unionist. Since I myself drafted the consultative paper, I am able to be quite clear that its terms were not intended to rule out people who believed in a united Ireland, provided they accepted the consent principle embodied in the 1949 Act. Cautiously and guardedly, Faulkner was holding out olive branches to the alienated and disaffected political minority.

Yet the sands were running out very rapidly. I have discussed elsewhere the events on 'Bloody Sunday', 30 January 1972 in Derry, and sought to show that the controversial events on that day were in no sense undertaken at the behest of the Stormont Government. The consequence, however, was the almost complete alienation from Government of even the most moderate and responsible members of the Catholic community.

Between the end of January and late March, Faulkner worked furiously to design and drive through his Cabinet the most comprehensive and wide-ranging proposals for change ever to be offered by a Stormont Government. To a striking extent, these proposals picked up themes to which all parties would return in time to come. In correspondence with the United Kingdom Government, Faulkner argued that great benefits would flow from a recognition from the Republic of Northern Ireland's right to self-determination. Such a recognition of constitutional realities could and should lead to much more effective cooperation in the suppression of terrorism, including dealing with the problem of fugitive offenders. The proposals placed on the table a willingness to participate with the Republic in an Intergovernmental Council, which would discuss matters of mutual interest, particularly in the economic and social spheres. There was also the suggestion that 'existing safeguards against religious discrimination should be re-enacted with greater precision as a Bill of Rights, with quick and effective access to the Courts to test any enactment or executive act alleged to have been in breach of its provisions'.

Whether such proposals, which only entered the public domain on the resignation of the Stormont Government, would have persuaded the SDLP in general and John Hume in particular to renew dialogue with the Faulkner unionists, must be a matter of doubt. Certainly Heath's United Kingdom Government now regarded the situation as so serious as to require what the then United Kingdom representative in Belfast, Howard Smith, was to describe as 'a discontinuity'.

Thus it was that, when Faulkner and colleagues met Heath and other British Ministers at 10 Downing Street on 22 March 1972, they could in theory have remained in office by accepting the terms dictated to them, including in particular the complete removal of all 'law and order' powers; yet British Ministers must have been aware that these proposals would be unacceptable and therefore precipitate the introduction of direct rule.

It has since been argued that, since Faulkner was prepared to take office once again, under new constitutional arrangements on 1 January 1974, as head of a Government without 'law and order' powers, it was strange that he could not accept such a proposition in 1972. This I believe to be a naïve analysis. Faulkner had witnessed at close hand the odium poured on the head of his predecessor for accepting the demise of the B Specials. To be asked to surrender such responsibilities from a basis of extensive powers was very different to the later choice between limited powers and an indefinite period in the political wilderness. In any case, the Cabinet had already made up its mind that it could not live with such a humiliation, and stuck to that line after the Downing Street meeting. One should reflect, too, on what the position would have been if the Northern Ireland Government had been prepared to accept Heath's proposals. Thereafter these allies in an ongoing war against terrorism would have been strangely uncomfortable bedfellows, with Faulkner bound to denounce the Heath initiative as a concession to violence.

So it came about that, after fifty years, the Stormont Cabinet was for the time being replaced by a Secretary of State for Northern Ireland and the Stormont Parliament was prorogued, never to be reconvened. The days of absolute unionist dominance through a single-party Government were gone for good.

In my judgement, the events of Faulkner's sadly brief premiership showed the misfortune of his belated accession to power. He had proved infinitely more energetic and ingenious than any predecessor in persuading Cabinet and party to go along with some radical new ideas. One wonders whether, if the British Government had realised that it was not facing a brief in-and-out involvement but a very long-term commitment to the Government of Northern Ireland, it might not have sought to build upon the Faulkner proposals and attempted to broker them with the Irish Government and the SDLP.

It is a sad reality that Faulkner's very brief premiership may be remembered more for the introduction of internment and the events on Bloody Sunday than for any other action of his Government. Too little consideration is given to the predicament of a Prime Minister who, seeing his community going up in flames, is advised that nothing more can be done.

In the days when I had to deal with the Belfast aircraft manufacturers, Short Brothers, I came to learn the jargon of 'extending the flight envelope'. No one was better placed than Brian Faulkner to extend the political envelope; the crucial question of judgement falling to the British Government was whether the maximum that unionism in office could deliver came close enough to the minimum its opponents would accept. Clearly the Heath Government had concluded that Faulkner's best efforts were not enough; but this would not alter my own judgement that he was incomparably the most effective and talented of the post-war unionist Prime Ministers.

Between 1921 and 1972, then, the history of Northern Ireland politics is one of action by successive unionist Governments and reaction by others. In March 1972, however, we entered the new era. The dominant power of a single party was challenged not only by new constitutional development but also by the emergence of other strong parties: the SDLP, DUP, for a time at least Alliance and ultimately PSF.

We now have to consider the very different scenario of the repeated attempts from 1972 onwards to find an acceptable basis for the restoration of the powers of government to elected representatives in Northern Ireland. In that process many different devices were to be tested: using the Secretary of State as chairman and *animateur*; shifting the focus to efforts by the domestic parties under the chairmanship of an eminent local person (Lord Lowry as Chairman of the Convention); hoping to grow constitutional development proposals through inter-party contacts within an elected consultative Assembly; and conducting talks under the chairmanship of a distinguished foreigner (ex-Senator George Mitchell). Some, at least, of these efforts were deeply prejudiced by the refusal of significant parties to take part. In what follows, we shall consider what acts of omission or commission by individual parties prejudiced the prospects of a successful and broadly acceptable outcome.

The initial approach of William Whitelaw was to encourage all the constitutional parties to bring forward proposals for constitutional change as the basis for a multi-party conference (ultimately held at Darlington).

The party proposals ultimately published as Annexes to the 1972 discussion document *The Future of Northern Ireland* revealed huge differences in perception and approach. While Faulkner's Unionist Party rested in large measure on a further development of its committee proposals and the later proposals swept aside by the Heath Government, the SDLP chose to entitle its submission *Towards a New Ireland*, called for an immediate declaration by the United Kingdom Government favourable in principle to Irish unity, and envisaged a role in an 'interim system of government' for joint British–Irish Commissioners alongside an Executive elected by proportional representation from members of the new Assembly. In the event only the Unionist, Northern Ireland Labour and Alliance Parties were willing to participate at Darlington.

While these efforts were going forward, a parallel development was the growth of the Vanguard movement launched by the disaffected unionist ex-minister Bill Craig. This had been formed early in 1972, at a time when the possibility of direct rule was being widely canvassed. The aim was to bring together as many 'loyalists' as possible under the umbrella of resistance to constitutional change. Craig, as already discussed, had long held the view that intervention by Westminster would be unconstitutional. The Reverend Martin Smyth and Captain Austin Ardill joined him as deputy leaders, and the new movement soon began to take a stance of threat and menace rather reminiscent of the early days of Continental fascist movements. Craig would travel to mass rallies in an open car, escorted by outriders from the so-called Vanguard Service Corps. At a massive rally in Ormeau Park, Belfast, in March 1972, Craig told an enthusiastic crowd of some 60,000 people that 'if the politicians fail, it will be our duty to liquidate the enemy'. On the last day of Stormont, Craig was to appear on the balcony of Parliament Buildings before a large crowd that had assembled, where he was joined by Faulkner to avoid an attempt by Craig to completely capture and manipulate the process. By May 1972 Vanguard was talking in terms of a possible need for Northern Ireland to 'go it alone'. Later on Vanguard was to develop into a distinct political party, in the process distancing itself from those of its sympathisers who remained loyal to the UUP. Craig's actions in 1972 could often seem as ludicrous as they were menacing, but his stance was in time to attract the support of such rising men as the young David Trimble.

Given an abortive and unrepresentative Darlington Conference and the clear gulf between the proposals of the main parties of unionism and nationalism (the UUP and the SDLP), the onus fell upon the British Government to make its own proposals and try to win support for them. While the 1972 discussion paper *The Future of Northern Ireland* was in part a deployment of options, it began in a subtle way to eliminate the unrealistic and to sharpen the focus. It was made absolutely clear that the constitutional guarantee would not be abandoned ('The United Kingdom Government is bound both by statute and by clear and repeated pledges to the people of Northern Ireland'); there was a strong hint that future Government would have to be participatory in character ('there is no hope of binding the minority to the support of new political arrangements in Northern Ireland unless they are admitted to active participation in any new structures'); and any settlement 'must also recognise Northern Ireland's position within Ireland as a whole'.

As the United Kingdom Government moved forward to firm proposals at the White Paper stage in March 1973, these concepts were given more definite expression. Henceforth the consent required for any movement out of the United Kingdom would be expressed by the people rather than the Parliament of Northern Ireland, and indeed a first (and so far only) Border Poll held on 8 March 1973 showed the support of 57.4 per cent of the total electorate for Northern Ireland's position within the United Kingdom, as against a derisory vote for Irish unity following advice from nationalist political parties to abstain from the polls. The White Paper now proposed the replacement of the old Northern Ireland Parliament by a new unicameral Assembly elected by proportional representation, the introduction of a 'power-sharing' executive Government (on the basis that 'the Executive itself can no longer be solely based upon any single party, if that party draws its support and elected representation virtually entirely from only one section of a divided community'); and a summoning of a conference at which the local political parties would join the United Kingdom and Irish Governments to discuss such matters as the formation of a Council of Ireland.

How, then, did the various parties play their respective hands once the broad intentions of the British Government had been made clear? On publication of the White Paper, Ian Paisley characterised its contents as very disappointing and Bill Craig as 'absurd'. Brian Faulkner reacted cautiously but constructively. He saw no problem in contesting elections to the proposed new Assembly, although he would want to negotiate with the British Government about the implementation of the details of the White Paper. The SDLP, too, while criticising the 'Irish dimension' of the White Paper as vague, agreed also to contest elections to a new Assembly.

The difficulty, of course, was that the elections were simply a stage in the process rather than its culmination. Parties would be seeking the support of voters in continuing uncertainty about the precise outcome of negotiations yet to come, and in the knowledge that any domestic understanding would remain provisional pending the wide-ranging conference, acknowledging the 'Irish dimension' to complete the process. As I have suggested in an earlier chapter, some would argue that any agreement subsequently reached by the parties should have been submitted for validation by the electorate. Yet events since the referendum endorsing the Good Friday Agreement have shown only too vividly that a 'yes' vote on a particular day, indicating support for what the voter supposes or assumes will follow, is no guarantee of continued support in changing circumstances and as the real outworkings of an agreement become clearer.

In an earlier chapter focusing on the role of the British Government, the proceedings at the inter-party talks chaired by William Whitelaw and the subsequent Sunningdale Conference have already been discussed. The most crucial issue, I have argued, was the nature of an 'Irish dimension', encapsulated in the idea of a Council of Ireland. As we have seen, the UUP had conceded in advance the desirability of a Council of Ireland with purely consultative functions. The critical question is whether the SDLP was wise to press so hard for a council with executive functions, or Faulkner to concede to that pressure. My considered judgement is that the SDLP, from whom the Irish Government was bound in considerable measure to take its lead, was over-ambitious in its insistence upon executive functions. It would have been better to join in efforts to create mutual confidence before all else. In a sense it was seeking to leap from introduction to marriage without the intervention of courtship. For his part, Faulkner – out of a decent and honest willingness to take real risks for political progress – allowed himself to be pushed into a politically unsustainable position.

With the formation of the power-sharing Executive on 1 January 1974, the willingness and ability of Northern Ireland parties to collaborate were to be tested as never before. The Executive itself was a strange mixture in human and political terms. Because of divisions within the UUP, Faulkner was supported by a team of rather mixed experience and ability. Of relatively long-serving Stormont Ministers, he could deploy only Herbert Kirk, a steady but uncharismatic veteran at Finance and the clever but essentially unreliable and opportunistic Roy Bradford at Environment. It was a strange aspect of the team-building negotiations that the Finance portfolio seems to have gone to Kirk without much competition. Because that department has a relatively low profile outside the system, people relatively new to Government could greatly underestimate its vast and indeed central influence within the system. At Education, Basil McIvor was a relative novice in Government, having entered the old Cabinet as Minister of Community Relations as recently as 1971, while the Agriculture portfolio went to Leslie Morrell, an upright figure with deep roots in the farming community but entering elective politics for the first time at the Assembly elections of 1973.

It always seemed utterly strange that the leader of the smallest party within the Executive, Oliver Napier of the Alliance Party, opted for the technical and low-profile portfolio of Legal Affairs and Law Reform, leaving his colleague Robert Cooper (albeit a member within the Administration but outside the Executive) to head the Department of Manpower Services.

Undoubtedly the strongest team of Ministers came from the SDLP. Gerry Fitt had tremendous bonhomie as well as political cunning and nous; he had good friends in Parliament, particularly in the Labour Party (so soon to return to power), and he was able to develop a sound working relationship with Faulkner, founded on mutual respect. Alongside him, his party colleagues brought various gifts to the Executive: John Hume with his entrepreneurial and marketing skills, command of languages, and excellent contacts inside and outside Ireland made a formidable head of the Department of Commerce; Austin Currie in his short tenure at Housing, Local Government and Planning showed the courage to address a rent strike advocated in different circumstances by his own party; Paddy Devlin represented some of the best if also at times the more abrasive qualities of the Belfast working class; and Eddie McGrady was then (as in times to come) a model of solid common sense, albeit saddled with a frustrating and largely meaningless Executive responsibility for 'Planning and Co-ordination'.

Nevertheless the fate of the Executive was to be like that of a frail new boat of radical and untested design sent out for its trials into the middle of a typhoon. I have described elsewhere the dramatic stages of its descent downhill: Faulkner's loss of the UUP leadership; the rapid devaluation of claimed advances on status or security; the untimely exposure to a General Election, with an overwhelming rejection by the electorate; and the final dramatic act of the UWC strike. Throughout this brief but stormy passage the parties forming the Executive behaved, on the whole, creditably and sensibly. There were few signs of radical differences in the approach to practical problems affecting all sections of the Northern Ireland community, such as unemployment, poverty and poor housing conditions. Sensible planning for the future had begun, but the time was far too short to be able to point to concrete results. Inevitably the human chemistry did not always lead to easy personal relationships; Bradford and Devlin in particular struck sparks from each other, and indeed towards the end of the Executive's life not a few of his colleagues saw in Bradford a possible defector, while Devlin had a resignation 'on the table' but not acted upon. It was a pity, but perhaps inevitable, that it took quite so long to persuade the SDLP that the Executive would sink unless some of the Council of Ireland ballast could be jettisoned. For all this, it is greatly to the credit of the principal figures in the Executive that they finally parted company without recrimination, and indeed with real regret.

On the day the power-sharing Executive fell, there was great rejoicing and triumphalism in Protestant areas of Belfast and the wider Province. Exultant women tricked out with Union flag-bedecked dresses or umbrellas literally danced in the streets like people celebrating the visit of some dictator in black Africa. The wider unionist community and the members of the Unionist Coalition now dominant at Westminster saw this as a great victory. They could not know that the failure of the Executive would be the precursor to further endless years of violence, or that some of those who had been prominently rejectionist in 1973–74 – men such as David Trimble or Reg Empey or John Laird – were to recommend later terms much less favourable to unionism, appreciating however belatedly the wisdom of making the best deal you can in a falling market.

From 1974 to 1994 there was to be a dreary period of repeated and ultimately abortive attempts to make political progress. These attempts were characterised by changes in the context of discussions, by the impact of decisions by individual parties to boycott political initiatives, and by significant changes in the strength and leadership of parties and the interplay between them.

For five years, from 1974 to 1979, the leader of the UUP in succession to Brian Faulkner (whose rump party, the UPNI, failed to flourish) was Harry West, who had been in active politics since 1954. He aligned the UUP with the DUP and Vanguard to form the UUUC in contesting the Westminster General Election of February 1974. At that election he won the seat in Fermanagh/ South Tyrone, which he was to lose against an independent anti-partitionist, Frank Maguire, in the second election of that year. Gerry Fitt remained the de jure leader of the SDLP, although it was becoming increasingly clear that the real intellectual power-house and ideological centre of the party was to be found in John Hume. Ian Paisley, of course, remained leader of the DUP, with a politico-religious ascendancy over his followers to be compared to that of the Ayatollah Khomeini. Craig, who had also won a seat at Westminster under the umbrella of the UUUC, led the Vanguard, which had evolved from a movement into a political party.

Wilson's Labour Government had now decided to remit directly to the elected representatives of Northern Ireland the vexed question of what (if any) provision for the Government of Northern Ireland would be likely to command the most widespread acceptance throughout the community there. The vehicle for this was to be a constitutional convention, to which seventy-eight members would be elected, like the Northern Ireland Assembly, by the method of the single transferable vote.

An analysis of the outcome of the Convention Election of 1975, and a comparison with the Assembly Election of 28 June 1973, demonstrates a striking shift in opinion. In 1973 pro-Faulkner and anti-Faulkner unionists had divided the unionist community pretty well down the middle in terms of first preference votes cast and seats won. At the Convention Election, the three principal parties of the UUUC were to gain forty-five of the seventy-eight seats (nineteen for the West-led UUP, fourteen for the Craig-led VUP and twelve for the Paisley-led DUP) as compared with a derisory five for Faulkner's UPNI. On the other hand, support for the SDLP remained strikingly stable (22.1 per cent of first preference votes in 1973, and 23.7 per cent in 1975). The Alliance Party had done slightly better, improving from 9.2 per cent of the vote in 1973 to a 9.8 per cent share in 1975, when indeed it gained more Convention seats than the UPNI. These results made it all too clear that, in the absence of some wholly unexpected development, Faulkner was now out of the reckoning as a significant player in local politics, despite his outstanding abilities.

Meeting under the chairmanship of Lord Chief Justice Sir Robert Lowry (supported by two outstandingly able and experienced special advisers in John Oliver and Maurice Hayes), the Convention opened with a re-statement of irreconcilable positions. The old Executive partners continued to urge the merits of partnership government, whereas the UUUC resisted institutionalised power-sharing and fell back upon the committee proposals made years before as the best they could offer in terms of participation. Improbably – and greatly to his credit – it was Bill Craig, that intensely enigmatic political figure, who sought to break the deadlock. He continued to oppose in principle the entrenchment of institutionalised or mandatory power-sharing, but he acknowledged that Northern Ireland faced an emergency comparable in seriousness to wartime conditions, and should therefore consider seriously a 'voluntary coalition', a kind of Government of all the talents. But this suggestion did not only fail to win the support of the partner parties within the UUUC, but led to defections from Craig's own ranks, with a group led by Ernest Baird breaking away to form the United Ulster Unionist movement. Thus the Convention petered out in March 1974, after its majority report failed to carry any conviction that its proposals could meet the essential criterion of 'widespread acceptance'.

Against such a background Roy Mason, appointed Secretary of State for Northern Ireland in September 1976, saw it as fruitless to launch any early renewed effort to achieve a political breakthrough, and instead decided to concentrate on improvements in security and strengthening the local economy. He had, however, to face the reality that some at least of the local politicians had not abandoned a willingness to achieve political ends by coercive methods. In May 1977, in alliance with loyalist paramilitaries, political leaders, including Ian Paisley and Ernest Baird, joined with representatives of those organisations to attempt a re-run of the successful UWC strike of 1974. The abject failure of this attempt to confront lawful authority can be attributed to at least four causes: the absence of a single motivating factor comparable with Paisley's 1974 warning that Dublin was 'only a Sunningdale away'; the absence of crucial support from the power workers with their potential stranglehold over the economy; the lack of backing from either the UUP or Vanguard; and the robust determination by Mason himself not to yield to coercion a further time.

In May 1979, under Margaret Thatcher's new Conservative Government, Humphrey Atkins was appointed Secretary of State for Northern Ireland, essentially to fill a gap in her team left by the assassination of Airey Neave. Atkins resumed low-key efforts to explore the possibility of political progress, but the value of his Constitutional Conference, which sat from January to March 1980, was greatly diminished by the UUP's decision to boycott it, leaving only the DUP, SDLP and Alliance around the conference table. Although Harry West was to remain leader of the UUP until 1979, an increasing spotlight was bound to fall – in the absence of devolution – upon the leader of the group of MPs at Westminster, and following West's defeat at the General Election of October 1974, this mantle fell upon James Molyneaux, an MP since 1970. Another very important and growing influence was to be that of the extraordinarily gifted and spellbinding parliamentarian, Enoch Powell. Powell, who might without hyperbole be described as a deeply flawed great man, a wonderful orator and immensely skilled in the parliamentary arts, had left his former home in the Conservative Party after a total breach with its leader Edward Heath. By 1974 Powell had been Conservative MP for a Wolverhampton constituency for some twenty-four years and for three years in the 1960s had been Minister of Health. Such a deeply political animal found his severance from active politics too hard to bear, and sought a new home in the UUP, where he won the election for the constituency of South Down in October 1974.

In 1979 Molyneaux, on the resignation of Harry West, was to add the leadership of the entire UUP to his leadership of the Parliamentary party. He was deeply impressed and, one might almost say, fascinated by Enoch Powell, whose counsels came to have an increasing influence upon unionist policy. Prior to the fall of Stormont, the major centre of influence in the UUP had always been there rather than at Westminster, and the unionist Prime Minister and his Cabinet colleagues were much more high-profile characters than their colleagues in the United Kingdom Parliament, even in those distant days when the unionist benches included some congenial and clubbable people, capable of making friends in the Conservative Party in particular, rather than their often unlikeable and abrasive successors. Even Harry West had been essentially a Stormont figure, coming relatively late and briefly to Westminster.

Molyneaux, on the other hand, had never sat at Stormont, loved Parliament and its traditions and procedures, was gratified to become a Privy Counsellor in 1983 and was relatively happy to retain Westminster as the centre of the political world. Then there was the growing influence upon his leadership of Enoch Powell. In some ways his translation to Northern Ireland was a great oddity, since he was essentially an English nationalist of imperialist leanings, deeply antipathetic to ideas of devolution and – since his defection – extremely hostile to a Conservative Party which he saw as willing to dilute national sovereignty and accept undesirable changes in the racial and ethnic make-up of the population. With Powell's encouragement, Molyneaux's first priority was to increase Northern Ireland representation at Westminster, which was indeed to be conceded by a fragile Labour Government looking for support wherever it could be found and prepared to shelve previous opposition to any increase in such representation.

So it was that the idea of 'total integration' came back onto the agenda. Historically, this had been the preference of unionist leaders in the run-up to partition. Devolution had been accepted at that time with a good deal of scepticism and reluctance, not least because the schema of the 1920 Act envisaged a growing together of the two jurisdictions in Ireland. Subsequently generations of unionist leaders had come to enjoy the power and prestige of local office. I had myself witnessed, when travelling abroad with Terence O'Neill in the 1960s, the magic appeal of the title 'Prime Minister', which opened so many doors likely to be closed to people with much more extensive responsibilities but more prosaic titles. After 1949, unionist leaders had been able to point to the Stormont Parliament as a bulwark of the 'consent principle' and the right to self-determination, since it was the consent of Stormont which would be required for any change in constitutional status taking Northern Ireland out of the United Kingdom. But the Constitution Act of 1973 had replaced the requirement of consent by the Parliament of Northern Ireland with a requirement for the consent of its people.

It was not only in the UUP that the year 1979 had brought about a significant changing of the guard, and a marked change in style and approach. The division within the SDLP between its socialist and populist faction, exemplified by Fitt and Devlin, and its 'new Ireland' faction, exemplified by Hume and Mallon, became more and more evident.

The crucial breach had come in the course of debate about Atkins' proposed Constitutional Convention. From the outset Fitt had wished the SDLP to attend and play a constructive part. Hume and others had initially opposed him, and although the party finally decided to participate, Fitt could see the prospect of a party giving priority to its nationalist aspirations over its socialist credentials. Paddy Devlin had already been expelled from the party in 1977 after complaining about the concentration, as he saw it, upon nation-alist rather than socialist priorities, and now in 1979 Gerry Fitt had become disillusioned and resigned the SDLP leadership. The inevitable election of John Hume as his successor was to be a fateful moment for his party and for Northern Ireland.

One approaches the question of Hume and his influence with some diffi-dence. Many serious historians would rate him as the most significant Irish political figure since Charles Stewart Parnell. He has been loaded with laurels; a Nobel Peace Prize, countless honorary doctorates, gold medals, citations, freedoms and awards. His voice has commanded respectful attention in the British and European Parliaments. There could be little doubt that, if he had chosen at any stage to contest the presidency of Ireland, he would have been elected with ease, and probably unopposed. He has influenced, and some would say driven, the Northern Ireland policy of successive Irish Govern-ments. He created links of incomparable strength with Irish America, with unprecedented ease of access to the State Department, Congress or the White House. He is an instantly recognisable figure all around the world. He and Ian Paisley were the dominant and enduring figures of Northern Ireland politics for decades.

It can seem almost blasphemous, then, to suggest that Hume's record is nevertheless open to analysis and, where it may be merited, criticism. He was throughout, within his own party, an exceptionally authoritarian figure. At meetings with the four SDLP MPs (while Joe Hendron joined Hume, Mallon and McGrady before his leader gave aid and comfort to Hendron's opponent Gerry Adams), it would often be crystal clear that the other three had little idea what the SDLP policy or reaction was to be until Hume had pronounced it. He clearly believed that the constant repetition of a limited number of well-turned phrases was the best way to communicate basic polit-ical messages, but on occasions the constant reiteration of what cynics called the 'single transferable speech' created a sense of intolerable ennui amongst not a few of his listeners. He was much more comfortable when operating at the level of grand concepts and broad, sweeping designs than when coping with the hard daily graft of politics and Government. Although he had, however briefly, been a highly effective Minister of Commerce in 1974 within the power-sharing Executive, he never thereafter showed any hunger for reassuming executive responsibility. Most damaging of all, he failed to win the liking or trust of the unionist community, who never lost the conviction that, for all his fine talk, his real objective was to deliver them into a united Ireland by the quickest available means. Above all, as I shall argue later, he showed every sign of regarding other nationalists, however unconstitutional their approach, as more acceptable allies than other constitutionalists, albeit unionist in political sympathy. For an end to the appalling polarisation in Northern Ireland it was necessary for the more constructive people in both sections of the community to seek allies towards the centre. In practice, the growing fragmentation in local politics, and the difficulty in convincing any significant number of voters to cross old lines of division, led to a contest on each side as to who could best advance its traditional values and objectives. The leadership of divided unionism was quite as guilty in this respect as its opponents; but they did not enjoy over many years a leader with capabilities or intelligence comparable to that of John Hume.

With the replacement of Humphrey Atkins as Secretary of State by James Prior, the domestic parties were challenged to respond to yet another version of the 'political initiative'. The inspiration for this approach clearly came from Brian Mawhinney the Conservative MP for Peterborough and himself an Ulsterman, who, as a member of his party's back-bench Northern Ireland Committee, had canvassed the idea of 'rolling devolution'. This was based on the premiss that if Northern Ireland politicians could be brought together again in an elected Assembly, albeit one endowed initially only with consultative and advisory roles, the inevitable proximity and the experience of working together for practical ends might foster an atmosphere in which political development could be fruitfully discussed, with the Assembly capable of moving in time (on the basis of widespread agreement) into the executive/legislative mode. It appears that Prior's first thought had been to appoint a local administration to assist him – rather as an American President appoints 'Cabinet Officers' – but he soon came to see that such appointees, even if willing to accept office, would be disabled by their lack of a democratic mandate. But Prior, a formidable political figure, still smarting from his exile from the economic centre of government by an antipathetic Prime Minister, was not content to be a mere caretaker who would preside over an unruly status quo in Northern Ireland, with the hunger strike at last petering out, but with violence and mutual animosity still rampant. He had come to be characterised – in the vulgar and offensive political terminology of the day – as a 'wet', although he could be tough and resolute when roused. But he was certainly of that school of Conservative politics which believed in compromise and the ability of reasonable men and women to reconcile their differences. He therefore adopted as his own the policy of 'rolling devolution', setting in train events leading up to the election by single transferable vote, on 20 October 1982, of seventy-eight members to yet another Northern Ireland Assembly. The response of the electorate and of the individual parties allows us to assess further movements and trends in Northern Ireland politics.

Unionist parties of various designations could still command a majority of seats (forty-nine out of seventy-eight) and of first preference votes (58.4

per cent), with the UUP still the largest party (at 29.7 per cent of the vote) albeit followed closely by the DUP (at 23.0 per cent). The SDLP continued to make a strong showing (with fourteen seats and 18.8 per cent of the votes) and Alliance benefited from late transfers under the preference system to win ten seats with 9.3 per cent of the votes cast. However, by far the most striking feature of this election was the decision by PSF to contest, for the first time, a 'Stormont' election, in which it was to win 10.1 per cent of the votes (although gaining only five seats), albeit contesting only seven of the twelve multi-member constituencies. The tally of seats was, indeed, unrepresentative of its voting strength; strikingly, Alliance had won twice as many, although winning a smaller share of first preference votes.

The willingness of parties to test the volume of their support at the polls did not, in every case, indicate any readiness to support the Prior initiative or to sit in the new Assembly. Both the major parties of nationalism, the SDLP and PSF, had fought the election on abstentionist policy. PSF concentrated on a call for 'Brits out', whereas the Hume-led SDLP expressed deep scepticism about the readiness of unionism to concede partnership in government or of the United Kingdom Government to concede a meaningful 'Irish dimension'.

The crucial provision embodied in the legislation setting it up was that the new Assembly could apply to Westminster for the transfer of devolved powers if 70 per cent or fifty-five of its members backed such proposals. In the meantime the Assembly could discuss local legislation and scrutinise the activities of the six Northern Ireland Departments through a series of departmental Scrutiny Committees. As the Assembly met for the first time on 11 November 1982 to elect James Kilfedder as its Speaker, the participating unionist parties (primarily the UUP and DUP) could command no more than forty-nine votes as a maximum, and this meant (and was indeed intended to mean) that devolution proposals acceptable to Parliament in terms of the legislation would have to win the support of Alliance members, who could be expected to insist on 'widespread acceptance'. The prospect of progress towards an acceptable political settlement were to be further devalued by the boycotting of the Assembly, on one pretext or another, by the UUP for lengthy periods of its life, leaving the DUP and Alliance to work the system as best they could. Because of its evident failure to be broadly representative, the Assembly was to be widely derided, and yet its Scrutiny Committees applied themselves conscientiously to a degree of oversight of Northern Ireland departmental activity which had long been missing.

Yet those parties which decided to boycott the Assembly, either throughout its life or for sustained periods, not only stood in the way of a widely acceptable 'home-grown' political agreement, but also fuelled a growing conviction in London that the local parties could never deliver a settlement, and that the British Government should therefore seek – in conjunction and cooperation with the Irish Government – essentially unboycottable arrangements which would break out of the enduring stalemate. This is precisely what the SDLP wanted to happen, and from the start the failure of both nationalist parties to participate made it impossible to reach the thresholds of support set for broadly acceptable devolution arrangements. Not for the first or the last time, the UUP shot itself in the foot by allowing the blame for failure to produce a 'home-grown' solution to be shared. It was easy to understand the growing impatience felt by British political parties with the disputatious Northern Ireland factions; yet it remained the case that any imposed settlement, reached over the head of some or all of the local interests, could never achieve that growth of mutual confidence and understanding without which political arrangements would be an empty shell. As already described, the conclusion of the Anglo-Irish Agreement of 1985 drove the unionist parties into furious disaffection, and left the Assembly limping along until June 1986 as nothing more than a megaphone for unionist protest. In its better days it had done genuinely useful work in its scrutiny role, but it had proved quite incapable of shaping a broadly acceptable future as the agendas of the opposing political parties diverged rather than converged.

Meanwhile, a striking and significant development was the rise and rise of Gerry Adams. A member of PIRA's delegation at talks with William Whitelaw in 1972, and previously an internee, by 1983 he had become President of PSF as its northern faction took firm control of the organisation. As early as 1979 he had been speculating about the prospect of advancing republican objectives by political as well as military means. He had been elected to Parliament for West Belfast in June 1983 and was proving himself to be a formidably articulate, shrewd and single-minded exponent and executor of republican objectives. His acceptance by others as a politician flowed both from his electoral mandate, which was incontestable, and from the purported distinction between PSF and PIRA, which seemed to many to be false. The riotous reception regularly accorded at a PSF Ard Fheis to unidentified 'volunteers' did little to build confidence that PSF was, or ever intended to be, a party committed to purely constitutional and democratic methods. In moments of ill-advised triumphalism the mask would slip, as when Danny Morrison, at the 1981 Ard Fheis, had spoken of republicans taking power in Ireland 'with an Armalite in one hand and a ballot paper in the other'. This reference to taking power 'in Ireland' was a reminder that republicans had never accepted the validity of post-partition institutions in either part of Ireland as expressing the true wish of the Irish people.

In the immediate aftermath of the Anglo-Irish Agreement, unionism of various brands flailed about in a state of utter outrage, both at the conclusion of the Agreement and their exclusion from the process which had led up to it. Massive street demonstrations and protests, physical assaults on the perimeter of the new Anglo-Irish Secretariat at Maryfield, and a total boycott of contacts with the Secretary of State and other British Ministers indicated the depth of their resentment. The initial meetings of the new Anglo-Irish Intergovernmental Conference held in Belfast had to run the gauntlet of angry crowds and be conducted under heavy police protection. The police, in the process of upholding a lawful decision by the Government which many of them as individuals found most unpalatable, exposed themselves to attacks, threats and in some cases abandonment of their homes. Their principled efforts at this time did less than they should have done to cement a reputation for impartiality in law enforcement. The political emotions and imperatives of the time drove the unionist leaders, James Molyneaux of the UUP and Ian Paisley of the DUP, together into a strange coalition, with the small, austere, patient and unflamboyant personality of the one harnessed to the loud, bombastic and rhetorical stance of the other. With painful slowness, beginning with exploratory discussions with civil servants and moving forward into 'talks about talks', unionism began to open a dialogue as to whether any alternative to, or replacement of, the detested Agreement might be possible. Intricate formulae, permitting dialogue with Government during a defined 'pause' in the operation of the Agreement, were discussed. These were essentially artificial and face-saving devices; even if the Inter-governmental Conference accepted a gap in its programme of meetings, the strengthened communication and consultation between the British and Irish Governments would continue, either through the Maryfield Secretariat or more directly. Nor could it be assumed – as the development of events was to underline – that any 'replacement' of the 1985 Agreement would necessarily be on terms more acceptable or favourable to unionism.

While the Northern Ireland community had to some extent been de-sensitised by the endless years and countless incidents of terrorist violence, the events in Enniskillen on 8 November 1987 were to have a singular resonance in Northern Ireland and around the world. This indiscriminate bombing attack, directed at a crowd in a small Fermanagh town gathered around the cenotaph to remember the dead of two world wars, struck most observers as not only callous but also blasphemous. The scenes of carnage after the event travelled around the world. The father of one of the dead, Gordon Wilson (himself wounded in the outrage), moved everyone who heard it with the dignity of his grief, uncontaminated by the slightest trace of bitterness or talk of revenge. In spite of utterly cynical efforts to dissociate itself, including ridiculous and implausible suggestions that the bomb could have been triggered by a security forces scanning device, PIRA stood exposed and condemned in the eyes of the world as an utterly ruthless, unrepentant and deeply hypocritical organisation. It was a very understandable reaction by any responsible politician to conclude that this could not be allowed to go on. It was also demonstrably the case that the commitment over many years of huge numbers of soldiers and police had failed to eliminate the threat of terrorism. Yet progress had nevertheless been made. A peak death toll of 497 in 1972 had fallen by 1985 to as low a figure as 61; and while 61 murders in a small community represented an unacceptable level of violence, far more people were killed in that year by road traffic accidents in Northern Ireland. Moreover, the number of 'civilians' (as distinct from members of terrorist organisations or of the security forces confronting them) had fallen over the same period from 108 to 21.

This was the background against which, in early 1988, Hume decided to open further private talks with Adams. He had come to the conclusion that the conversion of republicanism from 'the armed struggle' towards purely peaceful means could only be achieved by convincing its leadership that the ambivalent dual strategy was likely to postpone rather than advance the day of ultimate Irish unity. This could best be done by convincing Adams that the SDLP and a wholly peaceful and democratic PSF would be natural political allies, able to form with the Irish Government a most powerful nationalist alliance capable of moving forward the anti-partitionist agenda. Yet there were very great risks in attempting such a rapprochement. Not least amongst these were risks to his own party, the SDLP, whose policies and strategies he had so largely shaped. So far, that party had been able to point to a genuine and wide-ranging distinction between itself and PSF, as a liberal, internationalist, wholly democratic and peace-loving party, compared with Adams and his allies with their extreme reluctance to condemn or disavow violence and their all-too-close links with other notorious terrorist groups, such as ETA (or those members of such groups masquerading as politicians in their own country). If this distinction began to be blurred there would be a real risk of PSF presenting itself as more truly representative of the young working-class nationalist than the ex-teachers or other middle-class professionals of the SDLP. Hume would justify acceptance of any threat to his own party in return for a stimulus to peace-making as a preference for the greater good. Yet history has not been very kind to politicians who, in other countries during the 1930s, believed they could 'civilise' rivals who had thrust their way to prominence by brute force. These and later conversations were to be justified as part of a 'peace process'. Yet a certain kind of peace can be obtained anywhere at any time by subordinating oneself to the ruthlessness of another. No doubt Marshal Pétain persuaded himself that he was being as patriotic a Frenchman in 'making peace' (a euphemism for accepting defeat) in 1940 as he had been in standing against the Germans at Verdun.

The Hume–Adams axis was, however, open to an even more serious criticism. For far too long, Irish nationalism has been reluctant to accept that the holy grail of true Irish unity – most accurately characterised by Hume himself as a union of people rather than a union of territories – can never be achieved by efforts to subdue, subvert, outvote or outbreed the large unionist community established in the north-east of Ireland. This union can only be achieved, if at all, by patient efforts to convince unionists that their fellow-Irishmen of a different tradition are friends and allies, rather than opponents and enemies; that a pattern of unity could be devised which would respect their distinctive traditions and protect their essential interests; and that they would truly share in what Hume has often called 'a new Ireland' rather than hearing the cry 'We are the masters now'. None of this is to say that the nationalist sense of persistent disadvantage within Northern Ireland can be dismissed from the reckoning, although many unionists will observe that nearly thirty years have passed since they had the power to control things in Northern Ireland. What is incontestable is that the consolidation of society into politico-sectarian blocs can never lead to a united community, let alone encourage unionism to move forward from its defensive and beleaguered position.

I have written at length, in describing the role of the British Government, about the most recent push for a political breakthrough launched by Brooke and Mayhew, and carried forward to the watershed of the Good Friday Agreement by their Labour successors. Great credit is clearly due to Major and Blair, to Albert Reynolds and in particular to George Mitchell. Whatever their involvement or degree of encouragement or pressure deployed at crucial moments, no comprehensive agreement would have been possible without the constructive involvement of some, though not all, of the local political parties.

I have earlier suggested that Ian Paisley, in spite of his many remarkable and too often underrated qualities, must bear a not inconsiderable share of the blame for an appalling period in Northern Ireland's history. By the refusal of his DUP to participate in the talks process culminating in the Good Friday Agreement, he ensured that the true strength of unionism was under-represented at the conference table, leaving the heat and burden of the day to David Trimble's UUP and those fringe 'loyalist' parties linked with Protestant paramilitarism. This abstention from the process allowed him ample scope to complain afterwards (and not entirely without justification) that too much had been conceded to the aspirations of the nationalists and republicans. It was all rather as if, on the brink of a vital Rugby International to decide the destination of the Triple Crown, some of the most powerful team members had decided not to play because of a dispute with the Union or the team management. Perhaps this refusal to be selected was slightly more honourable than that of someone who opted to play but ran off to the dressing room just as the game reached its height. In close alliance with Paisley and the DUP, the able but abrasive QC Robert McCartney set new records for acerbity. These oppositionist politicians sought their justification in the argument that, before the process had got under way, not only the British but also the Irish Government had taken the line that entry to the talks, let alone to any Government formed as an outcome, must depend upon a complete and final renunciation of violence, a position from which they both resiled in the teeth of republican and loyalist obduracy.

The Paisley stance, then, was not without some degree of moral justification. But the eloquent cleric was also the able politician. If all representatives of unionism had declined to participate, the Anglo-Irish Agreement of 1985 might have been replaced, but very probably by a system conceding an even greater influence to the Government of the Irish Republic. Changes in the police and security arrangements, and other measures sought by the nationalists and Irish, would have moved ahead, and a territorial claim to Northern Ireland would remain today entrenched in the Irish Constitution. Talk of 'total integration' would prove a chimera, no unionist would enjoy any effective measure of executive power, and the blame for the failure to make any progress would be laid at the door of unionism, with calamitous effects upon the sympathy of the rest of the United Kingdom. To avoid these predictable evils, someone had to summon up the courage to take a calculated risk. As we shall see, that person was to be David Trimble.

In a very different way, and with very different motives, John Hume was also beginning to make it more difficult to achieve a political settlement acceptable to all. For the most honourable of motives, he had focused with his customary single-mindedness (some, indeed, would say tunnel vision) upon the 'peace process'. His prioritisation was justified in that the most immediate and crying need was to stop the killing. But if it was not only to be stopped but also to remain stopped, political progress would have to be made on terms acceptable to all, and combatants would have to move beyond a ceasefire or armistice to a genuine and unambiguous peace settlement. As we have seen, Hume had opened a line to Adams in early 1988, not long after the terrorist movement so closely associated with him had earned the odium of an appalled community. In the process he had offered a lifeline to militant republicanism at its weakest moment. As the political momentum gathered, particularly in the productive climate of good relations between John Major and Albert Reynolds, it was Hume who resisted efforts to make

PSF pay a meaningful price for entry into the process, and who lost no opportunity to press Major, through Reynolds, to become a 'persuader' for Irish unity. In his dialogue with Adams and Sinn Fein, Hume had the support and encouragement of some important clerical and other intermediaries, but as the wider community became aware in April 1993 that secret talks had been going on (confirmed by a statement on 25 April) unionist paranoia was entirely predictable. What promises and assurance, they wondered, were being delivered behind their backs to a man still holding over their heads the threat of endless violence? They were at that time unaware that, in its own secret contact with the Provisionals, the Major Government had clearly ruled out any prior objective of ending partition; the Union would continue to be upheld unless and until the people of Northern Ireland were to express a democratic wish for unity.

Undoubtedly Hume was a prime mover in developing the idea of a 'joint declaration' by the two sovereign Governments as the basis for further progress. By 1991 he was canvassing this idea with the Haughey Government in Dublin and it appears to have been discussed in principle between the two Governments for the first time at the Major/Haughey meeting in December 1991, and early in 1992 the British Government received both from the Irish Government and directly from Hume proposed texts with the thumbprints of the latter all over them, utterly nationalist in tone and sentiment and underlining the reality of a pan-nationalist front bent on persuading the British Government to coerce or abandon the unionists. At this stage, nationalism had still not abandoned the hope of persuading a British Government that there should be 'self-determination' by the people of Ireland as a whole, with the prospect of unionist dissent being overwhelmed by the nationalist plurality in the island as a whole. The impression of a growing alliance between Hume and Adams – to a degree embarrassing even to the Dublin Government – was reinforced by a joint statement issued by the two men on 25 September 1993, to the effect that they had made substantial progress, had reported on this to the Irish Government, and now regarded the whole issue as firmly placed on the intergovernmental agenda. Needless to say there was intense speculation about the thrust of this controversial document, although the deepest digging by interested journalists never produced a trace of it. It may very well have been the case that any report was made in a non-written form.

Throughout these developments, the unionist parties – without whose ultimate support no wide-ranging settlement would be possible – had been kept in the dark, baffled and infuriated by broad hints of secret dealings and confidential understandings. By this time Hume had become so persuaded of his own political rectitude as to resent growing evidence of Albert Reynolds' willingness, in dealings with the congenial Major, to make up his own mind. As the two Prime Ministers moved towards the mould-breaking Downing Street Declaration, Hume was to some extent sidelined.

When the first PIRA ceasefire was announced on 29 August 1994, Hume was certainly entitled to great credit for bringing the republicans in from the cold. Unfortunately they had entered the political arena with a ballot paper in one hand and an Armalite, if not in the other, at any rate handily under the table.

Following the Downing Street Declaration and the PIRA ceasefire (followed by a similar response from loyalist paramilitaries, accompanied in their case by an expression of regret for the suffering caused by their activities) the most crucial question was how the unionist leadership would react. There could be no doubt that the DUP would take its cue from Ian Paisley and insist that there could be no discussions including PSF in advance of republican paramilitary disarmament. If the UUP were also to follow that line, either PSF would be persuaded to change its stance (and this seemed unlikely), attempts would be made to form a political alliance excluding Sinn Fein (which Hume seems certain to veto), or direct rule would continue in an atmosphere of ever-closer cooperation between London and Dublin. If unionism held absolutely to 'no seats in Government without disarmament by the IRA', and the SDLP held equally resolutely to 'no Government without seats for PSF', political progress would in effect be vetoed by the intransigence of republicanism and Hume's reluctance to press them or to accept that they could be left behind.

The man who now faced the most difficult and unpalatable choices, David Trimble, had succeeded James Molyneaux as leader of the UUP in August 1995. His election, in preference to the wily and long-experienced John Taylor, had come as something of a surprise, but clearly had owed not a little to his flamboyant support for the Orange Order in its protest (thereafter to be annually repeated as an event in the dreary Ulster calendar) at Drumcree, near Portadown. Those who had voted for this one-time disciple of Bill Craig and defender of Orange interests found in time that they had not got precisely what they had bargained for. Trimble was, and is, a complex and interesting figure. A very intelligent academic lawyer, articulate to a high degree, with cultivated tastes in music and the arts, and a devoted family man with a most charming and likeable wife, Trimble can also be socially clumsy, shy and introverted, hot-tempered and abrupt. He was fortunate enough to enjoy the confidence and support of such able colleagues as Reg Empey, who had also travelled a long way from his early days in Vanguard. History will show how men such as these had the courage to face growing opposition within their own party towards the Good Friday Agreement, and their subsequent difficult decisions not to abandon the devolved framework without putting republican good faith to the test. Without the imagination to make a leap of faith, there could be no possibility of progress, and if this leap proved in the end to fall short of the farther shore, this did not diminish the courage of the attempt. In truth, Trimble at the Stormont talks must have undergone some of the conflicting emotions felt by Faulkner so many years before. To enter a deal triggering the release of convicted prisoners and initiating a fundamental review of policing and security without insistence upon matching progress to or towards the decommissioning of weaponry was to take an extreme political risk, but it was one entered into on the basis of assurances by the Prime Minister which proved to have little substance.

It has to be said that the role of PSF in these events casts the gravest possible doubt upon its democratic credentials. While insisting upon its separateness from PIRA, the rapturous welcome given at Sinn Fein gatherings to released prisoners underlined the reality not merely of close links but also of the essential unity of the whole republican structure. The notion that PSF was doing all that it had undertaken to do under the Agreement, and that PIRA alone could answer for its own conduct and policy, was deeply dishonest. While the people of Belfast, dazzled by his charisma, were giving a rapturous welcome to the American President who had presented Adams with the opportunity to be lionised and subsidised in America, republican militants were already laying plans for the outrage at Canary Wharf in London's Docklands which shattered the first ceasefire. PIRA representatives played intricate and cynical games with General de Chastelain's Commission established to oversee disarmament. Prospects, possibilities, 'modalities', inspections; everything short of actual disarmament or (to avoid any implication of surrender) 'putting arms beyond use'. International observers were able to confirm, because they had been taken to see a sample of them, that PIRA had bunkers stuffed with military materiel. The ordinary citizen had never doubted that such arms dumps existed, and in much larger numbers than republicans were prepared to admit. The revelation that foreigners had been allowed to see some of the weaponry was little more reassuring than a video of a Soviet missile silo would have been to Americans at the height of the Cold War. There were frequent arguments that no dissidents anywhere in the world had willingly handed over weaponry (patently untrue) and that the possession of weapons was of no account for as long as the gun 'remained silent'. These specious reassurances were of little value when set against the uninterrupted ferocity of 'punishment' beatings or shootings in turf wars for the protection of rackets and the maintenance of local control, and the readiness of republican leaders to imply that those considering a particular political course should bear in mind the reality of an army in waiting ('They haven't gone away, you know'). As police services ran down, military measures were reduced, convicted prisoners released and PSF members enjoyed the fruits of high Government office, the Sinn Fein leadership had the effrontery to justify their failure to put arms convincingly beyond use with a specious argument that others, and in particular the British Government, were failing in their obligations under the Agreement.

Nor was the record of the small loyalist political parties unimpeachable. The new politics had thrown up some figures of impressive eloquence and authority, such as David Ervine, but the ceasefires declared by the various loyalist paramilitaries appeared more and more nominal in character amidst deepening sectarianism and loyalist militancy, including murderous inter-factional feuds.

The Alliance Party (now frankly a diminishing force, particularly after acceptance of the Assembly speakership by its able leader John Alderdice) and the Women's Coalition used their relatively modest elected strength to concentrate on practical issues and prevent as far as they could the dominance of the old sectarian politics.

By his resignation from the office of First Minister, David Trimble made it clear to all that he would not allow the institutions established under the Belfast Agreement to survive without demonstrable movement on the decommissioning front. It is very doubtful if this threat could, of itself, have persuaded republicanism to make an acceptable move. Perversely, the terrible events in America on 11 September 2001, so full of threat and danger for the whole world community, may have had some constructive consequences in Northern Ireland. With a new awareness in the United States of the nature of global terrorism, coupled with the embarrassing arrest of republican activists in Colombia, the republican movement faced for the first time a distinct fall in the temperature of American tolerance. It was in this atmosphere that General de Chastelain was able to attest to a significant development in 'putting weapons beyond use'. Yet even this development did not offer Trimble a safe anchorage. His re-election as First Minister (alongside Mark Durkan as a new Deputy First Minister) was only made possible under the complex system of Assembly voting by the willingness of some Women's Coalition and Alliance Assembly members to accept temporary redefinition as 'unionists'. Although the UUC subsequently endorsed Trimble's stance, the very substantial size of the minority vote underlined the reality that the institutions of the Belfast Agreement did not command majority support within the unionist community.

As Trimble more and more narrowly survived challenges to his party leadership, as opponents within the party, such as the able Donaldson, contemplated and eventually completed defection to the DUP, as republicanism was tainted by association with punishment beatings, rackets and robberies, and so-called loyalism remained steeped in thuggery, it became ever more clear that he would suffer for his leap of faith. Policies ostensibly designed to reinforce the democratic centre led in practice to the inexorable rise of the parties of the extreme. So it came about that Trimble resigned the party leadership, the SDLP operated more and more in the shadow of Sinn Fein, and Ian Paisley and Gerry Adams ruled the political roost, with real power resting with the Secretary of State. In a final chapter I will consider what, if any, collaboration can be expected between these mutually antipathetic elements.

CHAPTER EIGHT

End-game or limbo?

In 2005 General John de Chastelain, chairman of the international body responsible for the oversight of paramilitary decommissioning, announced that, on the basis of personal observation by himself and his colleagues, he was satisfied that PIRA had honoured its pledge to put weapons and materiel 'beyond use'. Two clerics, the Catholic Father Alec Reid and the Methodist Reverend Harold Good, who had been present as observers during the decommissioning exercise, eloquently expressed their conviction that a crucial stage in the 'peace process' had indeed been reached.

This news was greeted with the greatest satisfaction by Governments in London, Dublin and Washington, and the hope was expressed that early inter-party dialogue would lead to the revival of the Assembly Executive, the return of devolved government, and the fulfilment of the promises embodied in the Belfast Agreement of 1997. These hopes were to be lowered if not dashed by a response from unionist politicians which was at best guarded and, in the case of the newly dominant DUP, sceptical to the point of hostility. The 'blame game' showed early signs of shifting from republicans ('Why do they retain their arms and persist in criminality?') to unionists ('Can we not now see that, whatever others deliver, they will never share power with nationalists?').

This grudging reaction to the satisfaction of a demand constantly reiterated can best be explained by the length of delay in the decommissioning process, a persistent unwillingness to trust the motives of the republican movement, the lack of any clarity about the future role (if any) of PIRA, a suspicion of continuing republican involvement in criminality and localised 'enforcement', and the continuing absence in the statements by Gerry Adams and others of any convincing element of regret or remorse. There was indeed a strong inference in such statements that victims of the violence in the Army or police had been wholly legitimate targets, combatants in a 'war'.

Yet the acts of decommissioning, following the earlier statement that the 'armed struggle' had been brought to an end, clearly represented a significant turning point in Northern Ireland's affairs. In the distant days of 1968 Terence O'Neill had used the imagery of 'Ulster at the crossroads'. Now, once again, Northern Ireland had reached a crucial turning point. But in what direction would it choose to turn?

It is timely, then, to return at last to those crucial questions formulated at the beginning of this book. Were the bloody and painful years of the troubles inevitable? As large-scale violence draws to a close, in what condition do we find Northern Ireland today? After all that has happened, where do we go from here?

In earlier chapters I have attempted to identify critical moments in which the descent into violence might have been averted. We are, of course, dealing here with hypotheses rather than certainties, but a review of the acts of commission or omission by the principal interests engaged suggests some broad conclusions. In criticising, as I will, the behaviour of various named individuals I am not to be regarded as necessarily questioning their good faith at the material time. Even those who adopt means most of us would regard as evil have usually convinced themselves that they are the best or sole means to achieve good ends.

I have sought to argue that a heavy responsibility for the developing state of affairs in Northern Ireland must lie at the door of the United Kingdom Parliament and Government. A sovereign Government cannot shuffle off its ultimate responsibility by pointing to the exercise of delegated or devolved powers. No British Government, faced with persistent evidence of misuse of power by a local authority in some populous metropolitan area, could be excused for shrugging its shoulders and denying all responsibility. Perhaps the reluctance of successive British Governments to involve themselves in the contentious areas of Northern Ireland for the best part of forty years flowed from a false parallel with the evolution from Empire to Commonwealth. Canada and Australia and New Zealand had become self-governing nations, and it was unthinkable that a British Parliament would question or a British Government interfere with their internal affairs. Northern Ireland, on the other hand, remained an integral part of the United Kingdom, with the sovereign authority of the British Parliament expressly preserved by Section 75 of the Government of Ireland Act 1920.

Yet, in what was virtually the first test of controversial use of its powers by the Northern Ireland Parliament, the British Government of the day first procrastinated and then retreated from the possibility of refusing Royal Assent. At the time of the 'Curragh Mutiny', uncertainty about the loyalty of some elements in the Army led to a failure to challenge in any way the armed preparedness of northern unionists, thus strengthening their resolve and inviting competitive militancy from Irish nationalists. This failure to assert the power of the State was to have its echo some sixty years later when the forces of the Crown stood idly by in the face of the UWC strike.

For much of the nineteenth century, British treatment of Ireland swung like a pendulum between coercion and concession. A history of substantial concessions to the demands of Irish nationalism threw into high relief the subsequent ill-considered executions of the leaders of the Easter Rising. An administration unswervingly stern in its principles and actions might have inspired fear and obedience; an administration consistently benign in its approach and methods might have inspired loyalty and affection.

Again, history was to repeat itself. One Government's recognition of 'special status', distinguishing terrorists from other criminals, undermined efforts to overcome subversion by due process of law, and sowed the seeds of an extreme reaction when a later Government moved to remove those privileges. At least William Whitelaw had the good grace to admit that his original decision had been a grave mistake, whereas Margaret Thatcher shut her eyes to the potential, and some would say inevitable, consequences of a later reversal of policy. Earlier Governments had clearly bowed before pressure; those who believed Margaret Thatcher would do so failed to understand her philosophy and make-up. The outcome generated a huge surge of sympathy in the Catholic community for the republican movement. In 1916 'England' had killed the republican heroes; all these decades later they had killed themselves by slow starvation. In both events Irish sympathy for the 'blood sacrifice' was to be dangerously stimulated.

The irony was that the 'Iron Lady', so adamant about the essentially subordinate issue of prison conditions, proved to be malleable on the fundamental issue of sovereignty. The insistence of successive British Governments that the Irish Government could claim no role in the internal affairs of a part of the United Kingdom – culminating in Mrs Thatcher's celebrated 'out, out, out' rejection of the formulations of the New Ireland Forum – crumbled under pressure from key elements within the diplomatic and political bureaucracy. At a crucial time in the negotiations leading to the Anglo-Irish Agreement of 1985, the key departmental ministers concerned were Geoffrey Howe at the Foreign Office and Douglas Hurd at the Northern Ireland Office.

The Foreign and Commonwealth Office has on all too many occasions argued for British withdrawal from what it regards as expensive and embarrassing commitments without much concern for the views and interests of those directly involved. Over a long official career I visited numerous embassies and consulates, and met many British Ambassadors, Consul Generals and their staff. In a great many cases I came to have the highest regard for their professionalism and acuity, as demonstrated by people like Nigel Sheinwald and Sherard Cowper-Coles – then promising young men and today stars in the Foreign and Commonwealth Office firmament. Yet I would also encounter traces of patrician arrogance. I remember in particular attending one meeting in London chaired by Christopher Mallaby, later Ambassador in Paris. He had just become Superintending Under Secretary for a Foreign and Commonwealth Office domain which included the Republic of Ireland Department. Although coming afresh to the topic, he presided over the discussions with ineffable self-assurance. Inevitably much of the meeting related to the affairs of Northern Ireland; I was the only person in the gathering who had lived and worked there for many years, and yet he showed no more interest in my views than if I had been an observer from Outer Mongolia.

At ministerial level, it was for Douglas Hurd to speak from the point of view of the Northern Ireland Office portfolio. But one has to remember here that he had only been a short time in Northern Ireland, that he had emerged from the stable of diplomacy (to which he would ultimately return as Foreign Secretary) and had formed his political attitudes as a close aide to Edward Heath, whose contempt for Ulster unionists, at Sunningdale and elsewhere, was marked. Since I was (very deliberately) excluded from the process, I can only surmise what was going on behind the scenes, but it is only too easy to imagine the arguments brought to bear on an initially sceptical Prime Minister: reminders of the Dublin Embassy burning and the need to make concessions to secure effective cross-Border security cooperation; and the desirability of removing the one remaining serious irritant in the all-important relationship between the United Kingdom and the United States.

Then, of course, there were the key officials. As Head of the Northern Ireland Civil Service, I found myself dealing with two successive Cabinet Secretaries, Robert Armstrong and Robin Butler. It was to be expected that the Cabinet Secretary, the closest official adviser to the Prime Minister of the day, would – not least in negotiations with another Government – regard himself as an executant of the Prime Minister's policy; and clearly Margaret Thatcher initially looked in the Anglo-Irish negotiations primarily for a basis on which the UK could secure more effective cooperation from the Irish Republic in confronting terrorism. On the other hand, her core convictions were essentially unionist, even jingoistic, and I would have little doubt that she felt profoundly uncomfortable about concessions intruding on UK sovereignty. I have a strong feeling that she embraced the final terms of agreement without enthusiasm and indeed with reluctance; and that she was brought to accept the outcome of the negotiations by the arguments of Ministers and ex-Ministers of the Foreign Office and by the judgement of Robert Armstrong that agreement on the lines negotiated would be in the national interest. At Sunningdale Edward Heath had treated Faulkner and his unionist colleagues with something approaching brutal contempt; in confronting the

UWC strike of 1974 Harold Wilson had excoriated a whole suffering community as 'spongers'. Armstrong had been close to both these Prime Ministers.

From the Foreign and Commonwealth Office itself the leading role was played by David Goodall (later High Commissioner in India). At once cheery and urbane, Goodall was a likeable individual, but with strong Irish connections and an Ampleforth education he was unlikely to have much affinity with the Northern Ireland majority.

Although these were clearly the predominant influences throughout, it was inevitable that senior officials from the Northern Ireland Office should also be involved, and these were the Permanent Under Secretary, Sir Robert Andrew, and the Deputy Under Secretary from the London Office, Tony Brennan. From the outset it had been made clear to Andrew that I, albeit Second Permanent Under Secretary at the Northern Ireland Office, was not to be involved. Since my relationship with Andrew was open and exemplary from beginning to end, it was not surprising that he allowed me on occasions to peer through the glass ceiling separating me from the ongoing discussions. I knew that British Ministers were keen to secure more effective security cooperation from the Irish Republic; that the Irish negotiators pressed for some quid pro quo for this; and that Margaret Thatcher was fundamentally uncomfortable with some of their demands. I would be confident that Andrew contributed a real knowledge and understanding of Northern Ireland not available to Cabinet Office and Foreign and Commonwealth Office representatives. But in terms of 'departmental weight' the Northern Ireland Office was a frigate in competition with battleships, and it is all too easy for cautionary words to be dismissed with the rationale that the speaker has 'gone native'. In the end, and not for the last time, strident opposition from the Prime Minister was to be succeeded by reluctant and grudging consent.

So the Anglo-Irish Agreement was concluded amongst much fanfare. In honour of the key negotiators, Robert Armstrong on the British side and Dermot Nally on the Irish side, a commemorative 'AN' tie was designed, to be worn as a badge of honour at celebratory events. Strangely enough, I probably knew Nally better than I knew Armstrong. For many years I made a point of keeping up regular informal contact with key officials in Dublin, first with the redoubtable Ken Whitaker and later with Dermot Nally. Since the centre of Irish policy (presentationally at least) has always been the bringing together of the two traditions in a new Ireland, it was perhaps a pity that it never occurred to Nally (even if it did not occur to Armstrong) that the presence at the talks of someone directly involved over the long term in Northern Ireland, and demonstrably sympathetic to the building of bridges which could bear the weight placed upon them, might have avoided some gross misjudgements about reactions and consequences.

There are those who still regard the 1985 Agreement as a landmark achievement en route to the Belfast Agreement of 1998. I have already argued that the underlying objectives of achieving stable devolution and inhibiting the growth of extremist politics were missed, not narrowly but by a mile. The brief, faltering life of an unstable Executive, operating without collective responsibility or much evident common purpose, has discredited rather than underpinned the idea of devolution. As the investment made in the Agreement by centrist parties failed to yield the expected returns, it was hardly surprising, if profoundly disappointing, that the electorate fled from the centre ground to the bulwarks of separated communities. In particular the unionist community were initially alienated by the self-evident unilateralism of the 1985 Agreement and the processes leading up to it. They saw a 'neutral' British Government face to face with a coalition between the Irish Government and the SDLP; an Agreement embodying very specific guarantees for the minority backed by the Irish Government, and with no reciprocity; and an entrenched right extending into perpetuity for the Irish to delve deeply into Northern Ireland affairs while ceding no opportunity to examine or question their own policies or actions. This overwhelming sense of alienation not only closed down channels of communication with Government for a considerable period, but contributed to a loss of confidence in British Governments generally and an attraction to policies of obduracy and self-protection.

I have earlier contrasted the unilateralism of the 1985 Agreement with the bilateralism of the later Downing Street Declaration. This could have provided a sound foundation for what would become the Belfast Agreement. I will consider later the part played by Northern Ireland political parties in the talks leading to that Agreement. Once again, though, I must emphasise the overarching responsibility of the Governments of the United Kingdom of Great Britain and Northern Ireland. They were, I believe, gravely at fault in at least three respects. I have already dealt with one of these: their consent to the creation in Northern Ireland of a form of devolved government lacking cohesion, stability or ultimate credibility. The other cardinal issues relate to the overall approach to terrorist organisations and their spokesmen and to the decisions taken in relation to prisoners jailed for terrorist offences.

Particularly since the 11 September 2001 terrorist outrage in America we have all lived with the rhetoric that terrorists must never be allowed to succeed. This has come in large measure from an America which year after year lionised the affiliates of gunmen and indeed invited them to the White House. Suddenly, after the bombing in London of 7 July 2005, even the Mayor of London, Ken Livingstone, has become an eloquent advocate of the need to stand together against terrorism; the same Ken Livingstone who over many years was happy to share platforms with those who termed themselves 'freedom fighters'. For too long, even British Governments had wrapped their relationships with the IRA with ambiguity. The line between 'never negotiating with terrorists' and talking to terrorists proved an extremely permeable one. Such discussions are usually rationalised by the argument that 'getting peace is all that matters'. During the Second World War similar thoughts seemed to have passed through the mind of Lord Halifax; while no doubt Marshal Pétain thought it better for France to bow the knee to the Nazis. I have described in detail how the Conservative Government began with the position that republicans could not be permitted access to the conference table, let alone be party to and beneficiary of any agreement, without clear and unambiguous declarations and evidence that violent methods had been abandoned for good and an irreversible and verifiable process of disarmament set in hand within a limited timescale. This position was shared, at the time, by the Irish Government. But the line drawn in the sand rapidly disappeared as the tides of compromise flowed over it. The able diplomatic former Senator George Mitchell was quite frank about the pragmatic approach adopted by himself and his colleagues. Without flexibility, he was persuaded, comprehensive talks would never get under way. But Sinn Fein and PIRA had reached the conclusion that, if they played consistent hardball, others would bend to their purpose. So not months but years would pass without a clear assurance that 'the war was over', criminality had been ended and the materiel of warfare surrendered, abandoned or – to the satisfaction of other parties – put 'beyond use'.

David Trimble and those in the UUP loyal to him consequently found themselves tied into a process which led to temporary and unstable devolution, regular suspensions of the institutions, repeated challenges to the leadership, estrangement from the party of significant political figures, and the final ignominy of massive losses to the DUP.

It was, I believe, a massive misjudgement to suppose that Sinn Fein would be lured into 'reasonableness' in order to remain within or re-enter devolved government in Northern Ireland. They would enter or remain in such government only if they were wholly comfortable with the terms, and throughout they kept their eyes firmly on the greater prize of political gains in the Republic and an ultimate role in government there. As conditions set by successive British Governments failed to be met without markedly adverse consequences for Sinn Fein, the unionist majority of the population progressively lost faith not only in the UUP but also in the United Kingdom Government as custodians of their interests. Long before the transcripts of honeyed conversations between Mo Mowlam and Martin McGuinness emerged into the light of day, suspicions of the tone and terms of exchanges between their

Government and Sinn Fein had begun to grow.

As Prime Minister, Tony Blair was deeply implicated in these processes of appeasement, with the experienced officials of the Northern Ireland Office frequently sidelined by the clandestine activities of Jonathan Powell. In one sense it was a healthy thing because at last a British Prime Minister had recognised the 'Northern Ireland problem' as a highly rated political priority. In this, as in so many other spheres, he proved himself to be an outstanding communicator and presenter. He felt obliged to intervene personally and directly in the campaign preceding the Northern Ireland referendum on the Belfast Agreement because he sensed – accurately I believe – that its principal local protaganists were doing a pretty ineffective job of selling it. Thus the 'Yes' campaign, asking voters to endorse efforts to unite a divided community, gave little evidence of true warmth and mutual understanding between the potential power-sharing partners. In this context the Prime Minister's personal intervention may well have been decisive in persuading around half of the unionist voters to put aside their reservations and vote 'Yes'. It is a sad fact that subsequently a large number of those who had voted in support of the Agreement were to feel strongly that this support had been obtained under false premisses. The clear sense of Tony Blair's 'assurances' to them, delivered with such panache in his own hand in front of the television cameras, was that without 'decommissioning' of PIRA weaponry, no Sinn Fein Minister would be allowed to serve in Government. There was, however, no such specific assurance embodied in the Belfast Agreement itself. Sinn Fein, with other parties, had simply bound itself to use its best endeavours to advance a process intended to deliver complete disarmament within two years. Of course, PIRA itself, supposedly and so conveniently a separate entity from Sinn Fein, had not given any undertakings to respond to these 'best endeavours' of political republicanism.

Great pains had been taken to distribute copies of the Belfast Agreement widely throughout the community, but it was highly unlikely that the mass of the population would pick its way carefully through page after page of bureaucratic prose. Voters at British elections are not in the habit of construing the fine detail of competing manifestos. They are, rather, influenced by 'sound bites' or key messages conveyed by the written or electronic media. Yet even those relatively few who had considered carefully the actual wording of the Belfast Agreement understood the sense of Blair's remarks to be that, if necessary, new legislation would be introduced in the event of a failure by republicanism to deliver the commitment to end conflict for good and stand down its 'soldiers' and weaponry. That was certainly the belief of David Trimble and those loyal to him.

It is a horrible experience for anyone temperamentally disposed to take things on trust rather than yield to absolute cynicism to find that in the event cynicism had been justified. Many of those who voted for the Agreement remained deeply cynical about the words, actions and motives of Sinn Fein. They were in little doubt that, if able to get away with it, it would suit Sinn Fein very well to remind all of us – as Gerry Adams famously said in a revelatory moment – that 'They haven't gone away, you know.' Those of us who not only said but believed that 'Ulster is British' could not credit that a British Prime Minister would fail to deliver on a solemn assurance offered as an inducement to vote as he wished us to do. Yet from that moment on we were to face year after year of procrastination, verbal and moral gymnastics, undelivered promises, meaningless gestures and small, unquantifiable concessions from republicanism. At the start of this demoralising process, appropriate words and actions from Sinn Fein might have carried some weight and contributed to mutual confidence; the excessive delay before ultimate action in 2005 led inevitably to demands that any actions subsequently taken should be demonstrable, transparent and verifiable. For a long time republican apologists continued to remind us that undefeated armies never surrendered. In 1998 Tony Blair was understood to stand by the parallel proposition that political parties with private armies behind them could not be allowed to serve in the Government of any part of the United Kingdom.

What cards, it may be asked, did the British Government have in its hands in the negotiations with Sinn Fein leading up to the Belfast Agreement? The prospect of places in a future Government of Northern Ireland did not, to the republican ideologists, represent in itself a great prize. For a great many years PIRA and its predecessors of the IRA had regarded both the Oireachtas and Parliament as institutions not entitled to exercise any authority in Ireland. This mindset is underlined by the recent reactions of republican apologists when asked whether they now accept that numerous murders carried out in the course of their campaign were crimes. Rejecting the assertion of the Irish Constitution that the Irish Army is the only legitimate army of the State, they have fallen back on the dogma that, since PIRA has in their view been the 'real army' of the Irish nation, deeds committed by it in pursuit of its ends were 'acts of war', and in that sense and context cannot be regarded as crimes. Presumably the Bosnian Serbs would mount a similar argument about the atrocities at Srebrenica and elsewhere. The decision not merely to contest elections for, but to take seats in, the Dail and a Stormont Assembly has been rationalised within the republican movement as a pragmatic step towards an ultimate goal; however, the several Sinn Fein members elected to the House of Commons continued to absent themselves from Parliament.

In my view the more important factors bearing upon republican negotiators included a growing war-weariness in a struggle proving to be costly and inconclusive; the realisation by republican leaders of the potential gains which could be won by their discipline and political skills; the development of a potential tripartite national alliance joining Sinn Fein to the SDLP and the Irish Government; and the exploitation of financial and political support in the United States.

However, the future handling of the numerous republican and loyalist prisoners convicted of terrorist offences by non-jury 'Diplock' courts emerged at the negotiations as a crucially important and sensitive issue. For republicans 'the men behind the wire' represented the elite shock troops of their 'army'. The proven willingness of prisoners to starve themselves to death rather than bow the knee to changes of regime equating them to ordinary criminals had done as much to energise the wider republican movement as the 'blood sacrifices' after the Easter Rising of 1916 had done for their predecessors. Many of the political leadership had themselves served prison sentences, and indeed the scary sight of the cold and ruthless countenance of Gerry Kelly within the inner councils of Sinn Fein left one sceptical about the real degree of distancing between 'politicians' and 'soldiers'. It was clear over many years that the republican political leadership, in determining on any new course, would want to sound out and weigh carefully the views of their comrades in prison.

In wider community terms, this was not a unilateral issue. With the decision by Ian Paisley's DUP not to involve itself in the negotiating process, David Trimble and his followers could look for support of wider unionist political interest only to the conference representatives of fringe unionist parties closely linked with Protestant paramilitarism.

It goes without saying, then, that the potential release of 'political prisoners' was bound to be an element in any successful negotiation. But this was an issue on which the United Kingdom Government would be in pole position. The Secretary of State for Northern Ireland was responsible for the prison and criminal justice system, and would for the time being remain so in the event of devolution being enabled by agreement. In these circumstances, it remains incomprehensible to me that the United Kingdom Government did not insist upon some direct link between the release of prisoners and the decommissioning of weaponry. A reasonably substantial first tranche of releases could have been offered as an act of faith and a gesture of goodwill. As clear and verifiable evidence emerged of a credible movement towards completion of the process within the envisaged two-year timetable, further releases could have been authorised *pari passu*. In practice, no collective obligation was imposed upon the sponsoring organisations concerned with particular groups of prisoners other than that they should 'remain on ceasefire'. Over time it was to emerge with horrible clarity that, as long as an organisation did not attempt to assassinate members of the security forces or devastate towns or villages with massive bombs, it could continue to act as a criminal mafia, terrorise and dominate entire communities, eliminate rivals, threaten and bully political moderates for 'offences', such as cooperation with the police; and offer a continuing implicit threat to democratic institutions. While an individual under the terms of his release could be returned to prison if involved in further offences, this did not prevent notorious ex-prisoners from appearing as a menacing presence at conspicuous flashpoints.

As the negotiations leading to the Belfast Agreement were in progress contemporaneously with my work as Victims Commissioner, I became acutely aware of how disconcerting, uncomfortable and in many cases nauseating it would be for bereaved and survivors to contemplate the return to their communities of people lawfully sentenced to imprisonment for crimes which had led to the grievous injury of themselves or close relatives or to the murder of those close to them. Nevertheless, not a few were prepared to accept an initiative on this front provided it was a genuine contribution to peace and stability. Yet as releases got under way, even those prepared to tolerate the unpalatable were in many cases appalled by what they saw on their television screens, as murderers swaggered free without any pretence of remorse, to be greeted with a clamorous welcome from hard-faced confederates at the prison gates, or received at meetings held by supposedly democratic and peaceful parties in an atmosphere of belligerent triumphalism.

The remission system in Northern Ireland prior to these releases was already generous, but people could not fail to note that while terrorist murderers gained conditional freedom, prisoners convicted of similar crimes for reasons of greed or passion stayed behind bars.

Of course the idea of phased and conditional releases prompts some inevitable questions. How should priorities for release be determined? And would not insistence on phasing tied to conditions have proved a 'deal-breaker'? In answer to the first question, I believe priority could and should have been based on considerations of the gravity of the offence and the time already served under the sentence imposed by the court. As everyone knows, a so-called 'life sentence' seldom means in practice imprisonment for life, and consideration can be given to review after a specific period. At the time of the Agreement, the prison population included prisoners who had already served a substantial number of years of imprisonment. It seemed odious that someone 'lucky' enough to have been convicted a relatively short time before the Agreement should serve an exiguously modest term for the heinous crime of murdering one or more people. Thus an initial tranche might have accorded priority for release both to people who had received long sentences but already served very substantial terms, and to those convicted for less serious offences such as the simple membership of a proscribed organisation.

A tougher line on the issue of prisoner releases might indeed have been a 'deal-breaker'. But if the United Kingdom Government had been as tough-minded and resolute as the republican negotiators, it could have presented a stark choice between a phased and conditional release process and the continuing detention of large numbers of paramilitary prisoners until completion of the sentences imposed upon them. Unhappily the United Kingdom negotiators showed that inherent irresolution which was to be shown later when appalling behaviour was deplored but not regarded as a breach of the 'ceasefire'.

Then there is the question of the Royal Ulster Constabulary. There was substantial common ground on the need for reform in policing arrange-ments. Whatever the historic reasons for it, the Protestant preponderance in the ranks of the RUC persuaded even moderate Catholics and nationalists that the force could not be trusted to take an even-handed approach. As for the republicans, both political and paramilitary, they saw the RUC as part of an enemy alliance seeking, alongside the Army, to defeat them. 'Loyalism', too, regarded effective policing as an impediment to their corrupt and brutal dominance of working-class Protestant communities. A long time had passed since the Hunt Report had promoted the paradigm of a civilianised and normally unarmed force; an ideal soon reduced to ashes in the crucible of persistent violence. The RUC itself had already begun an internal process of review and reform to make the force more fit for purpose in the future conditions likely to confront it.

Policing was to prove too complex and controversial a matter to be resolved within the timescale of the Belfast Agreement, and it was therefore remitted to a Commission headed by Chris Patten, one-time junior Minister at the Northern Ireland Office and later the last Governor of Hong Kong. There it had fallen to him to draw a line under systems and institutions which had done the citizens of the island and its territories some service. The Patten Commission approached its remit with energy and thoroughness, seeking evidence from far and wide across the community and holding well-attended meetings to listen to local views. Patten's colleagues included such able and perceptive people as Maurice Hayes, an amazing and inventive polymath. However, the outcome of any committee or commission of inquiry is inevi-tably to some extent predetermined by the choice of membership. Some have argued that the body did not include adequate or proportional repre-sentation of the view that, whatever its faults and failings, the RUC had served the community bravely over many years, sustaining numerous deaths and injuries in the process, and had maintained through difficult times a high morale and *esprit de corps*.

The Patten Report, when completed, was a complex document making a great many recommendations for the future. In particular it proposed special measures to deal with Catholic under-representation, a very substantial reduction in numbers both to 'leave room' for a better balance and to reflect more peaceful conditions, and a deeply symbolic replacement of the RUC by a new police service for Northern Ireland.

What was so extraordinary was not the nature of the Report itself, but the reactions to it. I reflected upon some well-remembered lines from Shakespeare's *The Merchant of Venice*:

> As who would say, 'I am Sir Oracle,
> And when I ope my lips let no dog bark.'

I had always thought it the role of committees or commissions of inquiry to make recommendations to Government, with its subsequent response open to scrutiny and possible amendment in Parliament, rather than to instruct the Government what to do. Yet when a Northern Ireland Office Minister showed any disposition to query or differ from Patten, there fell upon him from nationalist quarters (whether SDLP or Sinn Fein) extravagant denunciation. Peter Mandelson in particular incurred a high degree of wrath and odium, and since he has become such a hate-figure in so many quarters, it deserves to be said that, of all recent Secretaries of State for Northern Ireland, he sought to hold the best and fairest balance between the competing claims of nationalism and unionism.

The outcome of all of this was the easement into premature retirement of some of the RUC's most senior and experienced officers, an overall reduction in numbers towards a 'peacetime' level in a community still facing paramilitary mafias and sectarian animosity, and the consignment to the dustbin of a name and title rooted in history, carved on all too many gravestones, and cherished by people who had served us all, often in conditions of great and prolonged danger. This was, after all, the force which, in loyal support of Government in facing up to adverse reactions to the 1985 Agreement, had seen many of its members uprooted from their homes. I fear that the award of a near-posthumous George Cross to the expiring RUC was widely seen as a cynical gesture.

However, Sir Hugh Orde has provided a vigorous command of the successor PSNI (Police Service of Northern Ireland). He has given it robust and intelligent leadership in challenging times. In spite of the prolonged failure of Sinn Fein to support or participate in the new policing arrangements, the provisions for recruitment and the support and encouragement of the SDLP and the Roman Catholic hierarchy have led to a significant improvement in the sectarian balance of the force. Moreover, the modern PSNI must operate in an environment of unremitting scrutiny and supervision. The complex arrangements for accountability may at times seem oppressive, but there can be no justification or excuse for past misdeeds identified by the Police Ombudsman and no opportunity to repeat them. That said, while a minority of officers certainly behaved deplorably during perilous times, most RUC men and women served with honour and many suffered and died to protect us.

Let us, then, summarise the actions or inactions of successive United Kingdom Governments as they bear upon the contemporary state of affairs in Northern Ireland. Ireland as a whole might, just might, have reconciled itself to some form of continuing partnership with England, Scotland and Wales if the Act of Union had coincided with Catholic Emancipation. Its belated concession, the feeble reaction of British authorities to the Famine and a tardy approach to land reform fed a developing sense of alienation amongst the Catholic community in particular and promoted support for military action amongst the Irish diaspora. At sensitive moments the readiness of the Conservative Party to play 'the Orange card' encouraged in much of Ulster a growing resistance to government by an Irish Parliament, even one operating not as an autonomous entity but as a devolved legislature remaining under a United Kingdom umbrella. When even a Liberal Administration, representing that section of British opinion best disposed to Irish aspirations, failed to respond decisively to moves towards armed Ulster unionist resistance there was a loss of faith across much of Ireland in 'England's' willingness to take firm and decisive action. Yet, on the outbreak of war in August 1914 Irish democratic parliamentarism was still alive and well, and a great many Irishmen fought the war as volunteers in British uniform. Then came the Easter Rising of 1916. In one way it is easy to understand the sense of outrage felt by a nation struggling for survival in the worst of all wars when confronted by rebellion within its own jurisdiction. Nevertheless, the executioners effectively made martyrs of the leaders of the Rising and brought about a growing resistance in most of Ireland to any settlement involving continuing subordination to British power. Since the unionists would have opposed their submergence even in a devolved but united Ireland, it was inevitable that they would obdurately resist incorporation into the Free State emerging from the Treaty.

With Northern Ireland alone accepting and operating under the Government of Ireland Act 1920, a crucial issue would be the nature of the relationship between the national and sovereign institutions in London and the devolved institutions in Belfast. This was, of course, an entirely new scenario for the national politicians. Although the British possessions overseas were making the long journey from colonialisation, through burgeoning self-government towards Dominion and later Commonwealth status, it was a complete novelty to be dealing with entities termed a government and a Parliament in a part of what nevertheless remained a United Kingdom. As Britain did not possess a written constitution, important elements of its political and constitutional life rested upon convention, rather than upon a statute law which itself was not entrenched but amendable. On the face of the 1920 Act, the British Government possessed all the means necessary to ensure that its citizens in Northern Ireland would enjoy no lower standards of justice and democracy than their fellow-citizens in other parts of the islands. Section 75 of the Act, preserving as it did the supreme authority of the United Kingdom Parliament over all persons, matters and things in Northern Ireland, afforded the opportunity to legislate at any time in areas where the Parliament of Northern Ireland had been empowered to make laws, or to withdraw, amend or override those powers. Moreover, successive Northern Ireland Governments were to find it impossible to meet the reasonable needs of their population, let alone aspire to true parity of outcomes, without the availability from the Exchequer of funding in excess of the taxable capacity of Northern Ireland.

While I have discussed the degree of culpability of successive Northern Ireland Governments for the slide into conflict, I have sought to show that the degree of injustice and discrimination experienced by the Catholic and nationalist minority was on occasions exaggerated, and that nationalism itself was far from guiltless in the creation of a divided and mutually antipathetic society. Yet there were clearly identifiable occasions on which Unionist Governments – in terms of voting systems, manipulation of electoral boundaries, toleration of discrimination in housing allocations, blindness to the threatening character of sectarian police auxiliaries and other issues – could be seen to behave in a discriminatory way liable to produce resentment and the potential for a revolt amongst those adversely affected.

How much did British Governments know about this, and why, to the extent that they did know, did they not dip into the deep reservoir of their potential powers until very late in the day? There was, I think, a relieved sense in the early 1920s of 'Thank God, that's Ireland out of the way'. The settlement in Ireland, with the Irish Free State and Northern Ireland coexisting uneasily, might not be perfect, but if it were to be unpicked, what could be put in its place? If Sir James Craig and his colleagues were pressed too hard, might they not throw in their chips and leave the British Government to play again the tedious Irish game which had earlier occupied so much of the time and energies of British Parliaments and Governments? With a radio-borne

BBC still mired in an establishment complacency and with television yet to burst upon the scene, the electorate in Great Britain was not often troubled by forensic examinations of Northern Ireland policy or graphic pictures of its consequences. The television film of Gerry Fitt's batoned and bloody head, screened around the world, would have a thousand times more impact than the finest written journalism. With many other preoccupations in the inter-war period, successive London Governments did relatively little to keep themselves well informed about developments in Northern Ireland. Visits by senior British politicians were rare, and at official level responsibility for relations with Northern Ireland was tucked away in an inconspicuous corner of the Home Office. To the extent that United Kingdom Governments 'leaned' upon their Northern Ireland counterparts, it was largely at the behest of the Treasury in pressing Northern Ireland to reduce its reliance on subvention and increase its domestic contribution towards the cost of its own services.

At the end of the Second World War, the return of a Labour Government, with a traditionally favourable attitude towards the ending of partition, and with many Irish adherents resident in Great Britain, might have been expected to lead to a more distanced relationship between Stormont and Westminster. However, the attitudes of such as Clement Attlee, Herbert Morrison and Ernest Bevin had been much influenced by the experiences of the war, and the contrast between Northern Ireland's constructive involvement (albeit inevitably as part of the United Kingdom) and the neutrality of the Irish Free State.

So evident and so enduring was the convention (for it was no more) of non-intervention in spheres of activity devolved to Northern Ireland that it encouraged such local politicians as Bill Craig to believe that this stance was irreversible. Yet the ice of self-imposed restraint melted very rapidly when the graphic reporting of events by modern media, reinforced by the determination of sympathetic back-benchers to confront the policy of detachment, caused the Wilson Government to take a new direction. The subsequent involvement of James Callaghan as Home Secretary showed all too clearly what might have been done, and in my view ought to have been done, long before community relations in Northern Ireland had reached a condition of outright crisis. At this late stage we were to see at last all the potential mechanisms previously unused and neglected brought into play. A 'listening post' was established under the direction of Oliver Wright (to be succeeded later by Ronnie Burroughs and Howard Smith), the need for urgent change was forcefully impressed upon Northern Ireland leaders by the Labour Cabinet, and James Callaghan inexorably pressed, cajoled and bullied Northern Ireland Ministers behind the scenes to accept reforms which they could present as their own.

So a United Kingdom Government had at last acknowledged and lived up to its ultimate responsibilities in Northern Ireland. Unfortunately the mechanism of a credible Stormont Government was irretrievably undermined by the introduction of the Army as the primary agent of public order and the designation of the GOC (Northern Ireland) as the director of all security operations, whether conducted by soldiers or police. It would have been far better to introduce direct rule at that point rather than allow the authority and credibility of the Stormont Government under James Chichester-Clark to rot away, as his electorate looked to him for a restoration of order clearly beyond his powers. Thus it was that when the unionist politician with the best potential for leadership, Brian Faulkner, inherited the premiership, he mounted the bridge of a ship already taking on water, and was unable to discover any potential remedy other than the desperate gamble of internment. The release of contemporary Cabinet papers reveals that direct rule was not ruled out at the time of Army involvement, but that there was real concern as to whether the Northern Ireland Civil Service would remain loyal to authority in the event of direct rule. Such fears illustrated the lack of real 'feel', based on deep knowledge and involvement, for the local situation. There was also a more realistic fear expressed, relevant to the introduction of direct rule at any time, that it could prove a great deal easier to get into the situation than to get out of it again.

We then turn to the impact of the Heath Government. In the aftermath of his death at a great age, commentators have dealt at length with his personality and record. His Government's handling of the Northern Ireland crisis would represent a significant part of that record. Here the key political personalities would be Heath himself, William Whitelaw, Peter Carrington and Francis Pym. I was myself to see Heath in a number of different circumstances and settings. Accompanying Terence O'Neill, by then very close to the end of his tether, to discussions with the then Leader of the Opposition at his 'set' in Albany, I had admired the good taste of his surroundings and, in his splendid grand piano, the evidence of a cultural hinterland beyond the imaginings of his politically monomaniac successor in the Tory leadership. As a dispirited O'Neill retired to use what Americans term 'the facilities', I recall that Heath took me to one side and urged me to persuade him to stick to his task. Thereafter, as we walked together along the 'rope-walk', O'Neill for some obscure and rather embarrassing reason chose to tell Heath that I had obtained fourth place in the United Kingdom in the 1952 examinations for entry to the Administrative Class of the Civil Service. Heath observed, 'Oh, in my time I came first.'

Accompanying Chichester-Clark and Faulkner to difficult and tricky meetings at Downing Street, I could see that Heath's senior colleagues were in some awe of him, and likely to remain silent unless and until invited by the Prime Minister to speak. Indeed, when Heath paid a visit to Northern Ireland after the introduction of direct rule, I had a distinct impression that Secretary of State Whitelaw, normally pretty ebullient, was rather dreading the occasion and was distinctly relieved when it was safely over.

For myself, I believe that Heath was right to introduce direct rule when he did. Personally I had greatly admired Brian Faulkner's courage, willingness and ability to push his rather reluctant party in the direction of reform as far and as fast as possible, and indeed it is extremely doubtful if anyone else could have brought it so far. But it was never going to be enough to reactivate dialogue between the communities after the failure of internment, the calamitous reaction to 'Bloody Sunday' in Derry and the refusal of the SDLP to re-engage within the Stormont arena.

William Whitelaw's relatively short but extremely eventful and significant tenure as the first Secretary of State for Northern Ireland was characterised by success at the level of human relations (an area in which his Prime Minister, so adept at the piano, was tone-deaf), by a highly risky encounter with the republican leaders, by the decision to reintroduce proportional representation, and by a gross error in dealing with terrorist prisoners, which was to lead to tragic results for his successors in office and the whole community.

At the human level, Whitelaw was a figure of engaging bonhomie and a natural conciliator. While the Northern Ireland Civil Service could easily have felt neglected and discredited on the introduction of direct rule, Whitelaw and his sardonic but far-sighted Permanent Secretary Sir William Nield sought to engage senior members of that service in constructive thinking about the future. He showed consummate political skill in drawing the UUP, SDLP and Alliance Party into negotiations, and producing from those negotiations a conditional settlement pending the involvement of the Irish at the Sunningdale Conference in late 1973. He took a major risk in inviting IRA representatives to participate in clandestine (and in the event) fruitless negotiations in London, but his subsequent disclosure of this initiative averted the degree of adverse reaction which would certainly have occurred if prolonged efforts had been made to conceal a meeting which, in the contemporary circumstances, was bound to 'leak' at some stage from one source or another. The gross error was, of course, the fateful decision to grant 'political' status to paramilitary prisoners convicted of terrorist offences, which led to the establishment of the compound system at the Maze Prison as a university of terrorism, and carried the inherent threat or even likelihood of a disastrous counter-reaction if and when these unwise privileges were withdrawn or watered down.

The lack of firmness and consistency on the part of successive British Governments in coping with Irish terrorism has too often flowed from an exaggerated apprehension about the consequences of resolute action. For some time after the introduction of direct rule and the arrival of Whitelaw, resolute action by the Army to reduce the 'no-go' barricaded areas of Derry was regarded as unthinkably hazardous and provocative. After the horrors of the Bloody Friday atrocities in Belfast, Carrington as Defence Secretary was still inclined to advise a 'steady as she goes' line. Whitelaw, who at a memorable meeting almost levitated with rage, would have none of it. The deemed impossible became the urgent imperative. Operation Motorman was planned and set in hand, and achieved all its objectives without any sign of the apocalyptic bloodbath forecast by some of the pessimists. Of course the 'smack of firm government' does not always or necessarily succeed; unpredictable alternation between firmness and concession hardly ever does.

It is my judgement that the inter-party and inter-governmental negotiations of 1973 represented the best (and indeed last) hope to forge a constructive alliance between the moderate constitutional and democratic parties then commanding together substantial majority support. Since the collapse of the power-sharing Executive in May 1974, it has not infrequently been argued that, whatever the provision for an 'Irish dimension', substantial elements of the population were strongly averse to the presence in Government of any party seeking to advance towards a united Ireland, albeit by peaceful and democratic means. In the nature of things, one cannot be sure that opposition on these grounds alone would have failed to bring down the settlement. In the talks he chaired at Stormont Castle, concerned at this stage solely with the arrangements for internal government, Whitelaw recognised the sensitivity of this aspect by accepting that a unionist, Brian Faulkner, must head any Executive and be able to command a voting majority within it, in spite of his limited and vulnerable support within the wider unionist community. Whitelaw could more readily accept this since in reality an Executive so composed would have to swim or sink together. If either major party, as a consequence of being outvoted on a matter of substance, felt it could not continue in office, the statutory power-sharing requirement could no longer be met and the entire devolved structure would collapse.

It needs to be remembered that it was in this first phase of the 1973 talks, the inter-party discussions which Whitelaw chaired at Stormont Castle, that Faulkner was pressed to concede the principle of a Council of Ireland with some degree of executive power. The idea of some such council had already been included by Faulkner himself in his 'last gasp' proposals to divert direct rule, but all of us involved at the time in the preparation of those proposals had envisaged a council confined, at any rate in the first instance, to a purely consultative role. The significance of this concession I shall explore and underline later.

In the extensive coverage of the period following the death of Edward Heath, one is reminded of the sense of growing crisis then pervading the Conservative Government as it faced union militancy and its adverse effect upon the economy. These developments resulted in an illustration, by no means unique and perhaps not at all surprising, that the interests of Northern Ireland would always be subordinated to what the Government of the day perceived to be the wider national interest. No one was then in a position to weigh in the scales the wider damage which would be caused to British interests, and not just to their citizens in Northern Ireland, by the extent of the death and disorder which would persist over three decades. The removal of William Whitelaw from the Northern Ireland scene at this particularly crucial moment, with the edifice of agreement at Stormont Castle lacking the coping stone of the Sunningdale Conference to which the Irish Government would be a party, can be explained but not excused. Whitelaw had earlier proved a skilled and diplomatic manager of parliamentary business as Leader of the House and his successful conduct of the Stormont Castle talks had highlighted his gifts as a conciliator. It is hard to believe, however, that the ranks of Heath's Cabinet included no one else capable of filling credibly the office of Employment Secretary, and by his untimely removal Heath had deprived the British team at Sunningdale of the man who had won widespread confidence and even affection in Northern Ireland (other than in the ranks of the DUP and Sinn Fein), and who had great political 'feel' and judgement, based on his shrewd assessment of how far any of the participating parties could give without disintegrating.

Thus it was not to be William Whitelaw, but his successor as Secretary of State for Northern Ireland, Francis Pym, who accompanied Heath to the crucial conference at Sunningdale. Personally likeable and decent, but neither impressive nor charismatic, the unfortunate Pym was to be plunged into the Sunningdale maelstrom without any opportunity to explore the terrain of Northern Ireland's complex politics. The inevitable consequence was that the leading figures on the British side would be the Prime Minister and Sir Frank Cooper, who had succeeded Sir William Neild as Permanent Secretary at the Northern Ireland Office. Cooper was shrewd, able and forceful; Heath driven by ineffable self-confidence and a not always well-disguised degree of contempt for the Ulster Unionists as the kind of limited provincials unlikely to share his gleaming vision of a broad and radiant new Europe. There could be little doubt that in the course of the conference Faulkner and his colleagues were to feel increasingly beleaguered. It became clear to Faulkner, a man who relished office and executive power, and for the best of reasons, that he could either do his best to sell the flawed product on offer, or expect endless denunciation as the leader who lacked the courage and stature to make a great if risky leap forward. It is a sobering thought that in attempting to make such a leap several unionist leaders were to find themselves broken at the bottom of a chasm.

In a balanced agreement, every party would hope to make some gains and expect some losses. At Sunningdale, the Irish Government was allowed to give little and gain a great deal. There was to be no 'give' on what was widely regarded as a territorial claim to Northern Ireland inherent in the provisions of the Irish Constitution. The fudged and ambiguous formulations of the Agreement, when exposed to the processes of Irish law, proved to have no value. The vexed question of fugitive offenders and cross-Border justice was kicked into touch. Decisions about a Council of Ireland pointed to a growing harmonisation and integration of programmes and services. I find it hard to believe that Whitelaw, with his acute political skills and accumulated knowledge of Northern Ireland and its politics, would not have warned Heath of the great danger that these new structures could prove too frail to support the weight placed upon them.

To summarise Edward Heath's contribution to the history of Northern Ireland: he was almost certainly right to impose direct rule when he did, although this might have been done with greater advantage by his Labour predecessors; Faulkner had squeezed out of his Cabinet and Party the most extensive and radical proposals ever made or likely to be made by a unionist Prime Minister. Something had to be done to bring constitutional nationalism back into the political arena. It is, however, deeply ironic that the events persuading in particular John Hume, or affording him the opportunity he had sought to disengage from the Stormont Parliament, were almost entirely under the United Kingdom rather than the Northern Ireland jurisdiction. The shootings in Derry on Bloody Sunday, whether justified or not, had been carried out by soldiers responsible not to Stormont but to the Ministry of Defence and the British Government. The use of unacceptable techniques in the aftermath of internment had developed out of British experience in other conflicts overseas. Whatever the current and enormously expensive Tribunal may find, the deaths on Bloody Sunday were attributable to men under military rather than police command, and the very limited timescale afforded to the subsequent rushed inquiry indicated the determination of the United Kingdom Government to dispose of the matter, a most vain hope. The choice of William Whitelaw as the first Secretary of State for Northern Ireland was well judged. But developments on or after Sunningdale were to squander his inheritance. Faulkner was pressed too hard and Cosgrave dealt the easier hand to play. While Whitelaw tended to defer to

Heath (as he was later to do to Thatcher), it is hard to believe that he would have allowed so unbalanced a settlement to be shaped without reference to the realities of Northern Ireland politics. The replacement of Faulkner as leader of the UUP must have registered even with the most insensitive the fragility of the Sunningdale settlement. There is, however, no reason to believe that when Heath called his 'Who governs Britain?' General Election in 1974 the impact in Northern Ireland ranked high, if indeed it featured at all, amongst his considerations. The results of that election in Northern Ireland, with the power-sharing Executive having had no time or opportunity to deliver positive results, left Faulkner, Fitt, Napier and their colleagues in a most precarious position.

If it is my view, as indeed it is, that the Executive might well have collapsed in any event, why do I feel so strongly about the utter and abject failure of Wilson's Labour Government to support it? Internal strains and divisions within the Executive were already obvious. Paddy Devlin had a letter of resignation to hand; Roy Bradford was proving an unreliable ally to Faulkner; the SDLP Assembly party found it difficult to accept the need of their Executive members to compromise; and the outcome of the General Election showed all too clearly that the Executive had lost the support of the electorate.

I base my view upon the fundamental distinction between means and ends. Thus I regard it as perfectly legitimate to pursue the end of Irish unity by wholly peaceful and democratic means, but totally unacceptable to pursue that same end through violence, intimidation and criminal activity. Similarly I regard it as perfectly legitimate to bring the sentiments of the electorate to bear on a governing administration by wholly acceptable methods. If an administration is for a prolonged period wholly out of touch with the mood of its supporters in the country, one can expect – as constituents bring the pressure of their opinions to bear upon those who represent them – initiatives to reverse policy, defections from parties and other developments which may provoke resignations or a General Election. What is totally unacceptable is to reinforce political arguments with paramilitary muscle, to subvert and replace established authority, to move beyond appeals for support to demands for it, interfering in that process with the right of individuals in a democracy to make up their own minds and, if that is their wish, to go about their lawful occasions.

The utterly supine reaction of the Wilson Government to the UWC strike of 1974 had malign consequences extending well beyond the premature collapse of the power-sharing Executive. It discouraged future Unionist leaders, until the arrival on the scene of David Trimble, from taking any political risks to promote a definitive settlement. The extraordinarily ill-judged 'spongers' speech made by Harold Wilson towards the end of the strike spread scepticism amongst even the most moderate elements of the unionist community about the degree of sympathy they could expect from a British Government. Nationalists drew a different conclusion: that in the last resort they could not rely on 'the Brits' to stand up for them.

Overall, in addressing the degree of wider United Kingdom responsibility for the violence in Northern Ireland and the degradation of its politics, I would point to a lack of firmness in recognising and addressing the legitimate grievances of substantial numbers of people under their ultimate jurisdiction, succeeded by an ambiguous reaction to the subsequent violence, which has led ultimately to the disastrous radicalisation of Northern Ireland politics.

On the other hand, decisive intervention (occurring as it did fatally late in the day) would not have been necessary if Northern Ireland politicians had found a way of working harmoniously together in the public interest. The morbid defensiveness of the first generation of Northern Ireland Ministers can perhaps be explained, if not wholly excused, by the circumstances in which authority was devolved to them. The trouble was that not only was the same party successively returned to power, but also much the same senior personnel, led by Craigavon, continued to dominate the scene for the best part of two decades. They carried with them into the 1930s and 1940s a mindset shaped by earlier nationalist abstentionism, refusal on the part of many of the minority to accept the 1920 settlement even as a staging post, and the wholly negative attitude of nationalist politicians once they had entered the Stormont Parliament.

The accession of Basil Brooke to the premiership could have opened a new era. He had proved a pragmatic Minister, he had – despite his aristocratic background and manners – an extraordinary rapport with the ordinary unionist voter, and he was sufficient of a realist to accept the translation into Northern Ireland of the 'welfare state' reforms of the post-war Labour Government. But he was also a son of the borderland of County Fermanagh, forever influenced in his attitudes by the disorderly times of the 1920s when he had seen the B Special Constabulary as a last line of defence against a threatening nationalism. Such a man was never likely to overturn the established order by some grand reversal of policy; but it would have been possible for him, I would argue, to advance cautiously and step by step to a more equitable situation. In the event, under his rather passive leadership individual Ministers, such as Hall-Thompson, were not positively prevented from proposing some modest reforms; nor, on the other hand, could they rely upon the backing of their Prime Minister when facing an inevitable backlash from party backwoodsmen.

Of his successor, Terence O'Neill, I write with the diffidence of one who was a member of his 'court' and who drafted most of his significant speeches and statements, and must therefore accept a share of the blame for an ultimately unsuccessful premiership. His air of patronising haughtiness, his shy diffidence and lack of conviviality and his reluctance to till the ground before planting the seeds of reform all led to the eventual failure. His attitude to reform in Northern Ireland was emotional rather than strategic. He loved meeting Lyndon Johnson at the White House, exchanging banalities with Willy Brandt in Bonn, or reading some article headed by his name in the columns of *The Times*. Unhappily those who would determine his fate were not to be found in the White House, in the chanceries of Europe or in the editorial sanctums of Fleet Street, but in little Orange Halls in the backwoods of Antrim or Down or Fermanagh.

Writing this not long after the death of Sir Edward Heath, I see some similarities between two rather shy and lonely figures who did not find it easy to convert colleagues into friends. It is ironical that O'Neill's closest friend in the political world was the Ulster Unionist MP Robin Chichester-Clark, whose brother James's resignation was to precipitate O'Neill's fall and his own rather reluctant succession to the premiership. Above all else, O'Neill needed an ally who would complement his own positive qualities, which included the ability to create an impression of civilised and caring leadership in Great Britain and further afield. The ideal partner would have been the determined, able and articulate Brian Faulkner, much more identifiably a solid Ulster figure than the patrician product of Shane's Castle, Eton and the Irish Guards. At the time, perhaps inevitably, I shared to some degree O'Neill's rather paranoid notion that Faulkner was continually conspiring against him. Finding myself working later with a somewhat demonised figure, I came to have a very high regard for him, even though – while not shy in the same sense as O'Neill – he was a very private man. For whatever reasons the two men were never close, and the opportunity of presenting a formidable dual leadership was missed.

One can, however, attribute too much importance to the character and behaviour of individuals rather than the nature of the party they struggled to lead. Ill-disciplined, ill-organised, in reality more a series of local 'cells' rather than a centralised party, and heavily influenced by the presbyterian priority of individual conscience over central direction, the UUP proved over many years almost impossible to lead. Its extraordinary and creaking constitution incorporated influential voting rights within its supreme body for the Orange Order, many of whose individual members were in time to cast their individual votes for the party's rivals. The UUP has a melancholy history of reluctant and belated willingness to offer conformist concessions, which might have made a difference if offered earlier and in a less grudging spirit. What an irony it is that those leaders who were later prepared to take the risk of sharing office with Sinn Fein, David Trimble and Reg Empey, were to the fore in sinking the much less radical initiative of 1973–74!

O'Neill's successor, James Chichester-Clark, has been much under-estimated and denigrated by history. Admittedly he had the incentive of unrelenting pressure from James Callaghan to press ahead with some significant reforms, but in an exemplary alliance with Faulkner these were brought into force with exemplary efficiency and vigour. The Northern Ireland Housing Executive, for example, was to prove a huge success, not only in steadily improving the condition of the housing stock, but also in eliminating from the list of grievances real or perceived discrimination in the allocation of public housing. Nevertheless, this was a period when the authority of the Stormont Government – not always wisely exercised but hitherto largely unchallenged – began to disintegrate in the face of that Government's inability to maintain public order through forces under its own control.

When Chichester-Clark, tired and disillusioned, retired from the scene the premiership was at last assumed by Brian Faulkner. Outside the law and order area, his record in ministerial office was one of which he could be proud. His proposals to engage the Opposition in a more constructive way, and a readiness to accept within his Cabinet colleagues prepared to live with the de facto constitutional position and to participate in some form of collaborative association with the Republic: these and other initiatives represented the outer limit of what could be conceded without shattering his political base into pieces. As against this one must set the ultimate failure and malign consequences of internment. By then, the unfortunate Prime Minister was in a 'heads you win, tails I lose' situation. He could not realistically steer an untroubled route through the prevalent mayhem while assuring critics that nothing more could be done, and this unhappy predicament eased him towards the only major public order strategy as yet untried.

When, following the failure of internment and the tragedy of Bloody Sunday, the Heath Government decided that there should be a 'discontinuity' through the suspension of the Northern Ireland Parliament, Faulkner deserved real credit for his responsible, albeit inevitably resentful, approach. With Northern Ireland by then heavily dependent upon the Army for as much public order as could be maintained, Faulkner realised that it would be neither sensible nor responsible to lead his supporters into dissidence, in spite of the belligerent fulminations of other unionists inside and outside his party. His approach to the subsequent negotiations with Whitelaw and other participating parties was also responsible and constructive. He could point to an Assembly election giving him a reasonable mandate to negotiate, but this did not necessarily mean that he could carry all his erstwhile supporters into acceptance of any terms actually negotiated. Even at the time, one heard some arguments that he would be wise to seek support for the negotiated terms by referendum; later experience after the Belfast Agreement illustrates that support for underlying principles does not necessarily survive a failure to follow up those principles in effective practice. In the event, Faulkner's loss of the Unionist Party leadership, followed by the disastrous results achieved by himself and his allies at the Westminster elections of 1974, showed that he had been pressed to concede too much.

Faulkner's successors in the leadership of the UUP, Harry West and James Molyneaux, were above all careful not to rock the party boat. While West was only briefly an MP, and primarily a product of the Stormont system, Molyneaux was very much a House of Commons man, greatly under the influence of the spellbinding if manic Enoch Powell and unenthusiastic about any return to devolution other than under terms which had become unrealisable and even inconceivable.

Much has now been written about the enigmatic and faintly tragic figure of David Trimble. The history of that great American institution, the Supreme Court, reveals a number of occasions on which a President, making a nomination designed to swing the Court in a conservative direction, has found the performance of his nominee not quite what he had expected. Trimble's emergence as party leader ahead of the favourite John Taylor has been widely attributed to the assumption that his demonstrative support for Orange protests at Drumcree in Portadown promised a strict adherence to the hardest line of political unionism. Taylor's deserved reputation as a political weathervane may also have been a factor, although it must also be said that, in the aftermath of an attempted assassination and very serious injuries in 1973, he had shown himself to be a person of great personal courage and resilience.

In the famous review *Beyond the Fringe*, the incomparable Alan Bennett, in a wonderful parody of an orotund preacher, speaks to the text: 'My brother Esau is an hairy man, and I am a smooth man'. No one could characterise David Trimble as a smooth man. Testy, choleric and socially insecure, Trimble nevertheless brought to his position considerable reserves of political courage and self-belief. An academic lawyer by background, his speeches would be carefully argued but lacking in human warmth. Yet it was the Vanguard supporter of 1973–74 and the flamboyant loyalist of Drumcree who was to commit his party to the historic but perilous Belfast Agreement. This involved from the outset enormous political risks. He had a small nucleus of trusted and reliable colleagues – in particular Ken Maginnis and Reg Empey – but one always felt that John Taylor lifted his finger, like a golfer approaching a difficult green, to see which way the wind was blowing; while the ambitious and articulate Jeffrey Donaldson was to defect from his party's negotiating team at a critical moment.

In the days when the Department of Economic Development was the main shareholder in Short Brothers, the Belfast aeroplane manufacturer (since privatised under the ownership of Bombardier of Canada), I was presented by the company's Chief Executive, Sir Philip Foreman, with a copy of a book about the aviation industry entitled *The Sporty Game*. I learned from this that a 'sporty' proposition in this industry would be the launch of a major project which, if it did not realise its objectives, could prejudice the entire net worth of the sponsoring company. In that sense, Trimble's commitment to the Belfast Agreement was exceptionally 'sporty'.

The Agreement itself, I have earlier argued, was full of ambiguities and deliberate vaguenesses or omissions. The Prime Minister, Tony Blair, was quick to buttress the Agreement with reassurances; but could they, would they, be honoured in practice? Were they, indeed, capable of being honoured? It is inconceivable that a man with Trimble's legal background should not have scutinised the relative texts with critical care. His 'reward' would be a brief and rocky tenure as First Minister, the solace of a Nobel Peace Prize and appointment to the House of Lords, and the ultimate fragmentation of a political party which had dominated the scene for decades. Sinn Fein would claim that it had never breached the wording of the Agreement, but its dishonouring of its spirit left Trimble out to dry. Perhaps because he himself had fears and reservations from the outset, Trimble failed to sell the merits of the Agreement with any conspicuous enthusiasm. I suspect that, just as Brian Faulkner had done at Sunningdale almost a quarter of a century before, David Trimble took a great leap of faith with a heavy heart and many understandable and well-justified misgivings.

What, then, of the conduct of the other principal parties: the SDLP, the DUP, Sinn Fein and their leaders. In concentrating upon these I do not forget that other and smaller parties have at different times sought to bring a benevolent interest to bear, and occasionally have to a limited extent succeeded. The Alliance Party played a significant role in 1973 and 1974, although I still find it astonishing that its leader at the time, Oliver Napier, did not stand out for an Executive appointment of some real substance. Later the Women's Coalition would offer contributions of robust common sense to the political debate leading up to the Belfast Agreement. There were also the parties linked with 'loyalist' paramilitarism, although it is striking that the electoral support for these parties has always been modest. Only David Ervine made a real impact as the extraordinary reaction to his premature death indicated.

At its inception the SDLP seemed to offer the promising prospect of a moderate, centrist party appealing principally to Catholic voters and favouring the ultimate unity of Ireland, but ready to accept the constitutional status quo as long as this enjoyed majority support and to cooperate with other moderate and centrist interests in the good government of Northern Ireland. The Catholic and nationalist voters needed and deserved better representation than the rancid opposition of people like Eddie McAteer and other smaller groupings or individuals alongside the old-style and old-fashioned Nationalist Party. At its outset, the SDLP presented itself as a local form of 'rainbow coalition', bringing together anti-partitionist zealots like Seamus Mallon and democratic socialists with green edges like Gerry Fitt and Paddy Devlin. In the midst of this, the political role and reputation of John Hume grew and grew like some tall forest tree which can shut off all the sunlight from the places beneath it. Strongly influenced by the local circumstances of his Derry base, Hume's leadership of the SDLP out of the Stormont Parliament made British intervention inevitable, and was no doubt intended to do so. While he showed the qualities of an excellent Minister as a member of the power-sharing Executive in 1974, Hume never subsequently demonstrated much appetite for executive involvement in the government of Northern Ireland. Under his influence the party was to shed Fitt and Devlin, and thereafter to be led by Hume in an autocratic and authoritarian style. He set himself a number of goals which he pursued with great energy, persistence and power of persuasion. He sought to marshal and mobilise the great potential power and influence of Irish America; he deployed huge credibility with successive Irish Governments; and eventually he worked to create a powerful and effective coalition in which Irish-America, the Irish Government, the SDLP and Sinn Fein would work closely together to move towards, if not immediately to, a united Ireland. He regarded his prolonged parleys with the republican leadership as an entirely justified and necessary step to persuade them that, far from advancing the achievement of their goals, the prolongation of the 'armed struggle' was actually impeding it. However, it was clear to everyone that this could only be done by assuring Sinn Fein that, while of course disapproving of its violent means, the SDLP was sympathetic to its ends.

Some would argue that the PIRA ceasefire, followed by belated decommissioning, would never have come about without these efforts. That may indeed be so, but the entire process made more remote the prospect of that wider inter-communal understanding which would underpin real cooperation and a breaking down of barriers in a deeply divided community. I have argued above that David Trimble put the future of his leadership, and indeed his partnership, at risk by testing, if not accepting or assuming, the good faith of Sinn Fein. In a curious parallel, I believe that John Hume put the future of his own party at risk by blurring the previous clear distinction between a wholly constitutional and peaceful party and a political movement deeply routed in violence and criminality. The first sacrifice made in the interest of

Hume's new departure was the loss to Gerry Adams of the Westminster seat which Dr Joe Hendron of the SDLP had bravely fought for and won.

Moreover, Hume's linkage with Adams, following as it did upon Hume's efforts to mobilise the whole of nationalist Ireland in the New Ireland Forum, reinforced the laager mentality of the unionist community, which perceived an unholy alliance of 'green America', the Irish Government, the SDLP and Sinn Fein pressing a compliant British Goverment for ever-growing concessions to their interests and points of view.

It was amazing to witness in time the rapid fading of Irish America's enthusiasm for John Hume as 'the greatest living Irishman'; to see Adams and his cohorts lionised by anti-partitionist politicians and the kind of 'Provo-chic' celebrities who were happy to grace fund-raising dinners and receive with uncritical acclaim the heady rhetoric of the Sinn Fein leadership.

What Northern Ireland needed, before a single person had died in 'the troubles', was a willingness on the part of moderate and constitutional politicians on both sides of the sectarian divide to seek for common ground, to 'park' the constitutional issue as a matter to be determined ultimately by the will of the people, and in the meantime to work constructively and collaboratively together in growing mutual confidence. This would have required leadership of the most inspiring and charismatic kind, since the problem was not so much to identify what was desirable, as to bring the respective communities along in support of it. Perhaps understandably, analysts of the Northern Ireland situation sometimes look to South Africa and the constructive role played there by Nelson Mandela and F.W. de Klerk. There were, however, significant differences between the two situations. South Africa, with its substantial population, had a greater likelihood of throwing up substantial personalities than a small province of the United Kingdom, many of whose ablest sons or daughters would inevitably be attracted to larger opportunities and wider visions elsewhere. In South Africa the ruling oligarchy was greatly outnumbered by the majority community and was faced by extreme external and internal pressure for change. Yet even in tiny Northern Ireland, occasional people of substance and ability were drawn into politics. On the unionist side, one had Terence O'Neill exuding a general tolerant benevolence but insufficiently equipped for party management to move his party far or fast enough; one had Brian Faulkner, making valiant efforts to save a sinking ship but, for all his skills, incapable of carrying sufficient of his community with him; and one had David Trimble, testing the risks of inclusiveness with real courage but a visible lack of warmth.

In some senses John Hume richly deserved his Nobel Peace Prize. At the risk of hazarding the future of his own party, he sought to bring Sinn Fein out of the cold of conflict into the heat of the purely political arena. His advocacy had moved and impressed the Republic of Ireland, member states of the European Union and the United States. He had been the progenitor of a brilliant device to rebut republican insistence that the 'partitionist' institutions in Dublin and Belfast failed to respect or reflect the last vote of all the people of Ireland voting together at the General Election of 1918. This was the idea of parallel referenda north and south in the aftermath of the Belfast Agreement whereby he could point to an endorsement by majorities in both electorates and thus rebut the argument that new arrangements were being imposed upon the people of Ireland.

So it could truly be said that John Hume had done more than anyone to achieve comparative peace. But peace had prevailed through most of the 1960s. Peace alone would never be enough. There had been a time before the outbreak of 'the troubles' when there were some encouraging signs of a growing mutual tolerance between the two communities. As Northern Ireland heard at last in July 2005 that PIRA was bringing the 'armed struggle' to an end, it was a much more divided and embittered place than it had been in the mid-1960s. Discriminatory systems in local government elections, in drawing electoral boundaries, in allocating houses, in choosing people for employment, had come to an end. We had been endowed with a Human Rights Commission, an Ombudsman, a Police Ombudsman, an Equality Commission, an Oversight Commissioner for Policing and regulatory and supervisory bodies almost too numerous to mention. But what was the picture within this gilded framework? Communities in Belfast remained physically separated by formal barriers; insensitivity and intolerance dominated an ongoing debate about the right to parade and protest; the police service found itself in a society that was at one time relatively free of violent crime, coping regularly with intimidation and brutal thuggery.

Those who regard any degree of criticism of John Hume as close to blasphemy would argue that, as the long 'war' drew to its conclusion he had helped to bring it to an end and create the conditions for rebuilding. It remains to be seen whether, in the long run, what has been achieved is a lasting peace or a mere truce. The PIRA statement of July 2005, while encouragingly transparent in some respects, contained some significant ambiguities. While the 'armed struggle' was to be ended, it had been 'entirely justified'. They were 'very mindful of the sacrifices of our patriot dead' while merely 'conscious that many people suffered in the conflict'. Above all, there was no guarantee that their 'army' would disband; it would simply 'put its arms beyond use'. For what purpose, then, would the 'army' remain in being at all, rather than as an echo of Adams' earlier notorious reminder, 'They haven't gone away, you know.'

Let us, though, give the republican movement (or that part of it which has not already defected or may in future defect to irreconcilable elements such as the 'Real' or 'Continuity' IRA) the benefit of the doubt. How well placed are we now to build a stable and harmonious polity? The flip side of Hume's always well-intended efforts has been a flight from the centre and the reinforcement of the extreme wings of nationalist and unionist politics. Unionists too often see Hume as the subtle orchestrator of efforts to push them, by means more efficacious than violence, towards the destination of a united Ireland they do not wish to reach. They observe how John Hume, and his successor Mark Durkan, who developed in his shadow as his principal aide, have bolted shut the door to any devolved government which would not include Sinn Fein. Given the emergence of Sinn Fein as the leading party of nationalism and the second party in the jurisdiction, there is a certain logic in this argument; but the inexorable growth of that party owed not a little to the failure to draw a clear and distinct line between purely constitutional and force-based nationalism. It was the line taken by Hume which left Blair unable to deliver his commitment given during the referendum campaign to exclude from Government elements still associated with violence. On the other side of the community, this inability to deliver to unionists what they had been promised and expected led inevitably to the growing and finally terminal isolation of David Trimble and the swing of unionist opinion towards Ian Paisley and the DUP.

If John Hume's star, once so bright, has faded, one must acknowledge as a phenomenon of our times the endurance, ability and growing success of Ian Paisley and Gerry Adams.

First elected to the Parliament of Northern Ireland as long ago as 1970, Paisley has enjoyed continuous and inexorably growing electoral support as he stood at Stormont, Westminster or European elections. Comfortable middle-class liberals – people much like myself – made initially the gross error of greatly underestimating him. Conventional political oratory – with such striking exceptions as Tony Benn and Enoch Powell – had fallen away. Yet in Northern Ireland, outside the political sphere, there was a long history of support for vociferous and high-volume 'big tent' evangelism. Taking his time, assuring every single word of full emphasis, spicing his rhetoric with withering scorn, scathing humour and apocalyptic imagery, Paisley could be heard distinctly in the back row of the largest arena. People did not always like what he had to say, but many were convinced that he said what he believed. He appealed to the cultural Afrikaanerdom in much of Ulster Protestantism; the feeling that wagons should be drawn around the laager to keep out the forces of error and unbelief. While he clearly intended to lead both his Church and his party as long as he had breath in his body, he had a remarkable ability to attract to his cause people of force and intellectual ability, such as Jim Allister, Nigel Dodds or the efficient, if somewhat scary,

Peter Robinson. Rather like Margaret Thatcher, Paisley had the ability to maintain a front of apparent absolute consistency while bending, from time to time, before the prevailing wind. Belatedly he has come to be recognised at Westminster and elsewhere, both by people who approve of him and the larger number who do not, as a born leader. The figure of fun, lampooned by such media efforts as *Spitting Image*, has had to be taken seriously.

Where, though, is this undoubted leader leading us? Much of his initial support came from the members of his own Free Presbyterian Church – abstemious men with decorously hatted wives – and other followers of Ulster Protestantism's 'born again' sects. (One reflects that George W. Bush, if born in Northern Ireland, might well have ended up in the DUP!) The Moderator would be accompanied into electoral politics by such people as the Reverend William Beattie and the Reverend William McCrea. Inevitably, as a faction of zealots expanded into a mass party, the new recruits included people driven by ambition and pragmatism as much as by ideology.

Paisley's party fed upon fear and suspicion on two fronts. On the religious side, evangelical Protestants could too easily be persuaded that the see of Rome was seeking to impose its hegemony. Anglicanism had been involved in a prolonged dialogue with the Catholic Church, and even Presbyterianism was so divided between tolerance and dissent as to influence the annual elections to its Moderatorship. In his role as a church leader, Paisley was able to exploit apprehension about an imagined 'Romeward trend'. This apprehension on religious grounds spilled over into the political arena, at a time when no one could foresee the growing severance in the Republic between Church and State, fed in time by distressing disclosures of priestly misconduct.

On the purely political front, Paisley's consistent message was that each successive Northern Ireland Administration or British Secretary of State was involved in a 'sell-out' of the Protestant and 'loyalist' community. So it was that 'O'Neill must go' was succeeded by similar denunciations of all of his successors in authority. O'Neill had 'sold out' by inviting Sean Lemass to Stormont; Faulkner had 'sold out' by accepting the terms of the Sunningdale Agreement; Margaret Thatcher had 'sold out' by endorsing the Anglo-Irish Agreement of 1985; David Trimble had 'sold out' by accepting the Belfast Agreement of 1997. As one initiative after another failed to deliver the benefits expected of it, Paisley was able to gain credibility as the prophet of such failure, which he had not merely forecast but had also helped to precipitate.

Thus by 2005 Paisley brooded over the scene like a presidential head chiselled on Mount Rushmore. He could demonstrate final success in bringing a majority of the unionist community with him. In Peter Robinson, Nigel Dodds, Jeffrey Donaldson and others he had able and articulate colleagues, clearly capable in the right circumstances of exercising executive authority with efficiency and decisiveness. But could one truly see Ian Paisley himself joined in a stable and productive administration with the growing cohorts of Sinn Fein? He could, and frequently did, point to his record of assiduously pursuing in or out of Parliament the interests of all of his constituents, regardless of political or religious affiliation. Yet it was impossible to imagine the DUP as a comfortable home for a Catholic citizen supportive of the Union. It has to be admitted that the UUP itself has never made a marked effort to attract support from that quarter, but such a person as Sir John Gorman could live comfortably within it. Time and age may have taken some of the sharper edges off Paisleyite rhetoric, but it is difficult to foresee any developing warmth between himself and what is today a very substantial minority of the population. My own judgement is that, over the course of more than thirty years, Paisley's influence has been malign, and a major impediment to any convincing or enduring rapprochement between the communities.

Then there is the other currently dominating figure in our political life, Gerry Adams. We have seen over the years an amazing and spectacular transformation from the grim-faced, beret-wearing combatant to the sharp-suited, articulate politician. Adams and his principal lieutenants, and in particular Martin McGuinness, have demonstrated how innate ability and force of character can triumph over social and educational disadvantage. On many occasions Adams has played his media interlocutors like a particularly skilful fisherman bringing his catch to the shore. All too often he has been successful in persuading the British Government into trading actions for acceptable words or even the prospect of such words. A striking example was the treatment of a republican prisoner, Sean Kelly, originally jailed for his part in the appalling 'Shankill bomb' outrage, which led to the death of innocent people as well as his own confederate in the attack. Prematurely released from prison in the context of the wider releases following on the Belfast Agreement, he was liable to be returned to prison if reinvolved in unacceptable activity.

In 2005 then, and no doubt acting on firm information and advice from the security authorities, the Secretary of State ordered this offender's return to prison. However, on the eve of the PIRA declaration that the 'armed struggle' was being brought to an end, Kelly was once again released from custody. Yet as early as August 1994, PIRA had previously announced 'a complete cessation of military operations'. In the years which followed, it became painfully clear that this 'cessation' did not mean the ending of widespread crime and intimidation. 'The proof of the pudding', as the old saying goes, 'is in the eating.' Yet it became obvious that, in advance of any evidence of the practical effect of a particular set of words, the British Government was prepared to offer – in return for those words alone – a whole series of further concessions to republicanism, of which the release of Kelly represented only one element. Any rational person would suppose that releases post-1997 were on condition of no further involvement in unacceptable activity. Yet because the republican movement had given an untested and ambiguous pledge, the slate would be wiped clean in a way which played fast and loose with the judicial system. This willingness to trade actions for mere words was underlined by some most ill-chosen remarks from Tony Blair, which seemed to imply that PIRA had accepted boundaries to their campaign not observed by the Muslim fundamentalists.

Adams and his lieutenants have greatly flourished amidst this ambiguity about their particular variety of terrorism. In the United States the horrors of September 2001 and the attitudes of George W. Bush reined in the enthusiasm with which smart-suited apologists for terror had earlier been received in Washington, but it was truly beyond belief that a British Prime Minister should relegate to some subordinate category of guilt and opprobrium people who had set out to murder two of his predecessors in that high office. I would hope that the subsequent comments by Norman Tebbit on the condition in which PIRA had left his wife while attempting to assassinate Margaret Thatcher may have brought a faint blush to some cheeks, but frankly I doubt it. The republican movement would like us to believe now that they never set out to kill 'innocent civilians'. Leaving aside the question of the morality of assassinating some police constable on traffic duty, one asks by what definition those who died in Enniskillen or Claudy or at the La Mon Hotel could be other than innocent victims. Nor, as his bedroom ceiling fell around him in 1988, was I convinced that my eighteen-year-old son could legitimately be regarded as a part of anyone's war machine.

We have had to witness the grotesque charade of messages passing between Sinn Fein and PIRA on the pretext that these have been separate and distinct organisations. The reaction of Sinn Fein leaders to any challenge about the policies or actions of PIRA has been to portray a sublime detachment, a kind of cosmetic distancing. It is almost as if those who occupied the dock at Nuremberg, accused of presiding over an atrocious regime, had been allowed to offer the explanation: 'You had better ask the Wehrmacht (or the Gestapo or the SS) about that.' As Justice Minister in Dublin, Michael McDowell deserves enormous credit for refusing to be bamboozled by this claptrap; for pointing out the anomaly of the 'resignation' from the Army Council of people who had denied membership of PIRA at any level.

The question must be asked: would anyone in England or in Scotland or in Wales be content to see the Government of their country or jurisdiction conducted by people responsible for a prolonged and ruthless campaign of murder and destruction? Is it conceivable that powers for justice and policing should be devolved to a Stormont administration to be exercised by a Minister who had himself connived in atrocious crimes?

What, then, of the role of successive Irish Governments? This has to be considered against the continuing avowed political objective of bringing the thirty-two counties of Ireland together in a unitary Republic. One could well argue that this has, from the start, been a misconceived objective, and that any rapprochement between the two Irelands should have been patient and organic, with no predetermined destination. But, taking the underlying proclaimed policy as a given, have the actions of successive Irish Govern-ments advanced or retarded that cause to which they have apparently pledged themselves?

It is important not to be unrealistic in this analysis. When an area and a community have long been embodied into another state to which they no longer want to belong, it is perhaps inevitable that the first thrust of indepen-dence will be to emphasise and encourage distinctiveness. This is all the more likely to be the case where the jurisdiction enjoying a new-found indepen-dence is very much smaller in scale than the jurisdiction from which it has separated itself. It is understandable that the mere act of political severance needs to be emphasised and reinforced by emphatic statements of separate identity – from repainting the letter boxes or issuing newly designed postage stamps to matters of greater pith and substance.

Yet the actions of the infant Irish State too soon began to display a schizo-phrenia of aspiration. The founding fathers wanted to see their new Ireland not only free and independent but united; that is to say, including within its embrace all the people living on the island of Ireland. From time to time the new State asserted its independence by policies and gestures of what I might call 'non-Britishness', a stance not always easily distinguished from 'anti-Britishness'. This ignored the reality that it was precisely a sense of 'Britishness' which, in part at least, characterised the 'separated brethren' of the north. It can seem perverse to cry 'Come over and join us on the other side' while hacking down a good many of the existing bridges.

One also has to accept, of course, that this sense of 'Britishness' is only one of the characteristics of the northern majority. In the real world, communities of hundreds of thousands of people are seldom as monolithic in character as they may appear from the outside. In my own experience in a lifetime lived amongst them, the attitudes of the northern majority span a very wide spectrum, ranging from sheer sectarian hatred of Catholic neighbours north and south, through a suspicion that Catholic values still have a dominant influence within the southern polity, to a cool judgement that the retention of British status best serves the social, economic and political interests of the whole community, or to a deep and principled commitment to the idea of a United Kingdom of Great Britain and Northern Ireland. There have also always been a few Ulster Protestants drawn to the ideas of Presbyterian radicals like William Drennan who were prominent United Irishmen.

In spite of this spectrum of attitudes, it would be a gross error to suppose that a sense of 'Britishness' has not, to varying degrees, been a very important element in the culture and psyche of the northern majority. This was a very important issue faced by the unfortunate New Ireland Forum. No one could doubt for a moment the essential decency and integrity of Garret FitzGerald, the Taoiseach who had brought the Forum together. Yet one sensed that, not for the first or the last time, the driving force behind that initiative was the vision of John Hume, whose continuing influence on successive Irish Governments represented the main motive force of their Northern Ireland policy. Since the principal obstacle in the way of any movement towards Irish unity was the unionist fear of domination by a nationalist majority, a cosy alliance of nationalist parties north and south seemed a perverse way of offering them reassurance. Unionist parties were, of course, invited, but there was as much chance of their taking part as there was of persuading a life-long abolitionist to attend a conference to discuss the most humane ways of carrying out capital punishment. As individuals the McGimpsey brothers (one of them later an Executive Minister) sought to underline unionist realities, while economists of great experience raised the very valid question of how a hypothetical united Ireland would find the money to preserve public services in the north hitherto supported from the British Exchequer.

A reader of the Forum report will see that the participating parties struggled to acknowledge the distinctiveness of the northern majority; but to a large extent seemed to see any necessary protection of their interests within a new structure as principally a matter of safeguarding what might be called 'Protestant values'. For many years the SDLP in general and John Hume in particular had been arguing that no political settlement wholly and exclusively internal to Northern Ireland could be viable or acceptable, because any such settlement would fail to recognise the extent to which those who voted for the SDLP or other small nationalist parties felt themselves to be part of a wider Irish community. There was little sign at the Forum of any recognition or acknowledgement of a corollary. The implicit message was that the parties of nationalist Ireland would respect every essential characteristic of unionists other than their unionism.

Successive Irish Governments failed to understand the mentality of the Protestant and unionist community of the north. That community shared some of the better and some of the worse characteristics of Afrikaanerdom. It exhibited both pride and self-pity. It saw itself as relatively friendless and unappreciated. It came to believe that the British Government – any British Government – would happily wave goodbye to it tomorrow. It saw the policy of the most powerful country on earth, the United States, heavily influenced by a group of politicians unsympathetic to its ethos and aspirations, and essentially reflecting the views and prejudices of an Irish diaspora. In particular it became increasingly suspicious of the activities and influence of what came to be termed 'pan-nationalism'. It wondered what exactly was being said in the repeated exchanges over the years between John Hume and Gerry Adams. Was the argument, perhaps, along the lines of: 'We're winning, of course, but mine is a better route than yours if we want to get there quickly'?

Fine phrases about an 'agreed Ireland' came to appear increasingly hollow at the time of the Anglo-Irish Agreement of 1985. Any truly enduring agreement could only be reached as between Irish people, north and south. Yet here was an Irish Government prepared to negotiate with its British counterpart behind the backs or over the heads of those parties and people with whom any enduring accommodation would have to be reached.

It took far too long to convince Irish Governments of the significance and centrality of the consent principle. That failure was illustrated by the absurd 'status declarations' of the 1985 Agreement, soon to be stripped of any marginal value by the pursuit of the Boland constitutional case.

At a critical moment, the Irish Government at Sunningdale, as ever urged by the SDLP, had pushed the Faulkner unionists into the danger zone of a Council of Ireland with executive functions. It would have been better and wiser policy by far to allow mutual confidence to develop before taking such a definitive step forward.

So much for the record of the principal interests. Where have their actions and inactions left us, as we react at last to the belated act of PIRA decommissioning? Will we now move forward to a future which would include further decommissioning by loyalist paramilitaries, a scaling down of widespread criminality, the withering away of republican dissidence, and the formation of a stable and enduring and devolved government? It is all too clear that in the aftermath of the original ceasefire, 'war' was too often transmuted into crime; that whole communities remained in thrall to paramilitary thugs; that militant republicanism and militant loyalism themselves split into factions engaged in bloody rivalry for the spoils of local control; and that in too many areas the unionist and nationalist communities showed all too few signs of compromise or mutual sympathy.

A democratic process can throw up some significant evidence about the mood and temper of society. It is, therefore, revealing to examine carefully the results of electoral contests in Northern Ireland from 1983 (that is, before the Anglo-Irish Agreement of 1985) to the present day. The results of the parliamentary (Westminster) elections of 1983 threw up that clear majority for unionism which had existed since partition. The more moderate UUP and the more extreme DUP had received a majority of the total votes cast, with the UUP total of 259,952 well ahead of the DUP total of 152,749. On the minority nationalist side of the equation, the moderate SDLP received 137,012 votes, as against 102,701 for the more extreme Sinn Fein.

Let us remember here that a main motivation for the Anglo-Irish Agreement, as enunciated by one of its prime movers Garret FitzGerald, had been to reinforce the political centre-ground, to inhibit support for Sinn Fein, and to encourage power-sharing by moderate constitutionalists from both sides of the community. What, in reality, happened? A further thirteen years were to pass before elections to a local assembly could be held with any prospect of a productive outcome. The share of votes cast for Sinn Fein, which had been 13.4 per cent at the 1983 parliamentary elections, fluctuated between 10 and 12 per cent between 1985 and 1993, reaching its lowest point at the parliamentary elections of 1992. However, beginning with the local government elections of 1993, Sinn Fein's share of the poll rose inexorably, election after election, to a level above 24 per cent. So much, then, for the objective of inhibiting the rise of Sinn Fein.

In the parliamentary elections of 1987, for the first time the two major unionist parties failed to attract more than 50 per cent of the votes cast. Indeed, at the successive parliamentary or local government elections held between 1987 and 1993, the votes of the two 'moderate' parties (the UUP and SDLP) represented more than a half of the total votes cast as they did once more in 1997.

At the Forum elections of 1996, there was evidence of a shifting of the political tectonic plates. In that year, and in the elections of 1998, 2001 and 2003, neither broad unionism nor the 'moderate centre' could command a majority of the votes. In 2005, at local government and parliamentary elections held on the same day, the new shape of politics became starkly apparent with a clear majority of the population voting either for the DUP or Sinn Fein. These electoral trends are illustrated in Table 1.

There are those who would argue that these striking electoral changes will not necessarily prove an impediment to ultimate political progress; they would point to the development of the de Valera republicans into the democratic party Fianna Fail, to the hope that 'hardliners' may be better able to sell any settlement to the community they represent and to the expectation that a growth of mass support brings into the party new members sympathetic to its aims and able to be more pragmatic about its methods.

Nevertheless, one wonders if those who were so self-satisfied about their contributions to the Anglo-Irish Agreement of 1985 would have welcomed

Table 1 Performance of the four main parties, 1983–2005
Total votes (or first preference votes) and % of poll

	Date & Nature of Election	UUP	DUP	SDLP	SF
W	11 June 1983	259,952 (34%)	192,749 (20%)	137,012 (17.9%)	102,701 (13.4%)
LG	1985	188,497 (29.5%)	155,297 (24.3%)	113,967 (17.8%)	75,686 (11.8%)
W	11 June 1987	276,230 (37.8%)	85,642 (11.4%)	154,087 (21.1%)	83,389 (11.4%)
LG	1989	193,064 (31.8%)	109,342 (17.7%)	129,557 (21%)	69,032 (11.2%)
W	9 April 1992	271,049 (34.5%)	103,039 (13.1%)	184,445 (23.5%)	78,291 (10%)
LG	19 May 1993	184,082 (29%)	108,680 (17%)	136,760 (22%)	77,600 (12%)
F	30 May 1996	181,829 (24.2%)	141,413 (18.8%)	160,786 (21.4%)	116,377 (15.5%)
W	1 May 1997	258,439 (32.7%)	107,348 (13.6%)	190,844 (24.1%)	126,921 (16.1%)
A	25 June 1998	172,225 (21.3%)	146,989 (18.1%)	177,963 (22%)	142,858 (17.6%)
W	5 June 2001	216,839 (26.8%)	181,999 (22.5%)	169,865 (21%)	175,392 (21.7%)
LG	7 June 2001	181,336 (23%)	169,477 (21%)	153,424 (19%)	163,269 (21%)
A	Nov 2003	156,931 (22.7%)	177,470 (25.6%)	117,547 (17%)	162,758 (23.5%)
W	5 May 2005	127,314 (17.7%)	241,856 (33.7%)	125,626 (17.5%)	174,530 (24.3%)
LG	5 May 2005	126,317 (18%)	208,278 (30%)	121,991 (17%)	163,205 (24%)

Order of parties (majority of votes cast)
W 1983 (Unionist): LG 1985 (Unionist); W 1987 (Moderates); LG 1989 (Moderate);
W 1992 (Moderate); LG 1993 (Moderate); F 1996 (Inconclusive); W 1997 (Moderate);
A 1998 (Inconclusive); LG 2001 (Inconclusive); W 2001 (Inconclusive);
A 2003 (Inconclusive); W 2005 (Extreme); LG 2005 (Extreme).

W	1983	UUP	DUP	SDLP	SF
LG	1985	UUP	DUP	SDLP	SF
W	1987	UUP	SDLP	DUP	SF
LG	1989	UUP	SDLP	DUP	SF
W	1992	UUP	SDLP	DUP	SF
LG	1993	UUP	SDLP	DUP	SF
F	1996	UUP	SDLP	DUP	SF
W	1997	UUP	SDLP	SF	DUP
A	1998	SDLP	UUP	DUP	SF
LG	2001	UUP	DUP	SF	SDLP
W	2001	UUP	DUP	SF	SDLP
A	2003	DUP	SF	UUP	SDLP
W	2005	DUP	SF	UUP	SDLP
LG	2005	DUP	SF	UUP	SDLP

Note: W = Parliamentary; A = Assembly; LG = Local Government; F = NI Forum the thought that between 1983 and 2005 the UUP would lose some 50 per cent of its support, that Paisley's DUP would increase its Westminster vote to almost 242,000, or that the SDLP would by 2001 be overtaken by Sinn Fein.

The Government of Ireland Act 1920, in its long title, had spoken of peace, order and good government. One could argue that since 1994 there has been a partial, imperfect peace, albeit broken at Canary Wharf, unobserved by the perpetrators of the atrocious Omagh bomb, and ignored by those involved in internal feuds and the protection of criminal empires. Self-styled 'armies' continued to behave as mafiosi. No one could fail to welcome the sharp fall in deaths, injuries and criminal damage, but Northern Ireland remained far from a state of normality, as illustrated by the outrageous and daring Northern Bank robbery and the dubious activities of republican militants in remote and turbulent places like Colombia. At best we had witnessed an imperfect armistice. The combatants had never come to any conference peace table, and their political surrogates remained mired in doubletalk.

On the subject of order, it may be sufficient to say that the levels of criminality and real and potential danger in Northern Ireland made it a particularly unpropitious moment to promote the retirement from the police service of some of its most experienced officers.

Of course a central feature of the Belfast (or Good Friday) Agreement was the provision for devolved and all-inclusive Government in Northern Ireland. To accommodate this requirement departmental organisation was reviewed with the objective of creating as many ministerial posts as possible. Thus a Province already top heavy with public bodies (and all their attendant costs) found itself endowed with no fewer than eleven Government departments – the hydra-headed OFM/DFM (Office of the First Minister and Deputy First Minister) and ten other portfolios. Executive (or Cabinet) posts were filled on a formulaic basis, with other parties improbably accepting the control of the crucial spending departments, for health and education, by Sinn Fein Ministers, one of them self-confessedly a former active member of PIRA. We had the DUP taking up its 'share' of ministerial seats, while demonstrating its underlying contempt for the system by rotating party acceptance of those seats (with some of those occupants demonstrating conspicuous executive ability), and by refusal to attend meetings of the collective Executive alongside Sinn Fein. This system was patently unstable and incoherent. It staggered into repeated brief or more prolonged suspensions. Any sense of common purpose was lacking. If the 'moderate centre' parties could not demonstrate some sense of common purpose and growing understanding, one could hardly expect the most bitter of political enemies to work constructively together. I reflected on this as I sat in the stand at Lansdowne Road in Dublin watching the Ulster rugby team contesting (successfully) the final of the European Cup. Quite close to me the First Minister, David Trimble, and the Deputy First Minister, Seamus Mallon, sat glumly side by side, without exchanging a word or a smile. They seemed to me like inimical Siamese twins, cruelly joined together and perpetually uncomfortable. Save for the braking mechanism represented by the Department of Finance and Personnel and a Ministerial Code more honoured in the breach than in the observance, departmental Ministers seemed free to go their own way. The public sector was balkanised. In 1974 the short-lived power-sharing Executive had, as one of its first acts, decided to adopt the practices and principles of collective responsibility. A Government failing to do so would lack real democratic credibility and fail to face up adequately to those many complex issues of contemporary government only to be solved through close inter-departmental cooperation.

This terrible flaw in the arrangements for government was demonstrated by the decision of the Education Minister, Martin McGuinness, as one of his final ministerial acts, to rule out any academic basis for the selection of pupils entering post-primary education. I set aside entirely the merits of the case (although like many others I thought it a disastrous and utterly misconceived decision). What was so appallingly wrong and democratically objectionable about the process was that a single Minister could take and announce such a decision without any approval from Executive colleagues or the Assembly at large. This was the act of a commissar rather than a minister.

I hope that what I have written may give the reader some sense of the nature, extent and duration of the suffering endured for so long by Northern Ireland and its people. Back at the crossroads, after a long detour into arid and inhospitable country, where are we now heading?

The British, Irish and American Governments and the nationalist parties of Northern Ireland want to see a return as soon as possible to the inclusive, power-sharing, devolved government envisaged by the Belfast Agreement. This raises not merely the question of whether such a Government can be formed, but also the further vital questions of whether it could endure and be capable of providing efficient government in the interests of all the people. After the collapse of the Executive of 1974 I warned of the dangers of 'permanent impermanence', of systems where crises can bring down not just a serving administration but a whole system of government.

Sinn Fein and the SDLP will continue to press for the restoration of devolved government because they are confident that the inexorable tide of history is carrying them in the direction they want to see. For its part the DUP would like to exercise that substantial measure of power to which it believes its mandate entitles it, but neither it nor the UUP are confident about the bona fides of Sinn Fein as a partner in Government. I suspect that many who voted not just for the Alliance and other smaller parties but for the UUP and the SDLP do not look forward with enthusiasm to a devolved Government dominated by Sinn Fein and the DUP. As a citizen of the United Kingdom of Great Britain and Northern Ireland I ask myself whether I should be expected to tolerate government by people of extreme views and, in some cases, associates of criminals who killed without mercy and even after their premature release continue to defend their actions as legitimate and even praiseworthy.

It is, I suppose, not impossible that a hunger for executive authority may bring these strange bedfellows together within the framework and timetable contemplated by the St Andrew's Agreement of 2006. It is, after all, perfectly understandable for people of natural authority and capability to reach for the levers of power. But could a Government so formed operate for any time on an efficient and acceptable basis? Parties, I fear, would eye each other across the Executive table with unabated suspicion and distrust. It would take a great deal to persuade DUP Ministers in particular that moves proposed by Sinn Fein colleagues were not essentially in pursuit of their agenda to speed the achievement of a united Ireland. In the Good Friday Agreement it was agreed that 'Ministers will have full executive authority in their respective areas of responsibility, within any broad programme agreed by the executive Committee and endorsed by the Assembly as a whole'. Thus, while controversial legislation required cross-community support, there was no such requirement in respect of executive decisions. Now an Annex to the St Andrew's Agreement represents a movement towards conventional ministerial accountability, envisaging a Ministerial Code to

> place a duty upon Ministers. ... notwithstanding their executive authority in their areas of responsibility ... to act in accordance with the provisions on ministerial responsibility of the Code ... There will be arrangements to ensure that, where a decision of the Executive could not be achieved by a consensus and a vote was required, any three members of the Executive could require it to be taken on a cross-community basis.

Yet a dilemma remains. If controversial action can be blocked by an absence of cross-community support, may there not be a real and ever-present risk of deadlock as between factions hitherto deeply suspicious of each other?

If attempts to restore devolution fail, or if the institutions – once up and running – prove once again to be self-destructively fragile, the medium-term alternative can only be a further indefinite period of direct rule from London. One envisages that possibility without enthusiasm. I could too easily foresee a steady tightening of the financial screw on a Province still lagging behind Great Britain in too many of its public services, despite the ultimate responsibility for running Northern Ireland vested over many years in the United

Kingdom Government. Lurking in the background, a fear of this could be a covert inducement to accept devolution in the sense of Belloc's 'Cautionary Tale':

And always keep a hold of Nurse
For fear of finding something worse.

It is possible, as a resident of Northern Ireland hitherto always glad and proud to be a citizen of the United Kingdom, to feel at times like a party to a marriage whose partner no longer feels or shows any real affection, but who maintains an increasingly cool relationship out of a sense of loyalty. Vociferous as Peter Hain in the role of Secretary of State may now be about his support for the 'consent principle', supporters of the union cannot blot out of their minds his earlier support for the 'troops out' movement. Nor can one ignore the fact that, amongst all the citizens of this supposedly United Kingdom, we alone have been afforded no opportunity to vote for a party now deeply entrenched in the Government of our country.

There are moments, I confess, when even I – the son of English parents, although born in Ulster, a graduate of Oxford University and a Knight Commander of the Most Noble Order of the Bath – wonder if we would not enjoy a more dignified position as a community within a united Ireland. The excessive grip of the Church upon the Government of Ireland has been greatly diminished by changing social and political attitudes and by the shame of clerical abuse. The Republic, with massive support from the European Union, has increased its GDP per head to one of the highest levels in Europe; yet the financial and economic challenge of assimilating a Northern Ireland so heavily dependent upon Exchequer support remains enormous. The struggle in a reunited Germany to assimilate the underdeveloped East is a matter of record. There is, too, the nightmare prospect of Sinn Fein, appealing as it does to the young, disaffected and marginalised, obtaining real leverage in the politics of the Republic by virtue of an electoral system which can confer excessive influence on smaller parties. Nor has confidence in the Irish democracy been enhanced by the revelations from a seemingly endless series of inquiries and tribunals of deeply entrenched political cynicism and greed. I find it a sobering thought that an Irish Minister who often faced me across the table at Intergovernmental Conferences has since been found guilty of appalling corruption and self-enrichment.

We shall need, I fear, better men framing better policies if we are to escape from this unenviable impasse. We live in a community where it was considered striking that a young Ulster unionist and former international rugby-football star, Trevor Ringland, should voice his support for the Tyrone Gaelic Football team as it travelled to Croke Park in Dublin to contest (and win) the All-Ireland trophy, the Sam Maguire Cup. There are, I know, very many people who share such sentiments, who seek to be bridge-builders, who want to provide an alternative to the politics of mutual distrust and animosity. Let them come forward, then, for that would be far and away the best tribute to those whose sufferings it was my painful privilege to record.

Select bibliography

Official papers

1953 December *Northern Ireland, the Channel Islands and the Isle of Man: A Treasury Paper*
1969 October   *Northern Ireland: Text of a Communiqué* (Callaghan visit)
1971 August   *A Record of Constructive Change*, Comd. 558
     October   *The Future Development of the Parliament and Government of Northern Ireland: A Consultative Document*, Comd. 560
1972 March   *Political Settlement (Statements of 24 March 1972 by Prime Minister and Government of Northern Ireland)*, Cmd. 568
               Northern Ireland (Temporary Provisions) Act 1972
     June   *Northern Ireland: Financial Arrangements and Legislation*, Cmd. 4997
     October   *The Future of Northern Ireland: A Paper for Discussion*
1973 March   *Northern Ireland Constitutional Proposals*, Cmnd. 5259
     July   Northern Ireland Constitution Act 1973
     December *Sunningdale Conference Communiqué*
1974   Northern Ireland Office discussion papers
     July   Northern Ireland Act 1974
     The Northern Ireland Constitution, Cmnd. 5675
1976 January   *The Northern Ireland Constitutional Convention: Letter from the Secretary of State to the Chairman*, Cmnd. 6387
1979 November *The Government of Northern Ireland: A Working Paper for a Conference*, Cmnd. 7763
1980 July   *The Government of Northern Ireland: Proposals for Further Discussion*
1982   Northern Ireland Act 1982
1985 November *Agreement between the Government of the United Kingdom of Great Britain and Northern Ireland and the Government of the Republic of Ireland*, Cmnd. 9657
1989 May   *The Anglo-Irish Agreement: Review of Working of the Conference*
1993 December *Joint Declaration by John Major and Albert Reynolds*
1995 February *Frameworks for the Future*
1998 January   *Joint Statement by British and Irish Governments*

April *'Good Friday Agreement'* and Agreement between the Government of the United Kingdom of Great Britain and Northern Ireland and the Government of Ireland

2006 October   St Andrew's Agreement

Works of history, biography and autobiography

Anderson, Don, *14 May Days: The Inside Story of the Loyalist Strike of 1974* (Dublin, 1994).

Arthur, Paul, *Special Relationships: Britain, Ireland and the Northern Ireland Problem* (Belfast, 2000).

Bardon, Jonathon, *A History of Ulster* (Belfast, 1992).

Barton, Brian, *Northern Ireland in the Second World War* (Belfast, 1995).

Bell, J. Bowyer, *The Irish Troubles, A Generation of Violence, 1967–1992* (Dublin, 1993).

Bloomfield, Kenneth, Contribution to *Faith in Ulster* (ECONI) (Belfast).

Bloomfield, Kenneth, 'Devolution: Lessons from Northern Ireland', *Political Quarterly* (April–June 1996) (Royal Institute of Public Administration).

Bloomfield, Kenneth, *Stormont in Crisis: A Memoir* (Belfast, 1994).

Bloomfield, Kenneth, *We Will Remember Them*, Report of the Victims Commissioner (Belfast, 1998).

Bogdanor, Vernon, *Devolution in the United Kingdom* (Oxford, 1999).

Brett, Charles, *Housing a Divided Community* (Dublin, 1986).

Buckland, Patrick, *James Craig* (Dublin, 1980).

Callaghan, James, *A House Divided: The Dilemma of Northern Ireland* (London, 1973).

Carrington, Peter, *Reflect on Things Past: The Memoirs of Lord Carrington* (London, 1988).

Carver, Michael, *Out of Step: The Memoirs of Field Marshal Lord Carver* (London, 1989).

Churchill, Winston, *The Second World War* (London, 1948–54).

Clinton, Hillary, *Living History* (New York, 2003).

Cole, John, *As It Seemed to Me: Political Memoirs* (London, 1995).

Coogan, Tim Pat, *The Troubles: Ireland's Ordeal 1966–1995 and the Search for Peace* (London, 1995).

Currie, Austin, *All Hell Will Break Loose* (Dublin, 2004).

Daly, Cahal, *The Price of Peace* (Belfast, 1991).

De Breadun, Declan, *The Far Side of Revenge: Making Peace in Northern Ireland* (Cork, 2001).

Delaney, Eamon, *An Accidental Diplomat* (Dublin, 2001).

Deutsch, Richard, and Magowan, Vivien, *Northern Ireland, 1968–73: Chronology of Events*, 2 vols (Belfast, 1973, 1974).

Devlin, Paddy, *Straight Left: An Autobiography* (Belfast, 1993).

Dillon, Martin, *25 Years of Terror: The IRA's War against the British* (London, 1994).

Dwane, David, *Early Life of Eamon de Valera* (Dublin, 1922).

Eames, Robin, *Chains to Be Broken* (London, 1922).

Elliott, Marianne, *The Catholics of Ulster: A History* (London, 2000).

Elliott, Marianne (ed.), *The Long Road to Peace in Northern Ireland* (Liverpool, 2002).

English, Richard, *The Armed Struggle: A History of the IRA* (London, 2003).

Faulkner, Brian, *Memoirs of a Statesman* (London, 1978).

Fay, Marie Therese *et al.*, *Northern Ireland Troubles: The Human Costs* (London, 1999).

FitzGerald, Garret, *All in a Life: An Autobiography* (Dublin, 1991).

Flackes, W.D., and Elliott, Sydney, *Northern Ireland: A Political Directory, 1968–88* (Belfast, 1989).

Flackes, W.D., and Elliott, Sydney, *Northern Ireland: A Political Directory, 1968–93* (Belfast, 1994).

Foster, R.F., Contribution to *Varieties of Irishness* (Belfast, 1989).

Foster, R.F., *Modern Ireland, 1600–1972* (London, 1988).

Gailey, Andrew, *Crying in the Wilderness: Jack Sayers, a Liberal Editor in Ulster, 1939–69* (Belfast, 1995).

Godson, Dean, *Himself Alone: David Trimble and the Ordeal of Unionism* (London, 2004).

Gordon, David, *The O'Neill Years: Unionist Politics, 1963–1969* (Belfast, 1989).

Gorman, John, *The Times of My Life* (London, 2004).

Hamber, Brandon (ed.), *Past Imperfect: Dealing with the Past in Northern Ireland and Societies in Transition* (Derry, 1998).

Hayes, Maurice, *Minority Verdict: Experiences of a Catholic Civil Servant* (Belfast, 1995).

Heath, Edward, *The Course of My Life: The Autobiography of Edward Heath* (London, 1998).

Hennesy, Thomas, *Northern Ireland: The Origins of the Troubles* (Dublin, 2005).

Hennessey, Peter, *The Prime Minister: The Office and Its Holders since 1945* (London, 2000).

Hermon, John, *Holding the Line* (Dublin, 1997).

Heseltine, Michael, *Life in the Jungle* (London, 2000).

Holland, Jack, *The American Connection* (New York, 1987).

Jackson, Alvin, *An Irish History, 1800–2000* (London, 2003).

Jones, Thomas (ed.), *Whitehall Diary, vol. III: 1918–1925* (London, 1971).

Joyc, Joe, and Murtagh, Peter, *The Boss: Charles J. Haughey in Government* (Dublin, 1983).

Kelly, Henry, *How Stormont Fell* (Dublin, 1972).

Langdon, Julia, *Mo Mowlam: The Biography* (London, 2000).

Latham, Richard, *Deadly Beat: Inside the Royal Ulster Constabulary* (Edinburgh, 2001).

McCann, Eamonn, *War and an Irish Town* (London, 1974).

McCreary, Alf, *Gordon Wilson: An Ordinary Hero* (London, 1996).

McCreary, Alf, *Nobody's Fool: The Life of Archbishop Robin Eames* (London, 2004).

McDowell, A.D., *The Life of Sir Denis Henry: Catholic Unionist* (Belfast, 2000).

McIvor, Basil, *Hope Deferred: Experiences of an Irish Unionist* (Belfast, 1998).

McKendrey, Seamus, *Disappeared: The Search for Jean McConville* (Dublin, 2000).

Mallie, Eamonn, and McKittrick, David, *The Fight for Peace: The Secret Story behind the Irish Peace Process* (London, 1996).

Major, John, *John Major: The Autobiography* (London, 1999).

Mallie, Eamonn, and McKittrick, David, *Endgame in Ireland* (London, 2001).

Mawhinney, Brian, *In the Firing Line: Politics, Faith, Power and Forgiveness* (London, 1999).

Moloney, Ed, and Pollak, Andy, *Paisley* (Dublin, 1986).

Mowlam, Mo, *Momentum: The Struggle for Peace, Politics and the People* (London, 2002).

Needham, Richard, *Battling for Peace* (Belfast, 1998).

O'Brien, Conor Cruise, *Memoir: My Life and Themes* (Dublin, 1998).

Oliver, John, *Aspects of Ulster* (Antrim, 1994).

O'Neill, Terence, *The Autobiography of Terence O'Neill* (London, 1972).

O'Neill, Terence, *Ulster at the Crossroads* (London, 1969).

Pakenham, Frank, *Peace by Ordeal* (London, 1962).

Patterson, Henry, *Ireland since 1939* (Oxford, 2002).

Pollak, Andy (ed.), *A Citizen's Inquiry: The Opsahl Report on Northern Ireland* (Dublin, 1993).

Rees, Merlyn, *Northern Ireland: A Personal Perspective* (London, 1985).

Robbins, Keith *et al.*, *Varieties of Britishness* (Belfast, 1990).

Rose, Peter, *How the Troubles Came to Northern Ireland* (London, 2000).

Routledge, Paul, *John Hume: A Biography* (London, 1997).

Ryder, Chris, *The Fateful Split: Catholics and the Royal Ulster Constabulary* (London, 2004).

Ryder, Chris, *The RUC, 1922–2000: A Force under Fire* (London, 1989).

Scouler, Clive, *James Chichester-Clark: Prime Minister of Northern Ireland* (Killyleagh, 2000).

Smyth, Marie, *Half the Battle* (Derry, 1998).

Smyth, Marie, and Fay, Marie Therese, *Personal Accounts from Northern Ireland's Troubles: Public Conflict, Private Loss* (London, 2000).

Smyth, Marie, Morrissey, Mike, and Hamilton, Jennifer, *Caring through the Troubles: Health and Social Services in North and West Belfast* (Belfast, 2001).

Stuart, Mark, *Douglas Hurd: The Public Servant* (Edinburgh, 1998).

Sunday Times Insight Team, *Ulster* (London, 1972).

Taylor, Peter, *Brits: The War against the IRA* (London, 2001).

Taylor, Peter, *Provos: The IRA and Sinn Fein* (London, 1997).

Thatcher, Margaret, *The Downing Street Years* (London, 1993).

Walker, Graham, *A History of the Ulster Unionist Party: Protest, Pragmatism and Pessimism* (Manchester, 2004).

Wallace, Martin, *Drums and Guns: Revolution in Ulster* (London, 1970).

Whitelaw, William, *The Whitelaw Memoir* (London, 1989).

Wilson, Gordon, with McCreary, Alf, *Marie: A Story from Enniskillin* (London, 1990).

Wilson, Robin (ed.), *Agreeing to Disagree* (HMSO, 2001).

Windlesham, Daid, 'Ministers in Ulster: the Machinery of Direct Rule', *Public Administration* (Autumn 1973 issue) (Royal Institute of Public Administration, London).

Index